MIRACLES

Geoff and Hope Price met at a Christian centre in North Devon. Geoff trained in agriculture, and Hope as a nurse and health visitor. As well as working in Britain, they spent four years in Rwanda as missionaries involved in rural development and forestry projects.

In 1983, Geoff became an Anglican clergyman, ministering in parishes in Essex and Dorset. Now he and Hope are working in three parishes in town and country in Shropshire. They have a son, Luke, and a daughter, Naomi, who both share their parents' Christian vision.

The whole area of miracles came to life for them following the publication of *Angels*. Geoff realized that miracles, too, are not only jfound in the Bible, but are part of God's on-going work today.

By Hope Price

ANGELS

GEOFF AND HOPE PRICE

MIRACLES

TRUE STORIES OF HOW GOD
ACTS TODAY

PAN BOOKS

First published 1995 by Macmillan

This edition published 1996 by Pan Books
an imprint of Pan Macmillan Ltd
Pan Macmillan, 20 New Wharf Road, London N1 9RR
Basingstoke and Oxford
Associated companies throughout the world
www.panmacmillan.com

ISBN 0 330 34782 9

3 5 7 9 8 6 4

A CIP catalogue record for this book is available from
the British Library

Typeset by SetSystems Ltd, Saffron Walden, Essex
Printed and bound in Great Britain by
Mackays of Chatham plc, Chatham, Kent

All Pan Macmillan titles are available from
www.panmacmillan.com
or from Bookpost by telephoning 01624 677237

To all those who wrote to us about how
God has acted in their lives today,
making this book possible.

CONTENTS

CONTENTS

CONTENTS

ACKNOWLEDGEMENTS

Our thanks go to our church family in Market Drayton, Moreton Saye and Adderley for their prayers, support and encouragement.

We would like to thank all who have helped us, especially Chris Simpson and Elizabeth Hardacre for their
research, and the church for lending us their computer.

Our deepest thanks to Luke and Naomi, our son and daughter, who have given their love and care in so many ways while we wrote this book.

Most of all we are grateful to God for the strength and peace He gave us to write.

The authors and publishers are grateful to the following for giving permission to use copyright material: Kingsway Communications Ltd, Lottbridge Drove, Eastbourne, East Sussex, BN23 6NT for permission to quote from *Awaiting the Healer* by Margie Willer; Hodder Headline Plc for permission to quote from *Unexpected Healing* by Jennifer Rees-Larcombe; HarperCollins Publishers Ltd for permission to quote from *Marie* by Gordon Wilson.

Every effort has been made to trace all copyright holders, but if any have inadvertently been overlooked, the author and publishers will be pleased to make the necessary arrangements at the first opportunity.

FOREWORD

BY

GORDON WILSON

Miracles, like angels and, indeed, saints, make us all feel a little bit uncomfortable. We might like to believe in their possibility, but most of us would be shy of admitting that they exist or that we have witnessed them. Of course, our view of miracles depends on what we call a miracle.

Geoff and Hope Price have taken an unfashionable subject and set it in the context of a practical modern Christianity. Their account of modern miracles eschews the headline-grabbing cures or melodramatic changes in life that leap to mind on hearing the word. Instead, they concentrate on the miraculous ways in which God reveals His presence to us. People who have rejected or ignored Him are suddenly confronted and challenged by His love. People who have suffered are borne up by His strength, and those who do love Him are shown how to spread that love and faith.

We can all learn from this book. In the experiences of people in places as far apart as Rwanda and Cambodia we discover the universal community of Christianity. The dignity with which Father Kolbe and Corrie ten Boom suffered the outrages of Nazi concentration camps, and brought God's word to their fellow-sufferers, is a model of the refusal of despair. And a young man afflicted with cerebral palsy reminds us that the greatest miracle is life.

Geoff and Hope Price have done me the honour of quoting my words after the bomb which took eleven lives in my town, including that of my daughter, Marie. I said then, 'It's part of a greater plan, and God is good.' That sentiment is echoed by many others whose sufferings are recorded here. They too have felt the great shower of prayer in times of hardship.

If this book fortifies others who doubt and suffer, then it will have achieved its own miracle, and the old catch-phrase 'this book changed my life' will for once ring true.

Enniskillen, March 1995

CHAPTER ONE

Divine Intervention

God moves in a mysterious way,
His wonders to perform.

William Cowper (1731–1800)
(*Christian poet and hymn-writer*)

HE GREATEST evidence that God acts today is found in the lives of ordinary people. From time to time, at certain places in people's lives, God acts in an extraordinary way. This divine intervention is called a miracle. One does not have to be a special person or a classical saint to experience the touch of God. Indeed, while Hope was writing the book *Angels*, we were overwhelmed by the evidence of the countless ways in which God sent His angelic messengers, and it was that which led to the writing of this book. At a retreat house in Chester, around a fire during the beginnings of winter, I shared with Hope my growing desire to write a book on miracles. Why? Because miracles are not to be seen only in the context of the Old Testament, or even that of the dynamic Jesus of Nazareth in the New Testament; but also in today's world.

God has always intervened in history. The escape of the Israelite families from Egypt (Exodus 12) and the resurrection of Jesus (Matthew 28) must surely be two of the greatest interventions by God on man's behalf ever recorded. In each subsequent generation, men and women have carried, within their hearts and lives, true experiences of a miraculous kind. These stories are not to be boasted about, so as to bring acclaim to the teller, but rather must point the reader to God, who is alive and well in the twentieth century.

If we view the world as a closed system, we may see the unusual, but refuse to regard it as divine intervention. However, for those who see the world as God's creation, who are open to His personal interaction, miracles become a reality. It needs faith to appreciate a miracle, and as C. S. Lewis wrote: 'The best is perhaps what we understand least.' A 'miracle' can be described as a divine surprise which, in terms of our present knowledge, cannot be explained in intellectual or rational ways, causing us simply to stand back in amazement.

Something quite remarkable happened to two friends of ours, Kevin and Olive Allison, who live in Dorset. Kevin writes: 'When Olive was twelve years old, she fell from a beam in the school gym, rupturing a disc in her spine. From then on she was in continual pain. For a time she was paralysed, but when we married in 1959, by which time she was twenty, she could walk fairly freely. A year later we had a daughter, Tracey, although during the pregnancy Olive's back again deteriorated, so she had to wear a surgical corset and later a plaster jacket.

'During the following years her back pain was constant and frequently acute. Sciatica was a particular problem and she had pain in her shoulders, neck, head, arms and hands, which meant she had to spend months at a time in bed. She had long spells of traction, spinal injections and enough pills to make her rattle. Over the years she underwent three laminectomies, which removed damaged discs from the spine. A progressive build-up of scar tissue put further pressure on the spinal cord, making further treatments more complicated. She was treated by five orthopaedic surgeons and two rheumatologists, as she had also developed arthritis in both knees.'

Kevin continues: 'Despite the problems, we have a very happy marriage. We made the most of the good times between major crises, and Olive was always cheerful and positive. She is good at managing money and the home, and is a wonderful mother. We have always had lots of friends who have delighted in Olive's superb cooking. She also worked from home, using a computer link, for a local company. But, by December 1985 her condition was chronic: she could only walk a few yards on crutches, and her right knee frequently gave way, causing falls which aggravated the problems. She was also having increasing difficulty keeping her body upright, due to poor muscle tone, and in order to get about she had to use an electric buggy or wheelchair.

'In sheer desperation, because of the pain, she went again to see the rheumatologist. As far as conventional medicine was concerned, there was nothing more that could be done, but he suggested she might like to receive prayer for healing at a group connected with the church he attended. When Olive came home and told me this, I heard a quiet but authoritative voice in my mind say, "You must not let her go for healing unless it is Christian." This was a surprise, because I had stopped going to church since my youth, and Jesus had dropped out of my thinking.'

Olive adds: 'I was horrified at Kevin's reaction. How dare he check the group out when he was not even a churchgoer. I now know that experiences in the RAF had made Kevin realize that healing can also come from an evil source which, in the long run, will do more harm than good, but at the time I had never thought about it. Nevertheless, we contacted a lady from our nearest church and she came to talk the situation over with us. Then she asked if she could bring someone who lived near by, who knew a great deal about Christian healing. He was Bishop Ban It Chiu, a retired clergyman from Singapore. When he came, Kevin spent the first two hours complaining angrily about the lack of belief in the church as he saw it!

'The bishop patiently answered his questions, and thoroughly convinced Kevin, so he was ready to give his life to Christ. After leading him in a prayer of commitment to Jesus, the bishop turned to me and led me in a prayer requesting forgiveness, which by now I realized I needed. He then said that if I wanted healing, I must ask the Lord directly for it. He anointed my head with oil, put his hands on my head and prayed very simply for forgiveness and for healing. I felt the pain going from my legs, back, arms, and head out into Bishop Chiu's hands. I didn't say anything for a while, because I wondered whether the pain had really gone, or just seemed to go because that was what I wanted. But it really had: it was incredible. There was much rejoicing that God had healed my back, which had caused the arm, neck and leg pains, although my knees remained as they were. The bishop felt there were things in my life which prevented my complete healing at this time, so he asked God to show me what I needed to confess and be set free from.'

Delighted, Olive was now able to leave off the steel back support, and her spine had straightened so that Kevin had to lengthen her crutches by two inches. She recalls: 'Although I was still disabled, Kevin and I started a new life together in Christ. During the next six months, so many things happened. I learnt to ask the Lord for help and to pray from my heart instead of my head. He showed me many things I had to say sorry for. At Pentecost we went to Salisbury Cathedral, and Kevin wheeled me up for prayer at the end of the service. The priest and his wife who prayed for me suggested I turn my hands upward to God when praying, showing that I was open to receive from Him. I continued to do this, and each time, my hands felt heavy, but my heart felt light.'

Olive continues, 'The next month we listened to a talk about how artefacts associated with other religions sometimes contained spirits of other gods. Kevin and I both immediately knew we must get rid of an ebony carved figure we had at home, and we threw it in the rubbish bin. The day the rubbish was collected, Kevin as usual dressed my thighs, where my legs were so swollen that they rubbed together and caused sores. He bandaged them and put my tights and shoes on for me before leaving for work. As he left, he suggested I clear out a chest of drawers he was taking to some friends that evening. The last drawer contained lots of transparencies collected over many years. I began taking out the boxes, when suddenly the label on one box seemed to be written inches larger than normal. It said, "Olive and the ghost stone".

'I immediately remembered the incident. We were in North Wales and had stopped at some standing stones alongside a Roman road. Kevin wanted to take my photograph and told me to put my hand on the stone. When I did, it burnt me! Kevin said the stone felt cold to him, but again it burnt me when I touched it and I said something very foolish about evil spirits. When we got the transparencies back, Kevin had gasped. The one with me with my hand on the stone had on it another standing stone, blazing orange, alongside it. It was uncanny. Other people we showed it to found it eerie, but then we put it away and forgot about it. I knew now I had to ask the Lord to forgive me for calling on the evil spirits, and as I started to pray I found myself crying. Suddenly I experienced a tremendous feeling, as if every part of my body was being washed. It wasn't frightening, but I didn't understand what was happening.

'When I stood up I found my bandages and tights hanging loosely on my legs, as the swelling had all gone down. I realized that my sores and my knees were healed, so I didn't need my crutches. As I walked towards the stairs, I heard a voice telling me I could walk downstairs: I knew it was God. I hadn't been able to do that for years, so we had had a stair lift installed. Knowing the Lord was with me I walked down and, once at the bottom, turned round and walked back up again. It was incredible – I really could not describe the feeling – but I had a certainty that I was completely healed.'

Concluding, Olive recalls: 'When Kevin came in at lunch-time, I was sitting down. I got up, walked across the lounge without my crutches and walked upstairs. When I turned round at the top, Kevin was at the bottom, crying. When I phoned Bishop Chiu I said, "The Lord has healed me." He replied that he had been waiting for my call. He came round and blessed each room in our home. My complete healing had been delayed until the other things were dealt with. Since that day, 25 June 1986, I haven't had a twinge or an ache. I can walk for miles, run, cycle, and pick up my grandchildren.'

God, men and angels interact in a spiritual dimension, challenging those who by nature look only as far as the material. We were meant to walk by faith, not only by sight. The fruit looked so tempting in the garden of Eden, as recorded in Genesis chapter 3, and mankind ate what was forbidden. Since that act of disobedience, man has tended to look only at the world around him, largely ignoring what is spiritual. Nevertheless God breaks in upon our human frailty, reassuring us of His presence and His care.

In ordinary places, in villages and towns, God is doing extraordinary things. The whole of Britain, from ancient times to the present day, has been soaked in the supernatural. Our Christian heritage strikes a chord which is heard across the landscape of city towers, village greens and river valleys. From early Christianity to today, we have been immersed in the belief that God is with us.

In the countryside, nature reveals the hand of God, allowing us to draw strength from His creation. Until the Industrial Revolution scarred the landscape, every town and village was surrounded by the beauty of nature, and men and women could see their God thus reflected. Not only does nature reveal a God of creative energy, but also the divine intervention of a Redeemer. This is summed up in a hymn by Melody Green:

There is a Redeemer, Jesus, God's own Son,
Precious Lamb of God, Messiah, Holy One.

Thank you, O my Father, for giving us your Son,
And leaving your Spirit till the work on earth is done.

We ourselves, and the stage of God's creation on which we live out our lives, are very closely linked. Genesis 3:19 tells us: 'From [the ground] you were taken, for dust you are and to dust you will return.' The intervening years of our life on earth are an opportunity for God to deal with the God-shaped gap in the human heart. Miracles are a part of God's dealings with us. This does not mean that God is only at work in miraculous happenings. The Bible's view of God is that of an ever-present, forever sustaining personality, speaking to us through what He has made.

While I worked at Lee Abbey in North Devon, I heard the story of a group of students, led by a communist, visiting the great Rhine Valley in Southern Germany. The view across the river into the Black Forest was stupendous. While they were taking in this sight, the leader of the group said: 'What you see is for man to exploit. It is material for our use.' As the party drifted away from the vantage point, one of the sightseers lingered behind. 'Surely,' she said to herself, 'there must be more to this view than just the matter that I can see.' This revelation moved her to begin a spiritual pilgrimage, on which she found the man who 'even the winds and seas obey' (Matthew 8:27), God's Son, Jesus of Nazareth.

C. S. Lewis, the great Christian author, wrote in his book *Miracles*: 'Unless there exists, in addition to nature, something else which we may call the supernatural, there can be no miracles. Some people believe that nothing exists except nature; I call these people naturalists. Others think that besides nature there exists something else; I call them supernaturalists.' Lewis's book concerns those who are witnesses to the supernatural. In a sense, they are people who have experienced divine intervention.

Theology is called the queen of sciences, suggesting answers to the question of how we should understand God. Often our view of God is narrow. We have been led to believe that He is present only in church buildings, or able to be 'called in' when there is a crisis. J. B. Phillips, a New Testament scholar, wrote a book entitled *Your God Is Too Small*. In it he wrote: 'The trouble with many people today is that they have not found a God big enough for modern needs . . . While their experience of life had grown in a score of directions . . . their ideas of God have remained largely static.' We need to break through the limitations we put on God, and see Him touching every aspect of modern life – from the commercial banker in the City, to the crofter on a distant island, making a living from the land.

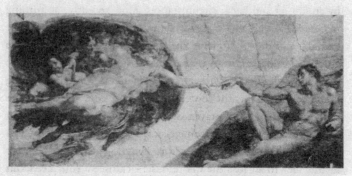

Sistine Chapel Ceiling: Creation of Adam
by Michelangelo (1475–1564), Vatican Museums & Galleries,
Rome/Bridgeman Art Library, London

The image of God seeking man is captured brilliantly by Michelangelo in the Sistine Chapel in Italy, where he depicted the relationship between God and Man in the form of two figures reaching out to each other. One figure is God, the other Adam, representing mankind. Their fingers are almost touching. For us today, it is a touch from God, which brings faith in Him alive.

If we cannot experience God in our lives, it is difficult to believe in Him, although the testimonies of others enable us to be more open to God reaching into our own lives. Rodney Bellamy of Shropshire has felt God's touch on his own life: 'On a number of occasions in the last ten years or so, I have felt a recognizable "touch" on my shoulder or back. These experiences have come at times when I have been distressed as a result of pressure at work.

'The "touch" has both reassured and renewed me, to an extent that I have felt burdens lifted, and I know all is well. It has shown me that, in spite of life's problems, God's guiding hand is available to us. As I have proceeded through life in my own self-motivated way, without considering the guidance which God provides through Christ, I have been overwhelmed at times by troubling and harsh circumstances. More recently, on turning to God for help, I have been saved by His guiding hand.'

Many of those who have known a miracle see a link between God's act and their own prayer. God has invited us to pray to develop a relationship with Him. St Thérèse of Lisieux, a young French nun who died in 1897 at the age of twenty-four, identifies the crucial element of prayer. She understood what Jesus taught when He said we must become like little children (Luke 18:17). Thérèse called her form of spirituality 'the little way'. She was saying 'no' to lofty, heavy religious teaching. We so need this 'little way' today, asking God openly and honestly to act in the context of our everyday life. In the *Story of a Soul*, St Thérèse wrote: 'When I turn to the sacred Scriptures, then all becomes clear – a single word opens out new vistas, perfection appears easy, and I see it is enough to acknowledge one's nothingness and surrender oneself like a child into God's arms.'

We commemorate those in Christian history who have been agents of God's miracles, or who have heroically defended the Faith, in many cases dying for their faith in Christ. Saints' days fill up the Church calendar, reminding us that God acted through men and women of the past. Sainthood is often associated with those who lived in another age altogether, and yet God is as relevant now as He was in days of old. When working in Dorset as a clergyman, I used to visit a delightful school in the village of Hampreston. One of my favourite assembly hymns ran as follows:

> They lived not only in ages past,
> There are hundreds of thousands still;
> The world is bright with the joyous saints
> Who love to do Jesus' will.
> You can meet them in school, or in lanes or at sea,
> In church or in trains, or in shops or at tea;
> For the saints of God begin just like me,
> And I mean to be one too.
>
> L. Scott, 1898

The media have, to a large extent, forgotten the countless people who quietly lead godly lives. They tend to emphasize the bad news, leaving the good news as incidental. For many people, God moves among them directly, working out 'coincidences', small pushes in the right direction that are valid interventions from God. The conditions which allow miracles to flourish are, first, trust in God's promises to mankind as found in the Bible and second, a childlike certainty that God is acting on our behalf. The word of God and prayer form the environment wherein God is willing to act for our good.

The greatest impact upon mankind and creation, in terms of miracles, was made in and through the person of Jesus of Nazareth. A Jewish historian, Josephus, (AD 93) wrote about the years AD 26–30: 'There was about this time Jesus, a wise man, if indeed we should call him a man; for he was a doer of marvellous deeds, a teacher of men who received the truth with pleasure.' Here, outside the Gospel records, Jesus of Nazareth is known to be an extraordinary man who performed miracles. It is because of the signs and wonders of Jesus, two thousand years ago, that Christians believe in the miraculous today. God became flesh through Mary, a truly divine intervention. C. S. Lewis stated: 'The central miracle prepares the way for this, or results from this.'

Throughout the Bible God gives meaning to the events that occur. When Jesus fed five thousand on a grassy hillside in Galilee, He took what was offered, five barley loaves and two fishes, a picnic for one boy. Giving thanks to God, the loaves and fishes were multiplied, and all those people were more than adequately fed. With this miracle, Jesus not only provided for the immediate need, food to eat, but later in the chapter Jesus explains He is more than physical bread, He is life itself. 'I am the bread of life; he who comes to me will never be hungry' (John 6:35). We are challenged to look further than the event of five thousand people being fed, to the One who can feed us spiritually and sustain us for ever. A miracle is not to be gazed at for its own sake. It is deeper than that. A miracle is a sign that God is at work, drawing us to Himself.

Just such a miracle happened to Arthur Milnes on 17 May 1994. That afternoon he had to drive to West Yorkshire to attend a meeting to do with his work, after spending the morning in the office in Wolverhampton. He was travelling on the A38, at Clay Mills south of Derby, and had just overtaken an articulated lorry, when his car was bumped on the rear nearside. Arthur remembers: 'Everything appeared to be total chaos. My car was spinning out of control. I hit my brakes and managed to correct the spin somewhat when I ran out of road. My car was hurtling down into what seemed to me at the time a bottomless hole. In fact it turned out to be a fifteen-foot-deep ditch. The car came to a juddering halt on its side. I was aware of the engine roaring and had the presence of mind to turn it off, to minimize the risk of a fire. I sat there for a few minutes, but it seemed like much longer. I realized that my glasses were missing and saw them, unbroken, on the back seat. I undid my seat-belt and retrieved them. I was then aware of the door being wrenched open and a voice anxiously asking if I was all right. I was helped out of the car and up the steep bank to the edge of the road.'

Several cars had stopped to help, and the driver of the lorry was most apologetic. He was driving a left-hand-drive vehicle and had not seen Arthur's car before starting to pull out into the outside lane. The driver of one of the cars had a mobile phone, so the police and an ambulance were called. When they arrived, neither service could believe that Arthur had escaped totally unscathed. His car was a write-off. Such was the general amazement that a local radio reporter was dispatched to interview him.

Arthur had been brought up in the Independent Methodist church, obliged to attend chapel four times every Sunday. From the age of about eighteen he had drifted away from the church, with no strong convictions about the Christian faith, although if asked, he would have said he was a Christian. Now, at fifty-two, he felt he had wasted those years and, following the car accident, a belief grew in him that he had been spared for a reason. On 16 October, he began to attend the parish church with his wife and daughter. In February 1995 Arthur wrote: 'I can honestly say I have found what was missing in my life. In these four short months, I have rediscovered my faith, and have come to know Jesus in a way I never thought possible – as a personal friend.

'I have also discovered another "family" in the congregation of St Mary's, and through our shared faith I now have a deeper and more loving relationship with my wife, Pam. How on earth she put up with me all these years I will never know – another miracle! My wife was already confirmed, but I had the joy of confirming my faith this month alongside Debbie, my daughter. My uncle, another Arthur, attended the confirmation service and said to me: "I have waited thirty years for this day." So have I, Uncle, so have I.'

Whenever God chooses to intervene in a person's life to change it, or to heal someone of a disease whether physical or mental, something of His glory is seen. Glory is literally an unveiling of God; in essence, what He is really like. The glory of God is expressed in miracles: God acts like a shaft of sunlight coming through the clouds.

Prilla Rowland, who lives in Sussex, had an experience like this. She writes: 'One autumn morning in 1983, we sat down to breakfast as a family before our three lively boys hurtled off to school and my husband, Richard, drove to his work as a GP. It was another normal day, except for the fact that depression, along with panic and anxiety, had dogged me for several months. Simple tasks like shopping at the supermarket became as daunting as Everest. Counselling had given support and valuable insight, and pills had helped, but I was still in a dark tunnel.' Knowing Prilla as we have for many years, we know how stable and cheerful she normally is, and just how foreign to her this depression must have been.

'Before the family dispersed each day,' Prilla continues, 'we always read a very short passage from the Bible and prayed together. Today it was my turn to read, from Luke 13. It was the account of how Jesus noticed a crippled lady across the crowd and called out to her that she was set free from her illness or "spirit of infirmity". As I read it aloud, it was as if Jesus were calling across the crowd to me that I, too, was being set free from my crippling depression. After the bustle of the family leaving the house, I sat down in the kitchen to think about that reading. It was so unexpected. Was it true that my healing had begun?'

Prilla recalls: 'A little while later, my mother-in-law popped in with a bag of bulbs to plant, and as I busied myself burying them in the soft dark earth, anticipating a marvellous display of hyacinths in the spring, I suddenly had a thought. These bulbs were like a visual aid from God. My healing had begun, but, like the bulbs, it would take time to appear; it would not be visible at first, but by the spring, we would have some evidence. And so it was. I received specific prayer for healing, and the gaps between the dark and anxious times got longer and longer. By the spring, I knew I was well. Twelve years have gone by since then, and there has been no recurrence of the depression.'

In each miracle, a person meets with the Author of creation. There is an authentic touch which remains on that person's life for ever. But there will always be sceptics. They will quite rightly examine the evidence before them. One cannot purport to have experienced a touch from God without some critical reappraisal of the facts. Fact must always be separated from fiction. Meeting God is an experience which produces in a person an inner conviction that resonates in the heart and mind and stands up to examination.

For instance, Alexander Solzhenitsyn, the great Russian writer and Nobel prizewinner, is a prophet of our day. His Christian faith was formed in the crucible of suffering. While serving as an officer in the Russian army in 1945, he was arrested for his opposition to the despotic Stalinist regime. Banished with millions of others to a forced-labour camp in Siberia, and suffering from inoperable cancer, his faith in God grew stronger. Miraculously healed, he has lived to speak a powerfully prophetic word not only to his own beloved nation, but also to the Western world.

Hope and I go away together twice a year to a retreat house, simply to escape the busyness of life and to be refreshed. One of the retreat houses we visit near Ascot is called 'Encounter'. This word sums up for me what happens to those who experience a miracle. It is an encounter with God which imparts a real sense of being known and loved by Him. People who have known God in this way are willing to talk about this experience: their encounter with God has profoundly influenced their lives.

CHAPTER TWO

Who Needs a Miracle?

Miracles are explosions of God's power, which defy
His normal laws of nature.

John Noble,
Everyman's Guide to the Holy Spirit

O ONE CAN BE forced to believe in miracles,
but to experience 'the real thing' is so stupendous that those who have not only believe, but
share it with others. Miracles challenge our
earthly way of thinking and believing; they
show us that God loves us to the point where He is willing to
step in and rescue us, even in life-threatening situations.

From 1978, Harvey Thomas was the public relations and
special projects consultant to the Conservative Party. His task in
the autumn of 1984 was to organize the Conservative Party
Conference in Brighton. In the early hours of 12 October 1984,
the last day of the Conference, an IRA bomb exploded in the
Grand Hotel where Mrs Thatcher and most of the Cabinet
members were staying. The bomb went off in Room 629,
immediately below Harvey's room on the seventh floor. 'The first
thing I knew,' remembers Harvey, 'was that I was going up.
Fortunately the ceiling went up ahead of me, so I didn't hit it.
Then the ceiling and I started coming down, and when I got to
where my room had been, it wasn't there any more.' While
travelling upward Harvey thought, 'Maybe it's an earthquake!'
but his next thought was, 'No, not in Brighton. Certainly not
during a Tory Party Conference!'

Harvey was alert, and instinctively put up his hands to form a protective air pocket for his nose and mouth. Convinced he was sure to die, he prayed quickly as he fell through three storeys. Harvey's fall was broken by a girder sticking out over a five-storey drop. Then a ten-ton load of rubble came down on top of him from the floors above. His eyes were shut and he could not move, except for one foot and that only slightly. A committed Christian, he recalls saying aloud, 'Lord, I've *really* got to trust you now.' Everything was still for a moment, then there was another terrific crash as a chimney fell past him, missing him by a mere two feet. Then he heard water gushing and fire-bells ringing. The water was from the fractured cold-water tanks in the roof, pouring down through the rubble, bringing with it bits of dirty masonry, which rained into Harvey's mouth and nose, causing him to choke. Fortunately his hands were in a position to prevent most of it going down his throat. There was such a weight on his chest, however, that it was difficult to breathe. With several feet of rubble on top of him, he could only wait for rescuers to reach him. 'All I had to do was lie still and wait, and God gave me the strength and peace to do just that.'

Harvey was not in serious pain. He did not feel numb and could tell he had no broken bones. He was glad that his wife, Marlies, was safe in London: she was expecting their first baby any day. The baby was already five days overdue, but Marlies would not hear a news broadcast about the explosion for several hours. The fire-bells rang on and on for more than an hour, then, hearing voices, Harvey yelled for help with all the strength he could muster. After the second yell, he heard a man shout: 'There's someone alive in there! Shout again! Where are you?' Two firemen, Mick Ayling and Ken Towner, kept up a conversation with him while they masterminded a rescue plan. Another eighteen firemen were helping to move rubble and fetch the necessary equipment for each stage of the rescue. Sheared electricity cables flashed and crackled in the pouring water. The precarious pile of rubble on top of Harvey could have fallen a further five storeys at any moment. Water was still pouring over him, making him cold, and the weight of the rubble became much heavier as it was saturated.

While under the rubble Harvey was thinking, 'I bear no personal bitterness towards the people who set off the bomb. In God's eyes they are fallen, just like anyone who does not know salvation.' As they got nearer, the firemen shone a torch towards Harvey, asking him, 'Can you see the light?' Ever-alert, Harvey called out: 'I saw the light long ago, brother, but I can't see yours yet.' They got a hydraulic jack and lifted the weight off Harvey's chest. At last he could breathe properly. Two firemen grabbed his arms, and other firemen held on to them. They all pulled while Harvey pushed, popping out like a rabbit from a hole, a few grazes sustained from the tight exit, but otherwise unhurt. He was released at 5.25 a.m.; the blast had been at 2.54 a.m. The last part of the rescue, having been filmed by ITN, was shown frequently on television during the day.

Harvey was taken by ambulance to hospital for a check-up. He phoned Marlies to ask her to come down by train, bringing him some clothes. He is eighteen and a half stone, and at that time of the morning there were no clothes available to fit him. Wrapped in a blanket, he answered questions at a press conference, which went out on Breakfast TV. He was filthy from all the rubble, and had to have six baths and wash his hair four times. After the first two baths, the nurses had to scrape the debris out of the bath – it was too much to go down the plughole!

When Marlies arrived from London there was a joyful reunion, then Harvey got dressed to go to the conference centre where he was given a warm welcome. Later Mrs Thatcher, in an interview about the bombing, said: 'Then, bless his golden heart, Harvey Thomas came into the room. He had been trapped under the rubble, but there he was. I was just so thankful that someone who had been through all those last terrible hours, could still be so remarkably cheerful and keep going.' The only things which were discovered intact from Harvey's room were his watch, found on the third floor, still ticking, and his Bible, battered but complete. Six days later, Harvey was in attendance when Marlies gave birth to their daughter, Leah Elisabeth.

On 6 May 1976 Satchitanand Rath, an Indian air-force pilot, also had a miraculous escape from a major accident. He was piloting a Dakota carrying thirteen passengers and crew and a full military consignment. It was a bright, clear day as the plane took off from Guahati to fly the five hours to Delhi. The plane was reliable, having been certified airworthy by the engineers and rechecked by the pilot. When all the vital checks had been made for take-off, Satchitanand said a brief prayer, as he always did before a flight: 'Lord, You be the pilot of this plane.'

All the instruments indicated that operations were normal, but, a few seconds after take-off, the plane started shaking violently and passengers shouted, 'Fire! Fire!' There was no indication of it in the fire warning system, but the co-pilot was able to confirm that there was a fire in the right engine. One propeller blade had suddenly come out of its hub and pierced the right side of the fuselage, breaking the fuel lines and catching fire. The pilot immediately shut off the engines and guided the plane back on to the runway. As the plane touched down, it behaved 'like a monster' and was most difficult to keep under control. The right wheel had burnt out, so the pilot struggled to stop the plane on the short portion of runway left, as it would easily have ignited the dry 'elephant grass' all around the runway.

Seeing the flames spreading, the passengers opened the main door while the plane was still rolling and jumped out, causing minor injuries. The navigator and the co-pilot also jumped clear the moment the plane came to a halt. The pilot was the last to leave the plane and, as he did so, there was a huge blast as it broke in two. It took nearly four hours for the fire brigade to get the fire under control. When the crew were able to approach the plane again, the front right half of the plane had been reduced to ashes, and the tail portion had melted due to the intense heat. The Hindu navigator, Ashok Chitre, poking through the ashes which had been their luggage, called out: 'We were saved because of this.' He brought out the pilot's leather-bound Bible which had survived intact. The aircrew suitcase, which was supposed to be fire-resistant, and everything else inside it, were completely destroyed. As the pilot knelt in gratitude to God, he opened the Bible and his eyes fell on the words 'The Lord bless thee and keep thee', the verse that had been selected for him when he was given the Bible at his baptism. The Bible was the only item of luggage which survived.

Owing to its low speed and low altitude at the time of the fire, the plane should have been sent into a spiral dive to the ground. In the twenty-six years of his aviation career, Satchitanand had not heard of anyone surviving a similar crash. He is convinced they were all saved by a miracle. The incident left him in no doubt that God is living, ready to save those who put their trust in Him. 'When you walk through the fire, you will not be burned; the flames will not set you ablaze' (Isaiah 43:2).

It was also in India that Luise Clutterbuck experienced a miracle. At the time she was with a team of about sixteen YWAM (Youth With A Mission) young people, talking about the Gospel in various towns. They had been in Madras and then felt they should go to another town called Chittor. They did not know where they would stay, but prayed they would meet other Christians. Luise remembers: 'After one night in a hotel, a lovely Indian Christian lady came up to us saying that God had told her, in a dream she'd had a few months previously, to expect a lot of white people, and that she should get her house ready for us. So we went with her and there was room for us all to stay. God was with us as we witnessed for Him, and many people in that town made a decision to turn to Jesus'.

It is easy to think that you will never personally see a miracle, but you may remember occasions when something unexplained has happened. C. S. Lewis in his book *Miracles* writes: 'God does not shake miracles into nature at random, as if from a pepper caster.' Miracles occur for a purpose. Coleridge wrote that 'chance is but the pseudonym for God in those particular cases in which He does not choose to give His own signature openly'. Miracles seem larger than life but are inside our day-to-day routine. When they happen, we are made to sit up and take notice.

When a man who has been a soldier and a policeman has an unexplained experience, it makes you stop and think. On 23 July 1993, Peter Starr was driving home from work in Reading along the M4 motorway at about 7 p.m. There had been torrential rain, so he kept his speed to about 50 m.p.h.

'I was in the inside lane,' Peter remembers, 'when, with no warning, my car made a sharp right-angle turn. Immediately I cried out "Jesus save me", which I had never done before. The front of my car just missed by inches the back of a car travelling in the middle lane. My vehicle turned two complete circles across the three lanes of the motorway and ended up in the fast lane, facing the hard shoulder, with the engine still going. There had been traffic all around me, but it was as if a giant hand had pushed all the traffic back, so there was a sizeable gap between me and the oncoming traffic. I started puttering towards the hard shoulder. As I approached the inside lane, there was an army Land-Rover bearing down on me, the driver frantically braking. (A flash thought was that this was where I would get killed by a former comrade!) The Land-Rover pulled up just short of me, at the moment my engine cut out. A second later a heavy pick-up lorry came thundering past on the hard shoulder, which I had not been able to see, behind the Land-Rover. If my car had kept going, I would have gone under it and been killed. The moment it was past, my engine started again spontaneously and I reached the hard shoulder in safety.'

Peter got out and walked around his car, which was not at all damaged. The car started again easily and Peter continued his journey without a problem. 'As I started to drive off, these words came very strongly into my mind: 'Now do you doubt My power?' The night before I had been expressing to my wife, Lynne, all manner of doubts about Christ's acceptance of me. This experience wiped away all my doubts. I am not one of these "super-spiritual" beings who seem to receive words from the Lord with ease. It had been a struggle for me to have faith in Jesus, since my turning to Him the year before. But these words were so strong that they stayed with me. I knew it was Jesus speaking to me.'

In a world where our spiritual antennae are dulled by materialism, all the memorable encounters of the Gospels stand as a symbol of the encounters Jesus wants with us today, bringing healing, forgiveness and new life. Jesus is forever seeking to draw our attention to the overriding truth that God loves us. Jesus could have caught our attention by throwing Himself from a high tower so the angels would rescue Him, as Satan tempted Him to do in Luke 4. Imagine the talk in Jerusalem that day! But Jesus repudiated these stunts, not wishing to do the miraculous for the wrong reasons. The focus of the Gospels is summed up in the entrance of 'the man who was God'. The great miracles of the Old Testament take on flesh in the New, through Jesus of Nazareth. The Red Sea was parted for the Hebrews to walk across; Jesus walked on water. Moses struck a rock from which water gushed for the thirsty Hebrews; Jesus turned water into wine at a wedding celebration.

In Africa, finding spare parts for vehicles to keep them functioning can be a real problem. Margaret Phillips, a Leprosy Mission worker, had a miraculous experience that she records in her diary on 23 June 1975. Margaret was working at Kumi Leprosy Centre in eastern Uganda during the time when Idi Amin's regime was making life very difficult for the British and, as a result, there were serious shortages all round. Margaret and a colleague headed for Amudat, a mission hospital 130 miles away, where all the missionaries were meeting together for a rare weekend break.

After a refreshing and encouraging time together, Margaret and her colleague set off to return to Kumi. They had not gone far when their Volkswagen car ran into trouble, so they turned back to Amudat. They prayed about the situation, but were not very optimistic of finding a mechanic in Amudat, which consisted of two rows of mud houses. They found a man called Daudi Cheptwai, who looked under the bonnet. Margaret says: 'I did not hold out much hope, since I had experienced Turkana tribesmen doing the same thing, and they were merely fascinated as they had never seen inside a car before!'

Daudi discovered that the distributor cap was cracked, and he disappeared into his mud house. When he returned he was dusting off a distributor cap which he clipped effortlessly into place. He had salvaged it from another car the previous week, and said they could give him a few shillings if they wanted to. The likelihood of there being the spare part needed for their particular make of car in this tiny remote village was for them a miracle. The car performed perfectly. Margaret continues: 'When we got back to the Centre, we made sure that the next person going to Kampala or Nairobi bought a new distributor cap, as we felt this one might not last long. Although we gave the details of the vehicle, the cap that was purchased in an actual VW garage in Kampala did not fit, and it was impossible to find one at all in Nairobi. A year later, when I left the Centre, the vehicle was still working well with the distributor cap which had been found in such an unlikely setting.'

Esther Lever from Southampton and her companions also had car problems when they were driving to Nagorno-Karabakh, to help and encourage the people there, in November 1994. It was Esther's fifth visit to Armenia, and on this journey she was with two Armenian drivers and a Czechoslovakian young woman. They had to cross three mountain ranges and it had been snowing heavily. Going up the second mountain range, the snow and ice were much worse.

Esther explains: 'Rounding a bend, we faced a very steep icy slope where several tankers had already halted. We watched as one after another tried the slope, only to slip backward, stopping in the deeper snow at the side of the road. We backed down to a safer place, deciding to drink some coffee and wait. Our driver was outside talking to other drivers when a large truck started up the hill. Near the top, this one also lost its grip and began to slide back. Soon out of control, it zigzagged dangerously, gaining speed and coming straight towards us. The two drivers leapt out of the cab. Our front passenger leapt out, and the young woman Vlasta and I, in the back seat, tried in vain to find the door-handles. It all happened so quickly, but I remember saying, "This will crush us . . . I can't get out . . . Jesus, help us." Then the truck stopped dead. It was the most amazing thing. One second it was about to hit us and then it stopped, just like that. The men came running to see what had happened, but there was no logical explanation. No rocks, no snow-heap, nothing in the way. The Lord had saved our lives.'

As Esther and her friends continued their journey, the weather and the state of the road steadily deteriorated. Four times the car stopped, resisting all human effort, but each time they prayed and it started again. As darkness fell, they arrived in Stepanakert, the capital city of Nagorno-Karabakh. The car finally stopped for good, within walking distance of the house to which they were going. They took aid to Christians there to distribute to others in need, and acquainted themselves with any new needs that could be met with the next delivery.

Unable to buy the necessary part to repair the car, they travelled back to Armenia by bus, which took sixteen hours. Two young men then bought the CV joint to repair the car and returned to it by bus. They replaced the part, but the car still would not start. They then found that another CV joint was needed on the other side of the car. They prayed, 'Lord, if You will start this car, we will drive it over the mountains and trust You to get us back.' The car started, they drove carefully and reached Yerevan, their destination, in eight hours. When the mechanics saw the car, they asked, 'How on earth did you drive this car? There is no way it could go, it can't be driven.' As Esther said, 'Well it did, and it was, and we were there to prove it.'

In another Eastern European country Anthea Disney was part of a team taking aid by lorry to Romania. When the team stopped at an orphanage, the driver inadvertently locked his keys in the lorry. With no spare keys, the driver was in a real dilemma as to what to do. He was an atheist, but knew Anthea was a Christian, and asked her to pray about the situation. After praying, Anthea felt she should try the front-door key of her house back home in Malvern. It seemed a crazy idea, as the lorry keys and the house keys were not at all similar. She tried the door key in the lock and it opened the lorry door easily, and the driver was able to retrieve the lorry keys.

The next day Anthea thought how unusual the solution had been and tried the same key again. It would not even fit into the keyhole, let alone turn the lock. On another trip to Romania, their lorry ran out of diesel; in Romania there are many miles between filling stations. With diesel, one normally has to bleed the fuel system before refilling, but they did not have time for that. They just tipped in more diesel and the lorry drove perfectly. Anthea knew that on both these occasions, God had intervened to help.

Another couple who had a miraculous experience on the road were Jim and June Rawson, who live near Salisbury, Wiltshire. They were visiting June's sister Flo and her husband Ron in Canada in 1987, and had a wonderful ten-day holiday. To get to

Toronto airport for the return flight, they decided to leave Ron and Flo's home around 6 p.m. to allow plenty of time for the drive to the airport and checking in. Just before leaving, they heard on the radio that there had been a major four-lane accident on the only route from their home to Toronto airport, called the QE1 motorway.

Ron telephoned the police for further information. The police confirmed the news, adding that there would be no possibility of driving to the airport that night. All emergency services were at the scene, and they insisted it would be hours before the motorway would be in use again. Then came a telephone call from Ron's son-in-law, who had just returned home along the opposite carriageway of the motorway. He was ringing to warn them of the pile-up in the other lane, saying there was no point in even trying to get to the airport.

Jim said: 'June and I went into the bedroom to pray, as we were anxious that we would not be able to catch our flight at 10 p.m. Then Ron said, "Let's go now." No one asked questions as we got into the car and headed for the QE1 motorway. What happened next was so amazing that, to this day, June and I still talk about it with wonder. We did not see any vehicle driving along the QE1 motorway. There was no sign of any accident and before long we reached the airport with time to spare. We said our farewells, then Flo and Ron drove home. We travelled uneventfully to England and the next day received an excited telephone call from Flo in Canada. On their drive home along the opposite carriageway of the same QE1 motorway, all four lanes were blocked by a major accident, with all the emergency services in attendance, exactly as the traffic news, the police and their son-in-law had reported earlier. Yet ,in between, we had travelled the same road traffic-free.

'We cannot explain how it happened: we only know how we felt as we travelled along the motorway. It was so silent and unusually calm, as if we were being transported in time in answer to our prayer.' It was a wonderful blessing for Jim and June, who are both committed Christians.

Michael Bromfield, rector of Hope Bowdler in Shropshire, also had an unusual experience while driving his car. One evening he was driving home past Wall-under-Heywood when he knew he had to stop. He asked 'What is it, Lord?' and, although he did not actually hear a voice, he felt he had to turn the car round and go back. Michael felt compelled to turn right and right again and stop outside a certain house. He did not know the occupants, and reasoned that it was not good manners to knock on the door of strangers after 9 p.m., but he felt he was being directed to do so. When the door was opened Michael said, 'I'm the new rector. I don't know why I've called, but I knew I had to come.' The couple looked stunned, but invited him in. They said, 'Well, that is remarkable. Exactly twelve months ago, to this very hour, our son was killed in a road accident.' The rector said, 'God wants you to know that He still loves you.' They had tea together, and a lovely conversation arose from that unusual inner prompting.

Sometimes a death can cause great suffering to other members of that person's family. Fraser Dickson was very distressed when his elder brother Francis was killed by a drunk driver at the age of twenty-three. Fraser was nineteen at the time, and for the previous four years had been very unhappy. He was a sensitive child who had not settled well at boarding school. He was desperately lonely, and had failed all his exams although he was intelligent. At seventeen he had run away and spent some time 'living rough' in London, though his family background was privileged.

Following Francis's death, it was discovered that Fraser had schizophrenia, and he was treated over the next eleven years in various psychiatric hospitals, often in locked wards, as he was a danger to himself. He was heavily medicated with tablets and injections, had sixty treatments of electroconvulsive therapy, suffered from hallucinations and heard imaginary voices. The effect of schizophrenia on the patient and their family can be most distressing, especially in acute phases of the illness. In two of these severe times Fraser tried to commit suicide by taking massive alcohol and drug overdoses. Each time he was admitted to an intensive care unit and would spend several days and nights unconscious. During these years his mother, a great aunt and his mother's oldest friend prayed regularly for Fraser's healing. The only surviving woman, the friend, Mrs May Griffith-Edwards, has confirmed Fraser's story. She wrote: 'As we lived in a different part of the country, I did not actually see him at that sad time, but his dear mother often made very distressing phone calls, telling me of his most irrational behaviour. Over that period he was in and out of psychiatric hospitals.'

At the age of twenty-three, Fraser met a lovely Christian cockney family in the East End of London and accepted Jesus into his life in their back parlour. However within two months, he was suffering an acute phase of schizophrenia. After another six years of various treatments he met, in Camberley, Surrey, an Anglican vicar, John Rawlings, who told him that God could heal him from schizophrenia, although doctors had not yet found a cure. John Rawlings' own wife, Helen, had been healed of it after seventeen years of suffering, and they both now exercised a ministry to others with mental illness, through the Acorn Healing Trust.

Fraser went to stay with John and Helen, and was prayed for several weeks. At times he was aggressive and paranoid, but he gradually received healing. He was also set free from evil spirits, which it was discovered had entered Fraser when he was a young child whilst staying with his uncle, a spiritualist. Fraser received much healing, but it was a battle, and it became too much for him. On his thirtieth birthday he ran away and travelled to Exeter. He was paranoid, and phoned the police, saying some Christians were trying to poison him. The police picked him up and, realizing he was mentally ill, they locked him up, until they were able to deliver him to the secure ward of a psychiatric hospital.

Several weeks later, when Fraser was much better, he discovered that another patient, a Christian, was regularly given a lift to a Christian fellowship at Countess Wear, near Exeter. Fraser went with him and was given much prayer and practical love over the following weeks. He gained greater understanding of how to praise God from Merlin Carothers's book *From Prison to Praise.* On 23 June 1977, while praising God, Fraser gave God all the years of his illness, saying that he could live with the suffering if it was His will.

Fraser recalls what happened next: 'I saw and felt a dark cloud rise from my head, saw a shimmering light and experienced a deep and intense heat in my head. It was the Holy Spirit at work in me. The consultant put my change down to a "mood swing", and would not cut my medication.' However when he was discharged from hospital five weeks later, Fraser believed he had been healed and that the Lord wanted him to stop all medication and treatment. Fraser's local doctor was willing to take him off the drugs on a trial basis, two weeks at a time, whilst closely monitoring his progress, and in August 1977 he ceased all treatment. While still in hospital, Fraser phoned John and Helen, who drove from Surrey the same day to visit him. They, and a group of Christians meeting together in Camberley, had continued to pray for him. Fraser was so renewed as a person that they hardly recognized the young man who strode into the room.

Since then, Fraser has been completely well, and has passed GCE O- and A-levels, City and Guilds exams, an RSA certificate and a diploma in Information Technology. He has married a lovely wife, Caroline, and they are involved in Christian ministry. Most recently he has passed his driving test which he thought would never be a possibility for him, because of the way his brother died and because of his illness. He has even been healed of after-effects of the ECT treatments and the massive overdoses he took, which could have caused lasting brain damage. He has had no recurrence at all of schizophrenia for the past seventeen years, and praises God for His healing power, love and grace.

David Lillie, the pastor of the Countess Wear Fellowship Fraser attended when he was in Exeter, wrote: 'I made the acquaintance of a man who had been a male nurse in the hospital where Fraser lived during those years and who was in close and constant attendance on Fraser. This man was an avowed atheist, yet when I told him Fraser had been completely healed, he exclaimed that his healing was nothing short of a miracle. He told me that Fraser was so severely affected, he was one of the last people he would have expected to recover from his illness.'

Mrs May Griffith-Edwards, who had prayed for Fraser all those years, wrote: 'Since his miraculous healing, I have seen Fraser several times, for hours at a time, and on each occasion he has been entirely normal. He has corresponded with me in the most intelligent letters and has a firm Christian faith.' The letters we have received from these sources confirm Fraser's own testimony of healing.

In their book *Requiem Healing: A Christian Understanding of the Dead*, Michael Mitton and Russ Parker help to put into perspective the death of a loved one. They write of the funeral of a young mother whose husband was a minister. 'The cortège entered the church with the husband and their five-year-old daughter walking side by side. The address was given by the widower who began his talk by saying, "I don't know why God let my wife suffer so much pain and die like she did in that car crash. I wish I did. I don't know why He let us move house only to have Ann die three months later. I don't know why." Then he went on to say, "But I do know this: that Jesus died for us all, and rose again. That Jesus promised eternal life to all those who trust in Him. And what I do know helps me to live with what I don't know." Here was hurt and hope being given equal expression.

'It is this voicing of feeling and faith which brings balance to the journey of dying and which gives us a better opportunity to let go of the dying and learn to free them into God's hands. It is this letting go at dying and death that prevents any unhealthy holding on to the dead.'

Michael Mitton and Russ Parker also give insight into the term 'the unquiet dead'. They write: 'It [the expression "the unquiet dead"] does not fit neatly into our established ways of thinking about death and the afterlife.' They draw on a report called *Deliverance* by Michael Perry, suggesting that 'appearances of the spirits of the dead [are] the souls of those departed this life who are not at rest, and are therefore said to be "unquiet".' We have found that in our own ministry we have developed a much greater understanding of our responsibility at a funeral service to commend the soul to God. This is like pushing a boat from this shore to the opposite side, releasing the deceased from this world for God to deal with for eternity. A funeral is not only ministry to the bereaved, but also the committing of a soul into God's hands.

The 'unquiet dead' may be those who have not received a proper funeral, passing them into the hands of God. They are not necessarily in an unwholesome or evil predicament. They could have died in battle, or as a result of famine when hundreds died and were thrown into communal graves. The souls of these dead are trapped in this world, trying to attract attention as a cry for help to be released.

Alternatively, someone may have been given a proper funeral, but they personally wanted to hang on to this life, because of 'unfinished business' before they died. The result is that these people may be 'dead but not departed', continuing to be part of this world, and so haunting the living. They may habitually haunt a particular place they were connected with, or harass later generations of their own family through hereditary illness or emotional problems. Some houses have been regularly visited by 'ghosts', because no one has realized that they need to be permitted to go on their way to eternity. This releasing of a soul can be done by a group of people praying, by name if it is known, to commit the soul into the hands of God, ideally with a priest celebrating Holy Communion at the place where the ghost has been seen.

For generations the Bermuda Triangle, an area of the Atlantic Ocean near the West Indies, has been known as a place where vessels of all sizes have regularly sunk without trace. Many people have reported that engines have mysteriously cut out when in this area, and inexplicable noises have been heard in the eerie stillness. Aircraft pilots have told of their navigation instruments going berserk when flying over the same portion of the sea, and some have been unable to regain control and crashed into the sea. The Bermuda Triangle was first described by Vincent Gaddis in 1964 who claimed: 'This relatively small area is the scene of disappearances that go far beyond the laws of chance.'

Dr Kenneth McAll was a consultant psychiatrist for thirty-five years, and in his book *Healing the Family Tree* he tells of his experience in the Sargasso Sea. In January 1977 Dr McAll and his wife Frances were passengers on a small cargo ship heading for Jamaica, which was caught in an Atlantic storm. To try to avoid the worst of it, the ship steered south, where the sea was calmer, but one of the ship's boilers burst. This sprayed those on deck with water from the funnel and delayed the progress of the ship for two more days. Dr McAll remembers: 'As we drifted gently in the warm and steamy atmosphere, I became aware of a continuous sound, like mournful singing. It was particularly clear when we were in our cabin. I thought it must be a record-player in the crew's quarters and as it continued through a second night, finally in exasperation I went below to ask if it could be stopped. However the sound down there was the same as it was everywhere else, and the crew were equally mystified. On the third day the engines were restarted and we slowly made our way to Jamaica.'

'The incident was forgotten,' Dr McAll reports, 'until, on my return home, I started to read about the Bermuda Triangle and the history of that area. By chance I found a book on the lawsuits of insurance companies against British sea captains in the eighteenth century, who had been found to have thrown live slaves overboard, emptying their ships in order to make quicker journeys back to Britain. They received more money from insurance claims than from selling the slaves in the cotton fields. It was an extraordinary and cruel affair.' Dr McAll read that it was especially those slaves who were ill after the long sea journey from Africa, who would be dispensed with as they would not fetch a good price in the slave market.

Dr McAll discussed the matter with other Christians and they decided to hold a Communion service, asking forgiveness of God for what their ancestors had done. Dr McAll says, 'This we did, and following the service, three bishops in the north of England publicized these events to encourage other churches to pray in the same way, and to pray for those who had died so cruelly, committing them into the hands of God. This was in June 1977. A few weeks after the service, an American newspaper contacted me, inquiring about what had made the instances in the seas and skies of the Bermuda Triangle suddenly cease. Six months later, there had been no further unexplained incidents. At the end of the year, the Bishop of Bermuda proposed a similar service to be held in the cathedral, and another was held out at sea. The bishop set up a scientific team to monitor any accidents. I contacted the Florida coastguard who informed me that up to June 1977 an average of one ship a month and one aeroplane every thirteen months had been lost. The last one to vanish had been a large Japanese cargo vessel in apparently calm weather.'

Ten and a half years later, the Australian Broadcasting Company researched a programme of unexplained happenings in the Bermuda Triangle, and found that there had been none since those Christian services had been held. Dr McAll concludes: 'If all those disasters could be explained by natural causes, why should a Holy Communion service apparently bring it all to an end? Surely it must be that those slaves who had had no funeral, and who had weighed down the ships that crossed the spot where they died, had at last been released into the hands of God.' It is now eighteen years since the last unexplained disappearance.

It has often been in the area of finance that God has performed a miracle. Numerous Christian organizations and individuals can testify to the fact that money for a particular project or personal need has been prayed for and exactly the right amount has arrived at just the right time.

When the present Archbishop of Canterbury, George Carey, was vicar of St Nicholas's Church, Durham, an ambitious plan was put forward to refurbish the inside of the church. This would enable the church, which stood in a strategic position in the city market-place, to provide a caring Christian centre. The vision was to share the Christian life with others, as well as to make the worship of God alive and relevant. Once the plan had been accepted, there was the matter of finance to consider. A Gift Day to be held on Easter Day was announced for St Nicholas's congregation only, before any appeal for funds was made outside the church. The congregation was not a wealthy one. A former churchwarden told the vicar, 'I recall that on many occasions I counted a total of seven or eight pounds in the collection.' As vicar, George Carey was only too aware of the diversity of the congregation; the hesitation of some, the poverty of many, the resistance of a few, as well as the dedication of others.

On the Gift Day, the congregation was asked to give through covenants, direct donations or pledges to be paid within a year. They had no idea how much would come in, but the future of the plan depended on what was received. The collection was counted during coffee after the morning service, and most people waited to hear the total. Voices were hushed when Geoff Moore, the churchwarden, announced: 'Everyone will be pleased to know that the giving this morning amounts to £99,942.' Gasps of amazement echoed around the church and the delighted members spontaneously started to sing 'Praise God from whom all blessings flow'. By the end of the day, the total had risen to £101,500. George Carey remembers 'the sense of awe, the wonder and jubilation! We now knew for sure that God wanted us to go ahead.'

Sometimes the Lord intervenes in a personal way. John and Christine Noble work full time in Christian ministry, based in Surrey with an organization called Pioneer. However in the early days of their ministry they had no organization or specific church supporting them, and they relied on God, through the generosity of others, to meet their daily needs. One morning Christine dressed the children, put them in the pram and made a note of all the food she would need to buy for the next few days. It was in the days before decimal coinage and all she had was a ten-shilling note. Christine tried to prune the list again, to limit it to the money available. It was an impossible task. So she went shopping with Jesus and a prayer.

In the grocer's shop, Christine made the necessary purchases, handed over the ten-shilling note and put the change she was given into her purse. She had no other money in her purse, but when she counted the coins to see how much she had left to spend, it still added up to ten shillings. She checked the coins again and again, but it was the same each time. She spent that same ten shillings several times over. Christine remembers: 'I still had the same amount in the greengrocer's, the baker's and the shoe-repair shop, and then the money ran out. I can't explain what happened, but I know God did it.'

Another couple who work for God and look to Him to

provide for their needs are Richard and Michelle. They are currently working for a Christian organization, 'Youth With a Mission', helping homeless people in London. They have often experienced amazing provision by God in the area of finance. In 1987 their car was in constant need of repair, and costing a lot of money. Feeling that this was not a wise way to use their money, Richard and Michelle asked God to give them a newer car. They hoped it would be a gift to them, so that the sale of their old car would help to finance a visit to Canada. Michelle's family live there, and they hoped to visit them at Christmastime. They already had two small children, and would by then have a third baby to show to the family.

A Christian mechanic offered Richard and Michelle a ten-year-old estate car, which he promised to make roadworthy for them. When the time came for Richard to drive to a conference, they hoped he would be able to use the newer car, leaving the older one for Michelle, who was by now in the late stages of pregnancy. Richard phoned the mechanic, but the estate car would not be ready for some time. As Richard replaced the receiver, he had a sense that this was not to be the car for them, but that God had another one in mind. Five minutes later the phone rang, and a lady they knew asked if they were looking for a car. Her husband had been given a company car, and they had been trying to sell their two-year-old car, but no one had responded to their advertisement. Would they accept it as a gift? It was an answer to prayer. They later discovered that the car was worth three and a half thousand pounds.

Richard and Michelle tried to sell their old car, but to no avail. Sadly, they decided they would have to give it away, sacrificing their trip to Canada. Within days of giving the car to someone, an envelope was delivered to their home containing an anonymous gift. It was enough money to pay for flights, insurance and spending-money for all five of them to visit Canada.

In 1986 a lady called Margaret, unemployed and particularly hard up, was worried about a fuel bill she could not pay. She prayed earnestly about it one night and felt compelled to turn on the light, open her Bible and read a verse that spoke about faith. Next morning there was a cheque in the post which exactly covered the fuel bill. It was an unexpected gift from someone, who did not know about the bill. Margaret had not been a Christian long then. She believes that the Lord has met this, and subsequent needs, because she has obeyed the Biblical instruction to give at least one tenth of her income to God's work. This she has continued to do, both in those days when she was hard up and now that she is in a more comfortable situation.

William Hayles was running his parents' pet shop in Prestatyn, and finances were tight. One Tuesday in November 1993 he needed £150 to pay for a delivery first thing on the Wednesday morning. From Monday morning to four o'clock on Tuesday, the takings were only £80. William looked like being in the embarrassing position of not being able to pay the supplier, so he looked to God to help him. Just then a customer came in, asking if a sack of dog food had arrived. William promised it would be there in the morning and was surprised when he was offered payment for it in advance. That had never happened before. William says, 'The atmosphere was electric over the next hour and a half, and I could feel the presence of God with me in the shop. During that time, five more customers came in for orders and each one paid in advance. When I tilled up, I had exactly £150, the amount needed for the delivery. As if to prove He is sovereign, God worked exactly the same miracle again three months later.'

Stephen Poxon is a member of the Salvation Army, currently training to be an officer at their London college. In 1991 his rather battered old car needed repairs estimated at £250, to pass its MOT. He needed the car for work, but had nothing like the money required, so he prayed. A couple of days later Stephen received a letter from John in Cumbria. He had once worked with John on a part-time basis, so did not know him well. In his time of prayer, the Holy Spirit had told John, 'Stephen Poxon needs money for car repairs.' His letter was to check with Stephen whether he had heard correctly. Stephen telephoned to say that this was spot on, but that he was reluctant to present him with such a large expense. John dismissed his reluctance and a cheque for £250 arrived by the end of the week, and the car was spared!

Joe Smith was born and raised in a gypsy wagon in Lancashire. Five years ago he became a Christian, and now makes regular visits with his wife to Eastern Europe with supplies and Bibles. Recently a friend, Jean Groves, asked how the money was coming in for the next visit in three weeks' time. Joe said that they had not received any money yet, but he was not worrying about it. 'It is God's work and He knows the need. He will supply,' Joe said. That same evening Joe was speaking at an Assemblies of God church in Leek, and was given a cheque for £550 – a quick answer to prayer!

Joe has seen other miracles since he became a Christian. Once he was in intensive care after a severe heart attack in which, he was told, three-quarters of his heart had been damaged. He had been smoking a hundred cigarettes a day, and the first thing he asked for when he came out of a semi-coma was a cigarette. He was told he could not smoke in hospital, and since that day God has taken away Joe's desire to smoke. Indeed, much to his doctor's amazement, he has not smoked at all since then. He still asks Joe if he is smoking again, but the Lord has removed Joe's dependency on cigarettes and his desire for them.

A lady prayed in her Bible-study group that she would be able to stop smoking. She had been smoking twenty cigarettes a day for eighteen years. The next morning Doris Spreckley opened the packet and laid a cigarette in her hand. She says, 'I looked at this strange object as if it was something from another planet, and yet I had been in bondage to it for so many years. There were no withdrawal symptoms, and I could even go into a room where people were smoking and God's protection was such that I couldn't even smell the smoke.'

Another reformed smoker is Michael Antonio, who used to smoke both cigarettes and pipe tobacco. One day whilst attending a Brethren church in Swindon, he heard the preacher say 'Your body is God's temple', and 'God lives in us.' At that point Michael felt that he should stop smoking. He says: 'I just didn't want to smoke a cigarette when God was living in me. I was abusing His gift of my body. Having smoked for ten years, I knew I was addicted to nicotine. I'd tried to give it up in the past for all the usual reasons – money, health and so on. After twelve hours I'd get withdrawal symptoms. My legs would feel like jelly and I'd be weak and bad-tempered, with flickering eyes and a dry mouth. I'd get a real craving to smoke again.'

Knowing he should stop, he confided in an elder of the church. The elder said, 'Go and pray to God, and He will give you the assurance that when the elders anoint you with oil and lay hands on you, you'll be able to stop smoking.' After praying for three weeks, Michael felt the inner assurance and told the elder. The elders prayed for him. Michael remembered he had two cigarettes left. His wife, Kim, crushed them for him. The elders prayed he would have no withdrawal symptoms, side-effects or cravings. Michael was miraculously cured. He had no desire to smoke at all, even when people at work tried to tempt him. He hasn't smoked at all since the day he was prayed for, 20 March 1984.

Don Goodwin of Grimsby received help of another kind. He was searching for God because nothing in his life was satisfying him. One Monday morning he decided to see if God was real, so he asked Him to do something that would prove His existence. Don swore in just about every sentence he uttered. He just couldn't speak without swearing; but after praying, when he tried to swear, he found he couldn't. Don heard God ask him,

'Why do you want to swear?' At that point he knew he must make a decision. Don said, 'I know You're there God — come on in.' Love and peace flowed into him; he felt as if he had been lifted off the ground. He had never felt anything like it before. The feeling lasted for three days.

When the feeling of peace left him, Don went to visit a Sunday-school teacher who was a friend of his daughter, and who had talked to him about the Christian faith. When he told her what had happened, she asked, 'Do you believe in Jesus?' Don replied, 'I know God exists, because He has stopped me swearing, and nothing in the world could make me do that except God. But who is Jesus?' He knew Jesus as a historical figure, but was He a madman, just a carpenter, or the Son of God? When the significance of Jesus' death was explained to him, he received Christ, because he knew for certain that God is true. This was after years of having rejected God, mocked Christians and sworn constantly.

David Waite was also lifted off the ground, but for a different reason. The brother of Terry Waite, David was doing Christian work in Austria for Open Doors, with his wife Alison, nearly twenty years ago. They lived in an old house and the shower was downstairs in a long utility room that also contained the washing-machine. David usually played a tape of Christian music while he showered. The water was extremely hot, but the trick was to get the temperature just right using the cold tap as well. David had to step down carefully into the deep shower tray, as he has a disabled leg.

David recalls: 'One morning everything went well until I had finished showering. As I turned off the taps, the unthinkable happened. The cold tap turned off at once, but the hot tap refused to budge. I tried straight away to turn the cold tap on again, but my hands were wet and I didn't succeed. The whole thing happened very fast and I knew that if I didn't move out of the shower immediately, masses of scalding water would come cascading down on my naked body. Yet I was unable to move quickly, as my disabled leg meant that I had to climb very slowly and carefully in or out of the shower tray. It was no use shouting for help. Ali couldn't possibly hear me upstairs above the music on the tape and the washing-machine. Instinctively I shouted 'Jesus, help!' Then the most incredible thing occurred. One moment I was in the shower, and the next I was lying at the other end of the room, watching the scalding water streaming down into the empty shower tray. I have no recollection of being lifted or carried; all I know is that I didn't get out of the shower by my own effort and I was not at all bruised or hurt by the sudden transportation. I was aware that God had broken into my life again, against all the rules, to save me from what would have been a severe scalding.'

Julie Sheldon was more severely disabled. For three years she was twisted into contortions by muscles that contracted beyond her control. Several times a day her body would go into such violent spasms that doctors feared her neck could break when her head was thrown backward. She was in extreme pain, and had to take a great deal of medication to sedate her, lessening the pain and easing the spasms and breathing difficulties. It was hard to cope with all these aspects of her illness, which was eventually diagnosed as generalized dystonia. Having been a ballet dancer trained at the Royal Ballet School, it was especially hard for Julie to cope with her now distorted body, when poise and beauty had been so much a feature of her life. Although there is no cure for dystonia, the doctors did all they could to minimize her suffering. Her husband Tom was devoted, but while he worked, their young daughters had to be cared for by a succession of nannies, which grieved Julie. She was confined to a wheelchair and could do less and less for herself, let alone for her family.

Hundreds of people prayed for Julie over the years, and a turning-point came when she was prayed for at her bedside in intensive care. From that moment, there was a definite improvement, and she was able to sit up, unaided, for the first time in months. The following day Julie was able to get out of bed and walk on crutches, having been bedridden now for a long time. The improvement came in June 1989, and by July, Julie was out of hospital for good and returned home. By early August she had no need of a wheelchair, crutches, splints or neck collar. The doctors were delighted, and called it a 'remarkable improvement from the disastrous state' she was in previously.

Withdrawal from the forty daily pills she was taking took much longer than Julie expected. She felt like 'a junkie', and the withdrawal symptoms were much worse than she could have imagined. As everyone around her rejoiced at the physical progress she was making, Julie was living with anxiety, terror, guilt, fear and feelings of inadequacy. The feelings were partly withdrawal symptoms, but were also caused by panic at coming to terms with normal life after being so disabled. Her elder daughter, Mimi, had become an independent eight-year-old, but when she needed help with her homework Julie would stare at it blankly or quickly lose patience, until Mimi retreated, looking crushed. Georgie, just five, also needed love and reassurance, yet her behaviour would provoke an outburst from Julie. Afterwards, or during the night, Julie would feel wracked with guilt and utterly worthless. Friends and family were a great support, but Julie was exhausted after weeks of restless nights and frustrating days, where a 'ballerina smile' and 'I'm fine thank you' seemed to be the easiest way of coping with all the adjustments to normal life.

Despite all the encouragement she was receiving, Julie felt empty, and was increasingly frightened. She had no peace, especially at night. After all she had come through she now felt like an able-bodied person *unable* to live, and became obsessed with thoughts of death as an escape. Regular counselling and prayer from Christian doctors and a church elder helped her through the depression. Her GP referred her to the Blackthorn Trust in Maidstone, who were especially helpful, restoring her dignity and will to live through their love and caring.

The final breakthrough arrived in October 1989 when a friend, Penny, came to visit Julie one blustery day, and they chatted for a long time. Praying with her, Penny broke the hold of evil that she sensed bound Julie's life. Then, Julie recalls, 'we walked with the children down into the orchard, and watched them running about, enjoying the wind chasing them through the trees, the leaves blowing in great billows into their faces. Silently Penny and I stood together under an apple tree. Time seemed to stand still. Suddenly I felt a great surge of power through me, a rush of warmth, light and freedom. I threw my arms into the wind shouting, "I've been healed!" I *knew* it at last. I was healed, not just in body, but right through, in my mind and in my spirit too. We hugged each other and rejoiced at the victory for God. The battle was over – I had been released. I felt full of light, and humbled by the knowledge that God loved and cared for me, even though I had wanted to end the life He had given me. He had never given up on me, even when I had almost lost hope in everything.

'I realize now that I was shown I could have a working ballerina body back again, but that physical healing was not all that was needed. God wanted me whole again, not simply to be out of a wheelchair and free from physical pain, but healed "inside and out".'

We cannot understand why God chooses to act in some circumstances and not in others. We must leave that question to Him. However what can be recorded is that when God does act, it brings joy and life to people living ordinary lives.

CHAPTER THREE
Miracles in our Family

It's easier to believe God can work miracles in other people,
than in ourselves.

Delia Smith
A Feast for Advent

A SERIES OF miracles happened in our family a
few years ago. At the time, we were missionaries in Rwanda with the Ruanda Mission,
CMS (now called Mid-Africa Ministry). When
our son, Luke, was just two he had malaria,
although we were all taking the recommended anti-malaria
tablets; it must have been an unusual strain which we weren't
protected against. When Luke became ill with a high fever,
malaria was the last thing we suspected as we knew he had
been following the treatment, so we concentrated on getting his
fever down.

By the third day Luke was having convulsions and hallucinations, which was very frightening for him as well as for me.
Geoff had to be away for two days, fetching European visitors
who were coming to discuss rural development projects. This
meant I had no car, and therefore no means of getting Luke to a
doctor, as they do not make home visits in Rwanda.

I prayed in desperation for God to send help. At once
someone knocked at the door. The man looked familiar from a
photograph, although I knew I had not met him before. He told
me he was Jon Henderson, a doctor with our mission, working
on the other side of the country. As he had to visit the capital

where we were doing language study, he thought he would call to meet us, as recently arrived missionaries. I welcomed him gladly and he examined Luke, and diagnosed malaria. He kindly drove to the pharmacy and brought back the right medicines for Luke, so he could begin treatment at once.

Luke recovered over the next two weeks, but the problem with malaria is that it keeps recurring. Once someone has been infected with it, it remains in the bloodstream for the rest of their life, flaring up maybe annually or every two or three years. The following year Luke had malaria again, but we recognized it more quickly and obtained medication, so he was only ill for one week. However at that time we heard of two missionary children in a neighbouring country who had recently died of cerebral malaria, in which the infection reaches the brain and is usually fatal. This worried us greatly, so we prayed specifically that Luke would never have malaria again.

Of course, after a prayer like that, you don't know for a long time whether God has answered it; we had to wait. Five years later I was at my nephew's baptism in St Albans. A girl I met at the gathering afterwards told me that her work was researching mosquitoes, investigating treatments for malaria. I suddenly remembered Luke's malaria and said, 'God answered that prayer – Luke has never had malaria again!' It was a wonderful realization. Now, twelve years on, that is still true, for which we thank God.

One of the most insidious illnesses is depression. I was a caring and level-headed nurse, and didn't think I was the type to suffer from depression. However after the birth of our second child, Naomi, in Rwanda in April 1977, a number of situations loomed large and conspired to make me become depressed.

Our son Luke, at just two, had his first attack of malaria. Naomi had colic, which made her cry with pain for four to eight hours each evening, from her first day until she was six months old. When Naomi was three weeks old, we moved house from

Kigali, the capital of Rwanda, where we had been studying the Rwandan language, to Gahini, where we were to begin rural development projects.

The house was in a bad state of repair, with fallen ceilings and goats wandering in through broken doors; it was like living on a building site for several weeks! There was a water shortage when we arrived, so we were limited as to how much we could drink, and we could not wash any clothes. Within two days I was having to breast-feed Naomi every hour, as my milk supply was affected by the water shortage. Naomi had been sick on all my clothes, all her own clothes and was now wearing her brother's! A young man we employed and trusted found the key to our safe, and disappeared with all it contained – a whole month's salary – and we never saw him again.

General Amin was causing havoc in Uganda, just forty miles away, threatening to bomb Rwanda. As a result of the war in Uganda armed gangs were attacking anyone who had property or vehicles, and many people were killed when they tried to resist. At night it was hard to sleep, hearing noises which we thought might be a gang approaching; our large mission house was quite isolated. One night we heard drums being beaten all night and were terrified; the next day we learnt that this custom announced a wedding day! I had a tooth abcess which was so severe that I needed pethidine for the pain, and meant the loss of the tooth. I also picked up an infection which had flu-like symptoms but which also left depression, even in people who did not have my catalogue of troubles. I soon sank very low.

God felt far away. My prayers seemed to bounce back off the ceiling; I did not feel in touch with Him at all. Geoff did all he could to help, but I was not getting any better. I leant very much on Geoff at this time. After three months we decided to pray and fast, with the other missionaries over a Sunday lunch-time, having given the children lunch and put them to bed for a sleep. The hospital, trade school and rural development projects all had staffing or financial problems, so we agreed that we needed to do something about them.

After praying for all the practical things, Geoff said: 'I think we should pray for Hope.' As our friends gathered round and prayed, God gave a special message for me through one of them, assuring me of His love and care. As the prayer ended, I gasped with amazement as I looked up. We were on the veranda, which looked out over a stunning view of a forty-five-mile lake, framed by mountains and tall trees. Everyone who visited the house had commented enthusiastically on the magnificent view, which I had weakly acknowledged. My eyes had been clouded by depression, so I literally had not 'seen' that view, although I had looked at it many times.

Now there was a dramatic difference. I looked up and said 'Oh, what a fabulous view.' In that moment, it was as if a huge weight like a heavy rucksack had fallen off my back. The moment the depression had gone I felt completely in touch with God again as my loving Father, and even the physical things I was suffering, like infected bites and a sore throat, immediately cleared up as well. It was an amazing transformation.

Two days later my parents arrived for their first visit to Africa. Mum had read between the lines of our letters and realized I must be depressed. She had asked a doctor friend to let her bring antidepressants and sedatives out to me. After a few hours together, she looked at me quizzically and said: 'I thought from your letters that you were depressed, but you're not.' She was delighted to hear of the miracle that had occurred only two days before, and the local hospital gladly accepted the tablets!

In the autumn of 1979 we returned to England on leave, at the end of a fulfilling and encouraging tour of three years. During the previous year I had had hookworm, carbuncles, infected bites and an operation to remove gallstones. I had been flown to England in September 1978 for the surgery, which removed about 130 small gallstones, and I had recovered well from that.

Geoff had driven right across to Rwanda with my X-rays to see if the operation could be done in the best-equipped hospital there, but the doctors had decided surgery in England would be the best option.

Returning to England for our leave in 1979, Geoff and I both had medicals. Geoff was tired, but I had a long list of symptoms including tiredness, lack of energy, itching from head to toe and nausea. They were all dismissed as the result of a busy tour in Africa which a break in England would soon put right. However after a month, although Geoff was fully recovered, I was feeling worse, so a series of investigations began. After five months of tests I was diagnosed as having chronic active hepatitis, which was treated with a high, twice-daily dose of a steroid drug called Prednisone. After having a biopsy and a scan, my liver, I was told, looked like that of an alcoholic and was twice its normal size. My liver functions were completely awry, and I could not tolerate any foods containing animal protein or fats, as they caused my liver to react. The disease, a very rare condition, was thought to have been caused in Africa by a virus.

We were due to return to Rwanda the following month to begin our second tour. The London hospital consultant treating me needed to monitor my progress for a further couple of months, so Geoff went on to Africa alone. The children and I stayed a few more weeks and then returned to Rwanda in June 1980. Initially I felt fine, full of energy and happy to be back among our African neighbours at Gahini. We prepared for the arrival of eight young people from England, who were coming to live with us for two months, to get a feel of missionary life and to do some practical work in the community.

My days were fully occupied with looking after our two small children, and ensuring there was enough clean drinking-water and nutritious food for our now extended family. We already had a forester, David, living with us from TEAR Fund, a Christian aid organization, so we were now feeding thirteen each day. All drinking-water had to be boiled, cooled and filtered, but they seemed to be constantly thirsty, so it all disappeared very fast each time they came in gasping for water again! Mealtimes were full of chatter and laughter, with supper extending well into the evening. Daytime activities for our children were shared with the children of another family. One mother would give lessons to the two five-year-olds, while the other provided play group activities to occupy the younger three for the morning. We took it in turns, and fortunately the other mother, Prilla, had trained as a teacher, which was a great help. We had many African visitors too, mostly during the afternoons.

All these responsibilities conspired to wear me out, and around nine o'clock each night I would fall into bed, exhausted. I would seem hardly to have slept before the children were bright-eyed again at five-thirty the next morning. It was the hot, dry season, so I was not surprised that, like the young people living with us, I was drinking a lot of water. I just hadn't noticed how much. One evening the youth project were having a meal at the home of the mission doctor, Rob, and his wife Trisha, so that we could eat just as a family. When Rob joked that one of the young men was on his third cup of tea, he replied, 'That's nothing, you should see how much Hope drinks!' Alarm bells started ringing in Rob's mind, as he suddenly remembered I was on a high dose of steroids. He sent a message for me to see him the next morning. I had no idea of the sequence of events which would unfold from that unexpected message.

When I saw Rob the following day, my urine was tested and it was found to contain a high level of sugar. It was not possible to have a blood test at Gahini, so Rob said I must go with him the next day to the government hospital laboratory in Kigali, the capital. A visit to Kigali took two hours each way, and so didn't happen very often, which meant there were always plenty of errands to be done. We went first to the laboratory, where my blood was taken for a test, and then we went to the post office to collect the mail, and to the pharmacy and shops to buy everything needed by those at Gahini. At about four o'clock we returned to the laboratory and Rob went in to get the blood-test result. I wondered why it was taking so long, but eventually he returned to the car together with the laboratory doctor, because he couldn't believe Rob's insistence that the patient was sitting in the car. Apparently with a blood-sugar level so high, I should already have been unconscious for two or three weeks!

A normal blood-sugar level was then measured as 80–120mg% and mine was 581mg%, so it was a miracle that I was calmly sitting in the car reading the mail we had collected. I was immediately hustled into the hospital for a huge insulin injection, and the two doctors decided I must have four insulin injections each day to reduce the dangerous sugar level. They also insisted that I take the next plane to England and stay there for a few weeks to stabilize the diabetes. I was most reluctant, since they had insulin in Rwanda, and we had so many people staying in our home.

I pleaded to be allowed to return to England in two weeks' time, when the youth project was due to leave. The government hospital doctor, to make me realize the severity of the situation, stated plainly: 'Without proper treatment for the diabetes, you could be dead by then.' It seemed I had no choice!

Armed with insulin, we set off for the airline office. Rob phoned the Mission to explain the situation and they approved the money to purchase the tickets for the flight. This was Friday evening and the next plane was on Monday, but already fully booked. The first available flight to England was the following Friday. Rob and I travelled back to Gahini to break the news to Geoff and all our guests, that I must leave for treatment in an English hospital.

Our children, Luke and Naomi, were only five and three years old and, as Geoff had to work and travel in my absence, we decided that it would be best if I took them with me. They could be looked after by my parents while I was in hospital and convalescing at their home. We would need three seats for the plane, as I was too unwell to have a child sitting on my lap for the fourteen-hour flight. As the weekend progressed, I began to feel weak. The Rwandan pastor came to visit and to pray for me, as he and his wife had noticed I was becoming ill.

On the Monday morning, Rob drove to the airline office to attempt to book seats for that afternoon's flight. He was prepared, if necessary, to tell them I was a medical emergency, which would mean we could take the seats of passengers who had already booked. This was a course of action we hoped to avoid, for the sake of those passengers, and also, knowing I was a medical risk, the airline would have insisted that a doctor accompany me. It seemed to us an unnecessary expense of mission funds to have Rob travel all the way to England and back, leaving the hospital unattended. So we prayed that three seats would become available.

At the airline office Rob was told there had been three cancellations just that morning. Rob drove straight back to tell us, and we had one hour to get ready before leaving for the airport. I flung two small suitcases inside a large one, so I could bring supplies back from England. I quickly packed a few toys and clothes for the children, some avocadoes and honey from our garden and Rwandan coffee beans. A few neighbours who had heard I was ill had gathered to hug us farewell.

Having said goodbye to everyone, Geoff drove us all to the airport. The children thought it all a big adventure. Once Geoff had seen us off on the plane, he drove into Kigali to use the only telephone to which we had access. He phoned my parents to break the news that, not only was I ill, but I was already airborne, so please would they meet me at Heathrow the following morning. It was quite a shock and, needless to say, they hardly slept!

During the flight, I had to give myself four insulin injections and look after two bouncy, excited children. By the time we changed planes, with an hour's wait at Brussels, I was feeling more drowsy and ill. When we landed at Heathrow, the other passengers and airline crew seemed to dash past us, but walking was now a huge effort for me, and it took over an hour for us to reach the arrivals desk. All the other passengers had collected their baggage, gone through customs and left. By now my parents were asking an airline official to phone Brussels to ask if we had made the connecting flight. I must have looked awful by the time I staggered up to them!

Immediately they had collected the baggage, my parents scooped us up and took us home to phone the hospital. The children were delighted to be back and settled in at once. A phone call to the London consultant brought the instruction that I must be admitted immediately. As I was giving my name and address in casualty, I slipped into a coma. As the doctor in Kigali had said, with a blood-sugar level as high as 581mg%, I should have been unconscious long before. Now, with three days of insulin injections four times a day, my blood-sugar level had been reduced to 279mg%, yet this was still danger level and I was unconscious for over twenty-four hours. God's intervention had kept me conscious, able to bring the children through two plane journeys and deliver them safely into the hands of their grandparents.

When the consultant came to see me, when I had regained consciousness the following day, he said I would not be able to go back to live in Africa again. This was a huge shock, as I thought I had only come for a few weeks. He was adamant, however, that my chronic active hepatitis was still a problem. With the added complication of the onset of diabetes, it was too serious to be treated in a small African hospital, two hours from a telephone or an ambulance.

The diabetes had been caused by the high doses of steroid tablets, so the drug of choice to treat the liver condition had to be reduced. To boost the effect of the lower dosage I was also given Azathioprine, a drug used for treating cancer. As a nurse myself, I had treated patients who were given this drug. Owing to the diabetes I had lost more than two stones in weight, and when I was well enough to be helped out of bed on to the scales, I weighed only 6 st. 12 lb. I remember sitting in the bath that day, looking down at my now puny legs, thinking, 'I've got cancer of the liver, and they haven't told me.'

On the consultant's next ward round, I confronted him with this thought. He replied that I didn't have cancer, but the liver condition was serious and not yet improving, although it had now been diagnosed for six months. The diabetes was unstable and was not responding to treatment as well as they had hoped. My blood-sugar levels were erratic and the hospital dietitian was finding it hard to decide on the best diet for both the diabetic and liver conditions. The diabetes was also affecting my eyesight, so I could no longer see to read, either with or without contact lenses, which was very frustrating, as I hadn't had time to read for ages and now had plenty of time!

I had grown up at Buckhurst Hill Baptist church in Essex, where the minister at the time was John Davies. When John came to visit me in hospital one afternoon, he said that he and the elders had been praying for me the previous evening. They felt God asking them to anoint me with oil for healing, as we are instructed to do in the Bible. James 5:14–15 says, 'Is any one of you sick? He should call the elders of the church to pray over him and anoint him with oil in the name of the Lord. And the prayer offered in faith will make the sick person well; the Lord will raise him up.' John said that they had prayed before for people to be healed, but had never used anointing with oil, which they now felt God instructing them to do. Since I was not being allowed by the medical staff to return to Africa, a telegram had been sent to Geoff advising him to come back to England once the youth project had left. He was expected back in a couple of weeks. We decided to have the prayer for healing after Geoff returned, in a Wednesday evening Communion service at the church.

One problem during those weeks in hospital was that I felt constantly hungry, but could not eat any snacks between meals as that would jeopardize the diabetes. I laughingly mentioned to John the minister during his visit that one of the few foods I could eat freely was cucumber. After he had left, I was taken off the ward for tests, and when I returned to the ward, I found that John had come back in my absence and left the biggest cucumber I had ever seen on my bedside locker!

After about two weeks' treatment, I was discharged from hospital with insulin to give myself by injection, now twice daily, and a carefully controlled diet. The Azathioprine tablets caused various side-effects. One was severe hair loss; my hair fell out in handfuls. That made autumn and winter very chilly for me, particularly after living in Africa for four years. A more serious side-effect was to reduce my white blood cells, so I had little resistance to infection. I was instructed to avoid contact with anyone outside my immediate family, which meant I could not take the children to school and playgroup, visit friends, go shopping or even go to church. After a few weeks I was fed up with this isolation and, during my weekly out-patient appointment, asked the consultant if there was an alternative drug I could use. The consultant agreed to stop the Azathioprine and increase the Prednisone, which had triggered off the diabetes, even though I still required a high dose.

When the date was set for the prayer for healing, Geoff and I phoned our friends all around the country. We asked them to pray on the same evening that God would heal me if that was His plan for us. That Wednesday evening service at Buckhurst Hill Baptist church was a special time for us all. The love and peace of God were felt by everyone present. When the minister and elders poured oil on my head and prayed for God's healing touch, I knew God loved me deeply and that whatever happened would be His best for us. Physical healing or not, I had complete peace.

The following morning I had my correct insulin injection and breakfast as usual. Then I went for an appointment at the chiropodist, since the feet are another vulnerable area for the diabetic. As I was leaving the chiropodist, I suddenly felt very dizzy and weak. I knew I could not manage the short walk home, so asked if I could phone my husband to come in the car to fetch me. As I was feeling very 'woozy' I instinctively knew I had to eat something sweet. I rushed into the greengrocer's next door, bought a banana and ate it as soon as I had paid for it. This corrected the hypoglycaemic attack I was having which happens when there is too much insulin in the body. Unless the diabetic eats or drinks some carbohydrate quickly, to rectify the imbalance, they become unconscious in minutes. Until that point, I had only experienced coma at the other end of the scale, when there had been too much sugar in my blood and not enough insulin.

Mid-morning, I had the designated coffee and biscuit, but then, an hour later, I unexpectedly felt myself going 'hypo' again and had to eat more biscuits. After lunch I was feeling fine, so we set out for a walk in nearby Epping Forest. Fortunately someone had some sweets in their pocket, because halfway through the walk the dizzy, weak feeling suddenly returned and I had to eat a sweet as I went wobbly at the knees. I had never had too little sugar in my blood before, and the symptoms were unfamiliar.

Returning from the walk, I had mid-afternoon tea as required in my daily diabetic programme. An hour later, at home cooking the supper, the same woozy feeling took hold of me again and I had to have a sweet drink to get me on an even keel again. By the time I discussed the situation with Geoff and my parents around the supper table, we all agreed that 'something' had happened during the healing service the previous evening. Suddenly I had much too much insulin in my blood. This meant my body must have started producing its own insulin again, in addition to the injections I had to give myself. Knowing that diabetics never normally regain their ability to produce insulin, this was a mind-blowing thought. I carefully wrote down everything I had eaten that day, as prescribed by my diabetic diet, and everything I had been forced to eat in addition, to correct the 'hypo' attacks, so that I didn't become unconscious. When I added up the carbohydrate values of the two lists, they were exactly the same amount.

I was due to see the consultant at an out-patients' clinic in four days' time, so each day I kept a careful record of everything I had to eat to stay conscious. The 'hypo' attacks happened five times a day, and every day the carbohydrate totals of the two lists were exactly the same.

By this time, Geoff had been offered a job as a lay pastoral assistant, looking after a church fellowship on a housing estate in the parish of Waltham Abbey, Essex. Geoff had moved from the African jungle to the concrete jungle. The vicar, Ken, and his wife, Margaret, owned a small cottage in Norfolk which they kindly offered to us for a weekend break just after the healing service. That weekend I had a monthly period for the first time since my daughter was born, three and a half years previously. This abnormality had been a matter of some concern, but hormone treatment which might correct it was inadvisable while I had other health problems. Geoff and I felt this was a further sign of God's healing from the Wednesday evening service, as my body was returning to normal in more ways than one!

By Monday, when we went to see the consultant, we were totally convinced by the evidence, that God had healed me of diabetes. The consultant was mystified: 'People don't get over diabetes; it can't be cured.' I assured him that although I couldn't be cured by medical means, I had been healed by God. He was afraid that stopping the injections would cause a return of the high blood-sugar level, but he did allow me to reduce the dosage of insulin by one-sixth of the daily amount. Each day that week, I continued with the prescribed injections and diet. Every day I went 'hypo' five times and kept a careful record of the extra carbohydrate I had to eat to correct each attack. At the end of each day, the total of the extra list was exactly one-sixth lower than the previous week.

When we saw the consultant the following Monday, I thought he would be convinced, but he remained doubtful. 'I can't understand it – a diabetic can't start producing insulin in their body again; I have no explanation.' He cautiously allowed me to reduce the insulin that week by a further one-sixth, but he fully expected me to be admitted to hospital in diabetic coma. I continued to keep a careful record and was relieved that the extra consumption of food was again reduced by a sixth; I was fast regaining lost weight!

This pattern continued for a further three weeks, each week the consultant wondering a little more seriously whether God had done this. When he said I could stop the injections completely I was delighted, but I had to continue to test the sugar level in my blood every day at home. The consultant still couldn't understand or explain the healing, but he knew that the evidence dated from the day after the healing service. He was a teaching professor, so each week that I went to see him, there was a different group of medical students I hadn't met before, sitting behind him. Each Monday as I walked into the room he turned and said to them, 'This lady believes God has healed her from diabetes, and I have no reason to discount her claim, because I haven't cured her, yet she is certainly better.'

The outstanding feature of the healing is that it happened while I was still taking a high dose of the very drug which had caused the diabetes. Owing to the unwelcome side-effects of the alternative drug, the liver condition continued to be treated with Prednisone, so the healing was even more miraculous than if I had stopped taking it.

The consultant continued to see me in out-patients each week, and I had to continue testing my blood sugar to reassure him there was no relapse. I never had another 'hypo' attack after ceasing to give myself the insulin injections. The liver condition had not improved significantly until the day of the healing service, but was improving all the time from then on, being monitored by a series of blood tests known as liver-function tests. Gradually I was feeling better and able to eat a more varied diet without my liver causing pain. Within eight months the blood assessments showed such progress that the consultant was able to pronounce my liver functions completely normal. This was as amazing to him as it was to me, since he had been certain that, given the damage caused to the liver, it would never function normally again.

At the time, we were very grateful to God that He had healed me completely of diabetes and chronic active hepatitis, both incurable conditions. I have never met anyone else who has chronic active hepatitis, but a few years later I read an excerpt from an autobiography *A Second Chance to Live* by American journalist Frank Maier, who had the same disease. He had all the same symptoms as me, and was told to expect haemorrhages in his liver, lungs, brain and heart, which were likely to cause his death in, at best, seven or eight years. I was amazed to read this, as I had never been warned of this likelihood. His case was diagnosed four years after mine, and maybe there were more documented cases by that time to establish a prognosis. Or maybe the doctors were reluctant to tell me of these possibilities, since I was only thirty with two small children.

When God healed me, He made a good job of it. Frank Maier was in and out of hospital and had all the best treatment, including a liver transplant, which was his 'second chance'. However he died five and a half years after his diagnosis, before his book was finished. What we did not realize at the time of my healing was the future God had saved me from: regular hospital admissions for repeated haemorrhages which were likely to lead to an uncomfortable death. How we praised God for this miracle.

The healing of my liver condition in July 1981 coincided exactly with Geoff's decision to become a clergyman in the Church of England. He had felt an inner call, and had also been encouraged to take this step by a number of people. The training involved two years' study at Oak Hill, the theological college nearest to us. I needed a job to finance the family, and my training had been as a nurse, district nurse and health visitor. My preference was for a part-time health visitor's job, and a tailor-made opening appeared at exactly the right time in our home town! You have to be healthy to work as a health visitor, so I had to have a medical with a health authority appointed doctor I did not know, as well as with the consultant who had been treating me. Both pronounced me entirely fit, only eight months after the healing service.

Geoff was immediately accepted by Oak Hill College, and the entire selection procedure for his acceptance by the Church of England took only three months, which is considerably faster than usual. This rapid series of events culminated in Geoff starting college, our youngest child beginning school and me starting work as a health visitor, all in the same week. It was God's perfect timing.

CHAPTER FOUR
The Miracle of Changed Lives

> To be a Christian is to be reborn and free, unafraid and
> immortally young.
>
> Joy Davidman in *Smoke on the Mountain*

N 1929, FOURTEEN-YEAR-OLD Joy Davidman
was walking through a New York park enjoying the effects on the maple trees of the snow
which had fallen that day. 'As I looked up they
burned unimaginably golden – burned and
were not consumed. I heard the voice in the burning tree: the
meaning of all things was revealed and the sacrament at the heart
of all beauty lay bare; time and space fell away, and for a moment
the world was only a door swinging ajar.' In that moment she
had discovered the spiritual realm as real as the material world
in which she stood. In the years that followed, Joy went through
much doubt, grasping various ideologies, searching for truth.

In her thirties, Joy Davidman was more widely read and
better educated than most people, and was also an accomplished
writer. On her own one evening she met God. 'All my defences
– the walls of arrogance and cocksureness and self-love behind
which I had hid from God – went down momentarily; and God
came in . . . God is infinite, unique; there are no words, there are
no comparisons. Can one scoop up the sea in a teacup? Those
who have known God will understand me; the others, I find, can
neither listen nor understand. There was a Person with me in
that room, directly present to my consciousness – a Person so
real that all my precious life was by comparison mere shadow

play. And I myself was more alive than I had ever been; it was like waking from sleep. So intense a life cannot be endured long by flesh and blood; we must ordinarily take our life watered down, diluted as it were, by time and space and matter. My perception of God lasted perhaps half a minute . . . I must say I was the world's most surprised atheist.' In that instant, Joy knew that God loved her; she repented and accepted His forgiveness.

'God came in, and I changed. I was aware simultaneously of the blinding presence of God and my own personality, black and smudgy, as I had never seen it before. I admitted my own arrogance, my intolerance, my prejudices, my vindictiveness. All in half a minute – it would have taken years of psychotherapy.' When her husband came home a few days later, Joy was a changed woman. He noticed a striking serenity that she had never shown before.

By comparison, the experience of Bob Murrant is in complete contrast. Bob was one of five children, living in Kingston-upon-Thames, where Dad was too fond of alcohol. Bob's mother had to work at several jobs to make ends meet. Bob remembers often being beaten by his father when he was the worse for drink. Bob feels his childhood was stunted, and he used to dream of being taken away from the estate where they lived.

Bob's mother sent the children to Sunday school, wanting her children to have some Christian teaching which she remembered from her own childhood. Bob really enjoyed Sunday school, partly because the leaders were kind to him. When he was about twelve, one of the elderly ladies of the church invited him to attend a Bible study in her flat. Her one-bedroomed flat was like a palace compared to his home; she had carpets and a lounge suite in good condition, even if old. Bob recalls: 'I did so enjoy those studies together, although I am not sure if I went to learn, or just because there was a good feed-up after the study.'

However when Bob was fourteen, two of his friends died, one of cancer and the other in a road accident; Bob's uncle also died of throat cancer, which knocked the little faith he had. A few weeks later, Bob was sexually assaulted by several older youths, and he needed someone to talk to. He tried to tell a minister he knew, who told Bob not to be a silly little boy. The experience of that rejection was very painful. Bob decided that there was no God who cared about anyone, and became an atheist. For the next nineteen years Bob thought Christianity was just for the unintelligent and easily manipulated members of society. Some years later, Bob agreed to the wish of his wife, Pat, to get married in church and later to have their first child baptized, but he did not believe anything the minister said.

Time passed. One day, Pat had taken their eldest child, Graham, to school and was walking home with Michael, then almost three, by her side and Emma, just six months old, in the pram, when a car mounted the pavement and came hurtling towards them. Pat pushed the pram one way and Michael the other, but did not have time to move herself. When the car stopped, there was a thumbprint indentation on the bonnet where Pat had reached out her hand, trying to protect herself. The pram went under the wheels of the car and Pat could see it was crushed and twisted. By some miracle this was the first time Pat had not strapped Emma into the pram, or she would have been killed. As it was, she was thrown about twenty feet and was crying, so Pat knew she was alive. However Michael could not be seen at all, until she looked beneath the car and found him under the exhaust pipe, lying motionless. Pat screamed and reached out to shake him, and then she heard a clear voice tell her that everything would be all right.

Just then, Michael opened his eyes. All three were taken to the hospital by ambulance. A neighbour who saw the accident phoned Bob to tell him what had happened and that she thought they were dead. In his mind Bob cried out: 'If there is a God, please don't let them be dead.' He rushed to the hospital, arriving even before the ambulance. His family's injuries were very few considering they had all been hit by a car which had burnt tyre marks into the pavement; Emma only had bruises, Pat had one broken thumb and Michael a broken leg and rib, and friction burns on his back. But Bob did not think to thank God that they were alive. Only years later did he realize what a miracle their escape that day had been.

Making progress in his career, Bob bought a butcher's shop, and one of his customers was Trish, a lady in a wheelchair. Pat got to know Trish by taking her eldest child to school, as it was difficult for Trish to negotiate the steep hill to the school, particularly with two other small children. Trish invited Pat to the Baptist church she attended and, after several refusals, Pat agreed to go. When she got up one Sunday morning, announcing she was taking the children to church, Bob decided to go too. They received a friendly welcome and could see that the preacher really meant what he was saying. Afterwards they were heading for a side-door, as most people were shaking hands with the minister at the main door. However the minister spotted them, smiled reassuringly and came over. Bob remembers: 'He told us they had been praying for us and we were, to say the least, gobsmacked. These people knew nothing about us; why would they want to pray for us? We could see that Jesus was real to them, not just a historical figure.'

One evening Bob and Pat were invited to the home of a couple at church who had become their friends. During the course of the evening they shared with Bob and Pat how they had become Christians. When they got home Bob and Pat talked for hours about all they had heard, and they prayed, pleading that they might have the same faith as their friends. When he woke next morning, Bob angrily decided nothing had happened, so there must be no God after all, and he went into the bathroom to shave.

Bob tells what happened next: 'I stood at the sink, seething with anger, and I started to shave and felt the blade cut into my skin. Suddenly I could no longer hear the children in the next room, or the traffic outside, because I was standing on a hill known as Calvary. In one hand I had a hammer, and the other was holding the arm of a man tight to a cross beam. As I hammered the nail in, He said, "I love you." Then the scene changed and I saw heaven. There was a throne and a figure on it that gave a feeling of timeless wisdom and understanding. By His side stood the man I had just seen, and hovering above was the Holy Spirit. Together the Father, Son and Holy Spirit said, "I love you." I did not deserve this love, but I received it as freely as it was given.

'I spent time talking and listening with the Lord before I found myself back in the bathroom. I emerged from the bathroom a changed man, not just changed but a new creation.' At first Pat could not believe the change in him, but two weeks later, Bob helped her become a Christian too. Since then, seven years ago, their faith has grown, and Christ is just as real to them today. We came to know them when Bob worked as an evangelist with us in a parish in Dorset.

A total life-change happened to Nora Brown because of a vision she had been privileged to see. She was seventeen years old and had been going for many months to Girl Crusaders, a Christian group for children and teenagers. She was 'trying to be good', but did not realize that she needed forgiveness through Jesus if she were to get in a right relationship with God. One night she woke up suddenly and saw a brilliant light between the cupboard and the wardrobe, the height and width of a man. She knew instantly that it was Jesus. Nora remembers, 'I scrambled out of bed, fell on my knees and, crying my eyes out, I asked Him to forgive and accept me, as I acknowledged Him as my saviour.' This conversion experience changed Nora, and Jesus has guided her throughout her life since then.

Someone with a very different story is Ralph Goldenberg, whose grandfather was the chief rabbi of the Sudan, having come there from Tiberias in what is now Israel. Ralph was born in Khartoum, into an orthodox Jewish family, and grew up speaking Sudanese Arabic, French, Italian and English. He was taught to read biblical Hebrew in preparation for his bar-mitzvah. His Jewish faith was of central importance in his growing-up years, but after he came to England to complete his education, he set aside Jewish practices, apart from fasting once a year on Yom Kippur, which he felt brought him nearer to God.

By the early eighties Ralph felt he had reached the peak of his profession as an ophthalmic optician. He had stayed in England, married Helen and had three sons, and owned a large house. His business was flourishing with two very busy practices, and yet, in spite of all the outward signs of success, there was a growing sense of spiritual emptiness within. This feeling increased when he spent time with some friends who had recently become Christians. There was something special about them, and the close relationship they had with God.

Helen, who had a nominal Christian background, had started to attend the local church, and one day Ralph felt compelled to phone the vicar, Christopher Blissard-Barnes, and arrange to see him. Ralph explained, 'I am a Jew but I want to find out about Jesus.' The vicar lent Ralph some books and challenged him to read one of the Gospels in the New Testament. The next time they met, Christopher asked Ralph if he could pray for him. Ralph says: 'I imagined he would read from a prayer book, but he simply prayed something like, "God, this man is searching for you; will you reveal yourself to him?" I thought it was like using a telephone, having direct access to God. Again Christopher challenged me to read one of the Gospels and I thought, if that will help me to reach God, I will.'

Ralph read one of the Gospels, and was immediately struck by how Jewish the New Testament was, just as if his grandfather was telling it. Ralph explains, 'It spoke to my heart. I reached the point where I accepted that Jesus could be the Messiah – and that's a huge step for a Jew – but one Saturday night I felt I really needed to know that Jesus was alive, not 2,000 years ago, but today. The next day I went to church with Helen, and Bill, the curate, led the singing of "Jesus is alive today"! It was mind-blowing; God's perfect timing!' That was the turning-point for Ralph and Helen, and they gave their lives to Jesus and became active members of the church.

Over the next few years, Ralph gradually felt God calling him to become a clergyman. In 1988 Ralph and Helen sold their home and business, moving to Bristol to attend a theological college for two years. Ralph found college a difficult experience in many ways, and three months before he was due to be ordained, he found he was having serious doubts about his calling.

Over the Easter break, Ralph was part of a mission team to Poole in Dorset. Only Ralph's wife Helen, his tutor and a close friend were aware of the struggle he was going through. One evening some members of the mission team met together and prayed for one another. Ralph asked for prayer for a service he was due to lead but Ray Fardon, the leader of the team, said, 'No, we must all lay hands on you, because God has something to say to you.' As they prayed for Ralph, Ray began speaking in tongues, or so he thought, but Ralph heard God's message for him spoken by Ray in perfect Sudanese Arabic, a language Ray did not know. In this way Ralph heard God's special message for him in his own mother tongue: 'My beloved son, I have called you; you are from the blood, the line of Abraham. I have called you into ministry, the Lord loves you.' Ralph knew God had performed this miracle especially for him, confirming without doubt his calling into the ministry. He was ordained in June 1990 and served as a curate in the outskirts of Bournemouth. He is now in a church in north-west London, where nearly half of the population are Jewish and there are several synagogues, including one of the largest in western Europe. Ralph is uniquely placed to reach out to his Jewish neighbours, who are asking questions, and some are finding, like Ralph has, that Jesus is their Messiah.

Afri Chandra owned a newsagent's business in Dagenham, Essex, and was from a Brahmin Hindu background. He felt his lifestyle to be meaningless, and was searching for purpose in his life. He remembered having once been given a Christian tract while he was in Calcutta, India, years before. He had a long conversation at the time with an Indian pastor who explained the Gospel to him. He did not become a Christian then, but now, ten years later, two of the Bible verses he had frequently reread in the Gospel tract came back to him: 'Come to Me, all you who are weary and burdened, and I will give you rest', and 'Whoever comes to Me I will in no wise cast out.' However Afri thought all religions led to the same God, so that Christ and the Hindu god Krishna must be the same. The more he puzzled about it, the more confused he became. He was restless and seeking the meaning of life.

One day Afri closed his shop early so he could go to visit Eric, one of his customers. Eric was a piano teacher who Afri knew was a Christian. Eric listened to Afri's searching and confused questioning and said, 'Perhaps you are not living the life that the Lord intends you to live.' Realizing that some areas of his life were wrong, Afri asked God to forgive him, but he still did not know who God was. Krishna or Christ? Soon after that, in the early hours of 29 October 1985, Afri saw a vision which left him in no doubt. He was already awake at four o'clock when he saw a blazing cross, and he remembers thinking: 'I am a hard-core capitalist who majored in accountancy – I am not into experiences of any kind!' He went back to sleep, but awoke again at six to see the same blazing cross, still in front of him. He knew then that Christ was God, and that he had found the truth he was searching for. It was a Thursday, and within an hour he had phoned Eric to say, 'Please get the water ready so I can be baptized today – I can't wait until Sunday.' So Afri was baptized that very evening at Becontree Baptist church.

In finding Jesus Christ, Afri had discovered that Christianity is not essentially about religion, but a relationship. He understood for the first time that, where other religions condemn sinners, God puts love into action. So Jesus died on the cross to take the punishment for wrongdoing, making a bridge for us to cross over to a new and transformed life. Afri realized that the founders of all other religions are dead and gone, whereas Christ rose from the dead and is alive. As his business was open seven days a week, at first Afri could not get to any church for fellowship and teaching. He believes God helped him when he sold his business in just one month, as he was eager to give his time completely to serving the Lord. He had already been trying to sell the business to help solve his restlessness, but God speeded up the deal which should have taken many months. Afri went on to Bible college and now works full-time as a church worker in Birmingham. He is happily married with two sons, and the peace Afri now knows has been totally life-changing.

Sometimes a difficult situation can move someone to look for answers to life's hard questions. This happened to Rosemary Marozzi, who has for years been looking after her husband, Silvio, who has Parkinson's disease. Through a friend she had recently met, she and Silvio were invited to attend a healing service in Folkestone, a few miles away from where they live. They did not enjoy the service, as the music was too loud, but when asked what they wanted from God, Silvio said 'help for the Parkinson's disease', and Rosemary said 'peace of mind'. Appearing to receive no help at the time, they found the experience rather upsetting, and tried to forget about it.

However two weeks later, on Friday 24 June 1994, Rosemary was writing a letter to the friend who had invited her to the service and had lent her some Christian books to read. She wrote that she felt she was 'on the brink of something'. At midnight she switched off the light and went to sleep. It was then she had an experience that was to change her life radically. Rosemary explains: 'I woke up around two in the morning and found I was weeping. I was immediately aware of a presence all around me, an extraordinary feeling of tremendous love and peace, such as I had never known before. I knew immediately it was God. I had a feeling of great sorrow, and a realization that my life was worthless, that I had turned my back on what was really important in life. I saw Silvio lying there, and was aware that I had not really understood his misery.

'Suddenly I felt all my worries and fears slip away from me, and I knew God had taken them all from me and that I wasn't alone any more. I realized how utterly blind I had been. I saw eternity stretching out before me, a glimpse of Heaven, and knew it was there for me. I had a feeling that this life on earth was transitory, so I could now cope with everything, while awaiting this glorious Heaven. I knew I could not turn my back on what I had seen and was now totally committed to God. I stayed awake nearly all night, afraid of losing that sense of great peace and love, which is still with me. As I write, five months later, I still feel it all with just the same intensity. I have been completely transformed. I lived a "worldly" lifestyle, and I would not have believed any of this was possible five and a half months ago. That experience of God has had a most profound effect on every aspect of my life.'

In 1989, Pat Reid was running a successful business with offices in Britain, America and Australia. A friend who worked for her kept inviting her to a supper party at the church she attended in London and, after many refusals, Pat eventually agreed to go to one with her husband. They were impressed by both the meal and the speaker, so they decided to see what a church service was like one Sunday. They were amazed to discover the place packed with about a thousand lively, enthusiastic people and, being in their late thirties, found they were among the older ones!

Several weeks later, Pat was on a business trip to California, and Annie, the friend who had invited her to the supper party, was working in the office there for a while. She had discovered a church she liked and invited Pat to meet her there next morning for the 10.30 service. Still jet-lagged, Pat did not wake until 9.55 a.m. Knowing that she would never be able to get there in time, she immediately abandoned plans to go to the church service and decided to go shopping instead. She showered, dressed, put on her make-up, had breakfast and was surprised to see that it was still only 10.25 a.m. As Pat drove the car out of the garage, she turned in the direction of the shopping mall. The next instant, she found herself driving into the church car park. The time was 10.29! She had only a vague idea of the way to the church without using a street map, but she knew it was at least a twenty-minute journey. How she got there, covering a route she did not know, in literally no time at all, amazed her. The impact of what had happened did not register until much later. Walking towards the church door, she muttered half jokingly, 'OK, so I'm meant to go to church.'

Pat was enjoying a career as a successful, even formidable, businesswoman, who revelled in her reputation for being strong, hard and uncompromising. However the effect of God's presence in the church, and the preaching, meant that she spent much of the service in tears. As she drove home afterwards, she was aware of a 'presence' in the car and knew that Jesus was sitting beside her, even though she did not actually see Him physically. He spoke to her about how much He loved her, and she understood for the first time that she could be forgiven for the many wrong things she had done in her life. Pat received the forgiveness Jesus offered, asking Him to come into her life. She felt peace flood her whole being. The experience was so powerful that she found she had stopped the car right in the middle of the eight-lane highway. Amazingly, no cars had hooted or bumped into her. It was as if she was intended to have that time, undisturbed, to meet with God. In the middle of a highway, Pat's life was changed for ever.

Within a few months, Pat's business collapsed in a totally unexpected way. She was devastated, and could not understand why God would allow such a thing to happen. However over the next three months, as she began to experience deep healing of her past, God showed her how distorted and damaging her current values were. For the first time, she began to see the effects her driving ambition, workaholic lifestyle and materialism were having on both herself and her family. Eventually she realized she had nothing left to lose by handing full control of her life over to God, which she did.

Within weeks, Pat was offered a job running a large hostel for young homeless women in central London. This required use of both her business and nursing skills, nursing having been her original career. God then confirmed for Pat, in an amazing way, that at last she was in the place He had planned for her to be. One of the girls in the hostel was a Christian, who had asked God to teach her how to pray for others. He told her to pray for the new director of the hostel, whom she did not yet know. He told her to show the new director the verse Joshua 1:9. The girl was reluctant to do so, since she did not even know Pat and had no idea if she was a Christian.

Eventually, after more inner prompting, she went to the deputy director's office and timidly said she had been told to give a verse to the new director, but was not sure if she could. The deputy director assured her Pat was a Christian and encouraged her to knock on her door. The hostel was so full of problems that Pat had been feeling very unsure about whether she was in the right place. A friend, Sarah, had come round to talk and pray about it with Pat. Sarah prayed that Pat would receive a positive sign that she should continue working there.

A moment later, the timid girl knocked on the door with her verse, Joshua 1:9: 'Have I not commanded you? Be strong and courageous. Do not be terrified; do not be discouraged, for the Lord your God will be with you wherever you go.' That was such a blessing to Pat; the right word at the right time, from a complete stranger!

Over the past four years, God has continued to challenge and change Pat, in every aspect of her life. He puts His finger on difficult and painful areas of her life that she would rather avoid, in order to deal with them. Nevertheless His loving patience, His provision for all her needs, His continued supernatural intervention in her life and the ways in which He is using her in leadership and ministry, all help make the transformation process worth while. Pat has come to believe that God takes the rest of our lives to work out His purposes, for our good in His mercy. She says: 'It is so good to know that God has done everything necessary to bring broken, wicked mankind back to Himself; all we have to do is accept.'

Back in 1926, a coalminer named Hugh Roberts was on his way home from Oakenshaw mine where he worked. There were no pit baths then, so all the men walked home blackened by coal dust. On the way, he would usually call in at the Working Men's Club for several drinks, which inevitably caused tempers to fray when he eventually arrived home. One evening, on his way home, Hugh noticed there was a mission being held in a tent, so he went there instead of the Club. He heard the good news of Jesus being preached, and he was soon soundly converted. He walked down to the front with his blackened face and gave his heart to Jesus. The following Sunday he called on his son, saying he would go to chapel with them. His daughter-in-law, Margaret, recalls: 'his face shone; he was a new man.'

Roger and Dianne Partridge experienced a series of coincidences which together made up one large miracle. At the time they were not Christians, so they did not recognize that God was working things out for them, as they can now see in looking back. Roger had a good job in Birmingham, where they lived after they were married in 1969. Dianne had a job she enjoyed, but she was very quiet and lacking in confidence, so she found it difficult to make friends. Dianne never enjoyed city life, and was homesick for Dorset where she had grown up, and longed to move back there. Two years after their wedding, Roger was diagnosed as having multiple sclerosis. The progression of the illness made the possibility of changing his job less likely, and increased Dianne's sense of feeling trapped. The birth of their son, Neil, in 1977 helped things for a while, but generally Dianne felt very unhappy.

A planned visit to Dorset in 1979 to celebrate Dianne's parents' wedding anniversary was postponed as her father was ill, so they actually visited them a month later in August. It was then that the series of 'coincidences' began. That weekend a casual glance by Roger at a 'situations vacant' column revealed an appealing job he was well qualified to do. When phoning the personnel department to make inquiries, Roger insisted on advising them of his multiple sclerosis, and was amazed that this did not affect their decision to interview him. The same day they offered him the job, which he was delighted to accept. That very weekend, Dianne's mother heard of a bungalow near by which was coming on to the market, which they were able to view immediately. Their offer on the bungalow was accepted, and their house in Birmingham sold in only three days, so they moved house only six weeks after that rearranged weekend.

At the time, Roger and Dianne did not acknowledge that God had had anything to do with these events, but their lives changed completely. Not just because they moved from Birmingham, which Dianne had longed for, but because they began a relationship with God through meeting Christians from the local Anglican church. Making Jesus the centre of their lives has given Roger and Dianne purpose and peace which they would not have thought possible. Dianne is now so outgoing, generous and lively that it is hard to believe she was so lacking in confidence during those ten years in Birmingham. Dianne says, 'What a wonderful God we have to do all that for us.'

Although she lives on a different continent, Mama Zawadi's story has similarities to others we have related. Originally Mama Zawadi lived in a small village called Digodigo in northern Tanzania. She belongs to the small Sonjo tribe, and was a teacher in the village primary school together with her husband. In 1983 Mama Zawadi bought a radio and started listening to Christian programmes broadcast in Swahili on FEBA Radio, a Christian broadcasting organization. She had heart and kidney problems, and lacked peace of mind. After listening to the radio programmes for some time, she found she wanted to know more about God. She decided to travel to Arusha, 400 kilometres away, to talk to the people at the radio station. The cars which passed that way were very few, but she managed to get a lift to Arusha. There the radio staff talked and prayed with her. She accepted Jesus into her life and was overwhelmed by the power of God. Her eyes shone after the prayer as she declared, 'Now I am sure that Jesus has saved me, and I feel that He has also healed me.'

As soon as Mama Zawadi returned home, her husband Frank could see a difference in her. Her face shone, and she kept praising the Lord. She was now so fit that she could fetch water from the well, which for years she had been too ill to do. She was so enthusiastic about the radio programmes that she inspired many others to come to her house to listen. Soon Frank decided to accept Jesus into his life too, since he could see how much knowing Jesus had changed his wife.

Together Frank and Mama Zawadi continued to listen to the radio broadcasts and to correspond with the staff at the radio station. As others joined them a large congregation began to meet in the primary school on Sundays. The tribal leaders objected to their not worshipping the spirits of their ancestors any more, and convinced the district official to transfer Frank and Mama Zawadi to a school in another area. They hoped that, without their leadership, the Christian group would cease to meet. In fact, the opposite happened, and the group grew in size and strength. The new leader, Masandu, was persecuted for not making offerings to ancestral spirits. However when there was famine in the area due to a severe drought, FEBA Radio was able to send several tons of food to the area. Masandu was in charge of distributing the food, and gained the respect of the people when they saw that he shared out the food fairly between the Christians and the other people of the tribe.

Frank and Mama Zawadi too have gone from strength to strength and are involved in church ministry in Ngorongoro, where Mama Zawadi teaches and Frank is the representative for all the teachers in the district at the district headquarters. They have been a great blessing to the church there.

In some situations, a person's life-changing transformation is seen to be the direct result of another's prayers. One such example occurred in 1984 when Jean Breach, in Sussex, prayed for her father in Kent. He was ninety years old, and had recently had a stroke. Jean had become a Christian a few months before, and was eager for her father to find Jesus and to know peace before it was too late. At a prayer meeting one evening near her home in Lewes, an urgent need to pray for him welled up inside her. She cried out, 'Oh Lord God Almighty, don't let my father die not knowing you.'

The next morning her mother phoned to say, 'Jean, your father has had me awake all night long, crying out to God saying, "Is it too late for an old man?" and endlessly going over the Lord's Prayer and the twenty-third psalm.' Jean immediately set out to drive the fifty miles to her parents' home, praying to know what to say. She kept hearing the words in her head: 'Tell him about the thief on the cross.' Jesus didn't say to the repentant thief, 'You should have turned to me earlier', but 'Today you will be with Me in paradise.'

Following their conversation that day, her father lived another three months, peaceful and confident that Jesus had paid the price for him to be sure of a place in heaven. Jean was able to stay in her parents' home the night her father died. She was fulfilling a business commitment near by which had been arranged several months before. Holding her father's stroke-paralysed hand, his fingers suddenly clenched hers with force and he sat straight up, with a look of joy on his face. He stopped breathing and Jean's mother, standing beside him, whispered, 'He's gone', and gently laid him down. It was at this moment that Jean's mother came back to Jesus with confidence, after sixty-five years of turning her back on Him.

A changed life is the greatest evidence that God is alive for us today. Jenny Glover of Market Drayton experienced the following intervention in her life: 'In 1993, while my husband Steve was away, I went in his place to the annual church meeting at the parish hall. I represented him in his role as caretaker and, much to my surprise, found myself elected on to the Parochial Church Council (PCC). The parish had no vicar at the time, and it was to be several more months before the new vicar and his wife came to the church. As members of the PCC, we were one of the first groups they met, and it wasn't long before they introduced us and our spouses to the Alpha course. They encouraged us all to take part in this discipleship course, which was to cover twelve weeks. I wondered what I was getting myself involved in!'

Jenny continues, 'I have never been a regular churchgoer, but have always considered myself to be a Christian and to lead a Christian life, as many people think they do. One purpose of Alpha was to bring us closer to Jesus, and to learn how to bring others closer to Him, in effect learning to become His disciples. During one of our Alpha meetings, while Geoff was speaking,

I suddenly realized, to my amazement, that everything we do in our lives is touched by God. This realization became stronger when I got home and, the next morning, I had to go round to the vicarage. Hope was at home, and I told her about it. She was glad that God had become real to me, and prayed with me. I still find prayer difficult, but now I am on the right road, knowing God loves me.'

The effect of the touch of God can be seen in the lives of countless people, a few of whom we have mentioned in this chapter. God is prepared to come to us when we cooperate with Him in making us more whole. As Martin Luther, the German Reformer of the sixteenth century, said: 'The greatest miracle of all is the miracle of a transformed life.'

CHAPTER FIVE

Miracles in the Bible

Unless it can be communicated, what is meant to be Good News for all men everywhere becomes a frozen asset.

J. B. Phillips,
God Our Contemporary

CLEAR understanding about miracles can be gained by getting to know the Bible. Nowhere in the Bible is a division made between God's constant power, sustaining His universe, and His individual acts among men and women. When the earliest biblical writers refer to 'the mighty acts of God', they consider of equal importance the miracle of creation and the miracle of the deliverance of the Hebrews from Egypt. The Exodus was brought about by the most significant act of God in the Old Testament. Psalm 135:6–9 describes God interacting with creation and man's affairs:

v.6   The Lord does whatever pleases Him,
         in the heavens and on the earth,
         in the seas and all their depths.
v.9   He sent His signs and wonders into your midst,
         O Egypt, against Pharaoh and all his servants.

The heavens, the earth and the seas are the three great domains of visible creation as perceived by the ancient inspired writers. Through Moses, God led the Hebrew people out of bondage, with great signs and wonders, and prepared them to become the nation of Israel. The Exodus (going out) was the key event in Old

Testament history, and took place early in the thirteenth century BC, around the time when Rameses II was Pharaoh of Egypt.

The cry of Moses was: 'This is what the Lord, the God of the Hebrews says: Let My people go, so that they may worship Me.' Pharaoh not only refused to let the Hebrews go, since his nation relied on the forced labour they provided, but he also tightened his control over them. In the face of Pharaoh's stubbornness, God took direct action. Over the next few months, ten harrowing plagues struck Egypt. All the water in the land turned to blood; frogs, gnats and flies tormented the people; boils broke out on everyone, a violent hailstorm destroyed all the standing crops; locusts ate up anything that was left and then there was total darkness for three days. And still Pharaoh hardened his heart and refused to give God's people their freedom.

Finally Moses announced that on a certain night the angel of death would strike the Egyptians' first-born sons. In order that the angel should 'pass over' their homes, the Hebrews were to mark their doorposts with the blood of a lamb killed in sacrifice. They were to cook the lamb and eat it that night with bitter herbs and bread made without yeast. They were to eat the Passover meal dressed ready to leave Egypt. Indeed, during the night Pharaoh agreed to let the Hebrew people go, and thousands of families, with their goods and livestock, began the journey to the east. Incredibly, the next day Pharaoh changed his mind, and summoned an army of six hundred chariots to bring the Israelites back. They had reached the Red Sea, which blocked their way of escape, and were thus trapped between the water and the rapidly approaching army.

God intervened once again. He opened a path of dry land right through the Red Sea, so that his people could walk across to safety. When Pharaoh and his army attempted to follow, the waters of the Red Sea flowed back over the seabed and they were all drowned. Every year the Jews mark the anniversary of this historical event as the Festival of the Passover. Christians also celebrate a great escape from death to life at Easter, a celebration remembering, on Good Friday, Jesus' death on a cross, followed by his resurrection, on Easter Day. 'For Christ, our Passover lamb, has been sacrificed. Therefore let us keep the Festival' (I Corinthians 5:7 and 8). Here Paul invites his readers to remember what Jesus has achieved.

Passing from almost certain death to life was the experience of Ann Scriven from Corfe Mullen, when she became suicidal. One Whitsun she had flu, which left her feeling very depressed. She went to see a doctor, who was unsympathetic. He addressed her with his back towards her and abruptly said, 'Well?' When she told him she thought she was losing her mind, he replied curtly, 'What do you want me to do about it?' He almost threw a certificate at her, and as she left, she thought, 'Whatever can I do if even the doctor won't help me?' Ann explains, 'As I got to the pavement edge, a car came round the corner. In a flash, I thought, "That's the answer; if I step out in front of the car I'll either be killed or end up in hospital where they'll find out I'm ill and help me." As the car was almost upon me, I stepped out right in front of it. It couldn't fail to hit me. The miracle was that I found myself on the other side of the road. The driver of the car had made no attempt to swerve, sound his horn or stop, but drove on as if he hadn't seen me, although I was only just in front of his wheels.' It was an amazing deliverance.

Throughout the Old Testament, the struggle between what is false and the truth was a real battleground. God was always willing to flex his muscles when necessary. After the Exodus under Moses' leadership, the Israelites soon grumbled against Him because there was no water to be found, essential to life in the desert. Exodus 17:1–7 has Moses crying out to the Lord: 'What am I to do with these people? They are almost ready to stone me.' The Lord told Moses to take his staff in his hand and to strike the rock at Horeb, which He would show him. When he did so, water poured out of the rock, for all the people to drink, just as God had promised.

A miracle comparable to the one God performed through Moses occurred a few years ago in the Marsabit diocese in Kenya. The Rendille tribe live in the Chalbi desert of northern Kenya. Kargi, where the people have a trading centre, had only one pump, with a very low yield of brackish water, which was totally inadequate for the needs of the people. In 1988 a team of Christians had come from Marsabit, eighty-five kilometres away, to explain to the Rendille people about the Christian faith through an interpreter, Gabriel Orguba. Orguba was from the Rendille tribe, but he had served a prison sentence for a crime committed in a tribal clash. While in prison he had heard the good news about Jesus from a Church Army evangelist, and after a few weeks he had responded to Christ. When he was baptized, he chose the name Gabriel. Now he had completed his prison sentence in Marsabit, Gabriel was glad to be translating for the team, telling his fellow tribespeople about Jesus.

Sitting under the big acacia tree, waiting to meet the team, the Rendille people were far less interested in hearing about Jesus than finding a good supply of water, and they asked the team for a borehole with a power-driven water pump. The team leader, Alexander Cendi, explained that boreholes and diesel pumps are very expensive, and that they did not have the resources for these things. He asked, 'Why don't you dig in this valley for water?' Indicating the harsh, featureless desert around, the people replied, 'We know there's no water near here.' Undeterred, Alexander replied, 'We will pray that you may find water here and can dig a well.'

A few weeks later, Alexander returned to Kargi where he found Gabriel now had a large congregation, all interested in hearing the Gospel. Seeing God at work had made the difference. In response to the team's prayers for water, they had dug where Alexander suggested and they now had five wells with a good yield of clear water. The people called them 'The Jesus Wells'. The next time Alexander went back to Kargi he took with him

Bishop Bob Beak (who wrote to us with this account), because the first twenty-nine adults were ready to be baptized as believers. Of course, the water used for the baptisms was from 'The Jesus Wells'.

We see further miracles in the Old Testament in the prophetic ministry of Elijah. During the reign of King Ahab in Israel, apostasy was rampant. Ahab and his wife Jezebel worshipped heathen gods and had killed God's prophets. Angered by these atrocities, God sent Elijah to tell Ahab that, because of his behaviour, He was going to bring a drought.

In the third year of the drought, Elijah returned to Ahab to see if he had repented. The King's response was to accuse Elijah of the drought and of Israel's troubles. Elijah's answer was to declare that Ahab was an idolater, challenging God by worshipping the god Baal, and he invited Ahab to send the prophets of Baal to Mount Carmel, where they would discover whether Baal, or the Lord, was the true God. If Baal could set fire to their sacrifice, then the people should worship him. However if God sent down fire to burn up Elijah's sacrifice, then He was the true God.

The prophets of Baal prayed, danced and cut themselves all day in an effort to make their god respond by sending fire, but without result. It was evening before Elijah had his chance, but as soon as he prayed to God fire fell and the sacrifice was consumed! 'When all the people saw this, they fell prostrate and cried, "The Lord – He is God! The Lord – He is God!"' I Kings 18:39.

Elijah knew God's protection throughout his life. It was foretold in Malachi 4:5–6 that Elijah would return. This prophecy was fulfilled as Elijah appeared with Moses when the disciples of Jesus witnessed Jesus' transfiguration. Jesus climbed a mountain (traditionally thought to be Mount Hermon in northern Galilee) with the disciples Peter, James and John. There, Jesus was transfigured by a heavenly visitation. 'As He

[Jesus] was praying, the appearance of His face changed, and His clothes became as bright as a flash of lightning. Two men, Moses and Elijah, appeared in glorious splendour talking with Jesus.' Luke 9:29–31.

One of the most striking aspects of the life of Jesus is the fact that He performed miracles. Even those who were against Him agreed that Jesus of Nazareth exercised a power beyond human capability. The miracles recorded in the Gospels include giving sight to the blind, enabling the crippled to walk, casting out evil spirits, stilling a great storm and raising the dead to life.

In the Gospels (the 'good news of Jesus'), miracles are described both as 'acts of power', as in the greatest miracle of all, when God raised Jesus from the dead (Gospel of Luke 24), and 'signs', notably in the Gospel of John. These signs demonstrated that the kingdom of God had come in Jesus, and enabled people to put their trust in Him, as when Jesus changed water into wine at a wedding reception in Cana, it is recorded in John 2:11: 'This, the first of His miraculous signs, Jesus performed in Cana of Galilee. He thus revealed His glory, and His disciples put their faith in Him.'

Gladys Ellam wrote to us from Emley, where she is a church-warden. On Sunday 17 April 1988, during Communion, they ran out of wine. On the way to the vestry she prayed, 'Lord, this happened to you at Cana and you saved the day with a miracle. I could do with one here today.' Gladys remembers, 'I thought no more about it, but as I knelt in prayer at the end of the service, the Lord said, "I turn the water into wine."

'At the back of the church, when we were saying goodbye to the congregation, my fellow churchwarden said, "You put water in both cruets this morning, Gladys." I remarked to my assistant warden that it was my fault we'd run short of wine, but as she was emptying the cruets, she said, "Gladys, this one is full of wine!" Then I remembered what I had prayed earlier. I just stood still, and my whole body seemed to be flooded with some sort of electric current that rooted me to the ground. When I managed to speak, I asked my assistant warden to show me the cruet. It was full to the brim with wine, not just below the neck to which point I normally fill it up.' Gladys's fellow warden was told what had happened and he came over. He held the cruet up to the window and assured them, 'This is wine, but there was water in there.' He was astonished too.

Miracles are also called 'wonders'. They stunned and amazed those who saw them. When Jesus healed a lame man, the response was: 'This amazed everyone and they praised God saying, "We have never seen anything like this"' (Mark 2:12). By these acts of power and signs and wonders, God was seen to be performing miracles through His Son.

John the Baptist was the connecting figure between the Old and New Testaments. He was the prophet who foretold the coming of Christ:

> It is written in Isaiah the prophet:
> 'I will send my messenger ahead of you,
> who will prepare your way' –
> 'a voice of one calling in the desert,
> "Prepare the way for the Lord,
> make straight paths for Him."'

And so John came, baptizing in the desert region and preaching a baptism of repentance for the forgiveness of sins. The whole Judean countryside and all the people of Jerusalem went out to him. Confessing their sins, they were baptized by him in the Jordan River.' (Mark 1:2–5)

When John questioned the authority of Jesus, Jesus replied in terms of miracles: 'Go back and report to John what you hear and see: The blind receive sight, the lame walk, those who have leprosy are cured, the deaf hear, the dead are raised, and the good news is preached to the poor.' Matthew 11:4–5. Malcolm

Muggeridge wrote of Jesus' miracles in his book *Jesus, the Man Who Lives*: 'In this sense, it may be said that Jesus was most human when, in performing His miracles, He seemed to be resorting to the supernatural, and that His divinity showed most clearly in what will have appeared to His contemporaries as most ordinary – His day-to-day evangelism and giving out of love.'

The frequency of miracles is far greater in the New Testament than in the Old Testament. There is no indication in the Old Testament that there were unrecorded miracles. However in the New Testament there are repeated claims that the miracles described in the Gospels were but a fraction of the number actually performed. 'Jesus did many other things as well. If every one of them were written down, I suppose that even the whole world would not have room for the books that would be written' (John 21:25). The key to all that Jesus did lay in the relationship that God the Son enjoyed with God the Father. In John 5:19, Jesus states: 'I tell you the truth, the Son can do nothing by Himself; He can do only what He sees His Father doing.'

Miracles did not stop happening when Jesus left this earth. He continues to use His power to heal people today. One example is Margery Steven of Wimborne, who enjoyed her work as a nurse in a military hospital during the Second World War. She later nursed at Wimborne Hospital and in a nursing home, but she was forced to stop work in her thirties, due to ill health. By the time she was forty, she had suffered from multiple sclerosis for five and a half years. She had lost the use of her arms and legs, gradually becoming weaker, until she had to be lifted daily from her bed to a wheelchair and strapped around with belts to keep her from falling forward. She had little control of her hands, so she had to be fed by one of her parents. She and her husband lived in her parents' home, so they could look after her while her husband was at work. Margery's sight was also affected, with her left eye becoming completely closed and in her right eye treble vision. She began to have blackouts and would sometimes lose consciousness for hours at a time. She had been a Christian since the age of six, when her father had been healed from a spinal complaint shortly after her parents had become Christians. Throughout her years of suffering Margery's faith remained strong, as she held on to God's promise: 'My grace is sufficient for you, for My power is made perfect in weakness' (2 Corinthians 12:9).

On 4 February 1960 Margery dreamed she was sitting on a chair beside her bed, and she put out her left leg, but she woke up to find it was a dream. Then she heard a voice in the room which she knew belonged to the Lord saying, 'Tarry a little longer.' She was encouraged by the account in the New Testament of Jesus raising Lazarus from the dead, which gave her hope that 'What my Lord can do for Lazarus He can do for me, if it is His will.' Yet although her hopes were high after the dream, she continued to deteriorate physically. Her speech became so badly affected that at times she could not make herself understood, even by her parents. She reports: 'In all this suffering was the realization that what Jesus could do for Lazarus, He could do for me. His message to me to tarry a little longer meant that, in His own good time, He would heal me. I left the future to Him; it did not matter if it took days or years for my Lord to deliver me; I knew He would in the end.'

Margery's account continues: 'Oh Monday 4 July, exactly five months after the dream, my Lord healed me, in the very chair of which I had dreamed! I had said goodbye to my husband at five minutes to six, a helpless woman. At six-fifteen my mother gave me a cup of tea. At six-twenty my parents lifted me from my bed, strapped me in the chair beside the bed, putting a bell in my good hand, to summon aid if needed. My mother went to get my washing-water and my father had gone to get a towel from upstairs. Then in a matter of seconds, my Lord Jesus healed me! I felt a warm glow spread over my body. My left foot, which was doubled up, straightened out; my right foot, the toes of which were pointed towards my heel, came back into a normal position. I grasped the handle of my bedroom door, which was beside me, undid the straps which were around my body, and said "By faith I will stand", which I did.

'Then I thought of my mother and the shock it would be to her if she came back to find her daughter standing after so many years, so I sat down and called for her. With that, both my parents came running into my room, thinking I was in need of them. I said, "Mum dear, take my hands, don't be afraid, something wonderful has happened." I put out my right arm and, as I did so, my left arm came out from behind me and joined the other. It was so wonderful a few minutes afterwards to find I could wear my wedding ring, which I had not been able to do for years, as the fingers of that hand had got so thin. My mother said, "Darling, how wonderful, your hand is warm and is well again." I replied, "Mum, it's more wonderful than that, I can stand." With that, holding her hands, I stood once more to my feet.

'Then, unaided, I walked from my bedroom, through the small dining room to the kitchen, my parents following mutely. When I reached the kitchen, I turned and went back into the dining room and, taking off my glasses, I said, "Mum, if I can trust God for my hands and feet, I can trust Him for my sight." With that, in a moment, my left eye opened and my sight was fully restored! In fact, Jesus did such a perfect job that I do not need the glasses I had before I was ill. To Him be all the glory.'

Margery and her family did not tell anyone of her healing until she had been examined by her doctor the next day. Since then, several doctors and nurses have been to see her and have gone away knowing that only God performed this amazing miracle. A friend of hers recounts: 'During the long years of her illness I have cried after seeing her poor twisted body, but have also come away marvelling at her wonderful faith in Jesus Christ.

I went to visit Margery with a few flowers on 6 July 1960, quite expecting to hear her mother say, "I'm afraid she's not well enough to see visitors today", as I knew she had been lapsing into unconsciousness for hours on end. Instead, I was met at the door by the smiling face of her mother, who was her faithful nurse through the years. She greeted me with the words: "Have you heard the news?"

'Margery's mother told me of her daughter's healing, but it just would not register – a dying girl suddenly restored to health – it could not be possible. The door opened and Margery walked in. I was astonished, amazed, speechless, after the crippled, skeleton-like body that I had known. In its place I saw a tall, well-built woman, with a sense of the presence of Christ about her. We knelt and thanked God for this wondrous miracle. Praise Him! I rushed out of the house, stopping all my friends, telling the marvellous news. Many people have come to know Jesus through Margery's testimony.'

Margery was in good health for thirty years. She travelled all over England and Holland, speaking about how God had healed her, giving the glory to Him. She was able to nurse her husband and both her parents until they died – her mother only in 1992. Margery is grateful for all the years of excellent health she has had, although now in her late seventies she has had an eye removed and has not been so well recently, but her favourite hymn is still 'Great is Thy Faithfulness'.

Miracles continued to be part of the life of the early Church after the ascension of Christ. J. B. Phillips, who translated the New Testament into modern English, entitles the book of Acts *The Young Church in Action*. The action included the working of miracles in the name of Jesus. The Holy Spirit came on the disciples at Pentecost, as Jesus promised it would, which enabled the early Church to carry on His work.

We are given a moving account of the young Church in

action when a man crippled from birth met two of the disciples, Peter and John, outside the Beautiful Gate in Jerusalem, and asked them for money. Peter looked the man in the face and said:

> 'Silver or gold I do not have, but what I have I give you. In the name of Jesus Christ of Nazareth, walk.' Taking him by the right hand, he helped him up, and instantly the man's feet and ankles became strong. He jumped to his feet and began to walk. Then he went with them into the temple courts, walking and jumping, and praising God. When all the people saw him walking and praising God, they recognized him as the same man who used to sit begging at the temple gate called Beautiful, and they were filled with wonder and amazement at what had happened to him.
> Acts 3:6–10

Miracles accompanied the apostles on their missionary journeys, as God's kingdom became available throughout the earth. 'Your kingdom come' was included in the prayer Jesus taught His disciples. Now it was actually happening, through prayer and the 'laying on of hands', in the power of the Holy Spirit. The 'laying on of hands' is used during prayer for someone in need. Those praying place their hands gently on the shoulder or head of the person, inviting God's Holy Spirit to come and minister.

The apostles realized that the greatest work of the Church was to proclaim the reconciliation of men and women to God, through faith in Jesus. When miracles occurred, they were marvellous answers to prayer. They were signs of God's compassion, confirming the truth that the ministry of Jesus was now active in His Church by the Holy Spirit.

Much healing happened through the apostles and other disciples. We read in Acts 5:12, 15: 'The apostles performed many miraculous signs and wonders among the people . . . As a result, people brought the sick into the streets and laid them on beds and mats so that at least Peter's shadow might fall on some of them as he passed by.' Even clothing was effective in healing. In Acts 19:11–12 'God did extraordinary miracles through Paul, so that even handkerchiefs and aprons that had touched him were taken to the sick, and their illnesses were cured and the evil spirits left them.' Not that these articles had extraordinary qualities in themselves, but the least item of clothing or shadow represented a direct means of contact with the power of Jesus Christ, which was still available through His followers.

The working of miracles was not merely the experience of the early Church, but has continued right into the twentieth century. In 1 Corinthians 12:10, Paul states that one of the gifts of the Holy Spirit is 'miraculous powers'. This power was not only for the first century AD but also for us, living in our modern world.

By far the greatest miracle of all was the raising of Jesus to life again, by God, after horrific Roman crucifixion. For us today, this speaks of God's desire to breathe new life into those who are spiritually dead. As the New Testament records, carrying our sins, Jesus died in our place, taking the punishment required for sin, and so securing forgiveness for men and women.

Audrey Anderson of Kent experienced such a 'resurrection' transformation. Audrey writes: 'Forty-three years ago a miracle happened to me which changed my entire life. I had returned with my husband from India suffering from depression, brought on by tropical anaemia and other illnesses, but more especially by feelings of guilt and fear that I had offended God with the wild lifestyle I had before marriage, and subsequent disobedience.

'Visiting Lincoln on our way down from Scotland, I was too frightened to accompany my husband to the cathedral. However on a day's outing with my in-laws to Norwich, I did not like to protest when they suggested we all go to the cathedral there. We went in, and, as they moved about with my husband, looking at the different plaques, I went and stood alone by one of the huge pillars. I silently cried to God to help me. As I did so, something shot through my body. In a split second, I was aware that I had a heavenly Father who loved me intimately and tenderly. All the fear was gone, and I was filled with this wonderful love, longing to let it flow out to others.

'As we emerged from the cathedral into a café, I could only give my feelings expression by pouring out countless cups of tea for my in-laws and my husband! I kept the secret to myself, basking in the wonderful knowledge that God really loved me. But after we returned to the suburb where we were to settle, the transformation in me took on a more practical expression, and I started visiting deprived families in the area. I also joined a local church, where the vicar was very helpful. Six weeks later a friend explained how to become a Christian, by asking for forgiveness and inviting Jesus into my life, which I gladly did.'

The resurrection of Christ is not to be held up as a supernatural event for its own sake. For Audrey, resurrection life began suddenly, in an extraordinary way. Today she writes: 'Though I have sometimes been conscious down the years of failing Christ, He has never failed me, and I know that I can trust Him fully, right through to eternity.'

CHAPTER SIX

Miracles of Healing

The Bible has many a recipe for our health.
More importantly, it tells us of the source of
that power needed for our healing.

Bishop Morris Maddocks

F ALL MIRACLES, it is those of physical healing that hit the headlines. Other equally astounding acts of God may go unnoticed. Healings of a dramatic nature are sometimes subject to close scrutiny when they are brought to public attention, inspiring belief in some, while others remain sceptical.

This is what happened when Jesus healed the sight of a man who was born blind. Investigators questioned the man's parents as to whether their son had been blind at all! The man's parents were asked: 'Is this your son? . . . Is this the one you say was born blind? How is it that now he can see?' 'We know he is our son,' the parents answered, 'and we know he was born blind. But how he can see now or who opened his eyes, we don't know. Ask him. He is of age; he will speak for himself' (John 9:19–21).

His parents' response is tempered by fear, for already the Jews had decided that anyone who acknowledged that Jesus was the Christ would be put out of the synagogue. However they summoned the man who had been blind and said, 'Give glory to God . . . We know this man [Jesus] is a sinner.' He replied, 'Whether he is a sinner or not, I don't know. One thing I do know, I was blind but now I see!' (John 9:24–5).

Jesus' miracles of healing have not only an individual local significance, but also an eternal, spiritual meaning. In the case of the healing of the blind man, we learn that God's Son can heal spiritual as well as physical blindness. We can enter into the miracle and glean truths for ourselves. What is evident from all the letters sent to us is that what other people have experienced cannot be taken away from them. They are certain enough to commit to paper what God has done for them; for others to scrutinize, because they know their experience is real. 'One thing I do know. Once I was blind but now I see!' echoes through many of the testimonies of healing, we have encountered.

In the strict sense of the word, healing means the restoration to full health of a person who has been ill in body, mind or spirit, and includes both gradual recovery resulting from medical treatment and the immediate cessation of a condition of illness or disease. In the Old Testament, God says: 'I am the Lord, who heals you' (Exodus 15:26). God still heals today, and He enables trained people to be agents of His healing. It is still a 'calling' for men and women to be instruments of His healing, as members of the caring professions.

Sometimes healing comes through medical means, along with an additional element of unexplained restoration, which leaves the medical team delighted but baffled. In these circumstances the doctors know they have done all they can, but it is not enough, and then God takes a direct hand and completes the healing Himself. This is what happened to Gillian Edgar, whose doctor said she had the worst case of full-blown myalgic encephalomyelitis (ME) that he had ever seen. Gillian sets the scene in February 1984: 'My first marriage had broken down, causing much pain on both sides; I had had an abortion, a serious head injury and a cancer scare; because of financial difficulties, I was working full time as a nursery school teacher, as well as doing two part-time jobs. I was also in another relationship which was not going well. When I went to see my doctor complaining of lumps under my arms, I was just beginning to recover from a flu-like virus which had left me feeling extremely weak. My doctor, knowing the kind of life I was leading, put my illness down to stress.'

Gillian continues, 'I carried on teaching, but the flu symptoms kept returning, sapping more of my energy each time. I also lost my home in a serious fire soon after I had become ill. Eventually my job became impossible to manage and I was forced to give it up. I was considered depressed by the medical profession. After extensive tests in various hospitals, I was eventually diagnosed with myalgic encephalomyelitis.' With ME it is necessary to get plenty of rest at the onset of the disease, but since it had taken two years for Gillian to be diagnosed, and she had not known of the need to rest, she had almost complete body collapse by this time, from which she was told she would never recover.

Gillian describes her condition at the time: 'I was registered severely disabled, and spent my time either in bed or in a wheelchair. Since ME affects the brain, my concentration was limited, I found speech difficult, and could not cope with conversation. I became allergic to sunlight and most foods, so I was on a very limited diet and my weight dropped below six stone. My muscles deteriorated and I experienced an irregular and rapid heartbeat which made me frightened and exhausted. Muscle twitching, pain and insomnia were problems too, but worst was the constant feeling of having severe flu. At one time I was taking thirty-five tablets a day, plus Tertroxin for an underactive thyroid gland.'

All this changed on 7 November 1988. Gillian explains: 'I felt awkward when it was suggested that two Christians come and pray for me, but I had nothing to lose, so reluctantly I allowed them to visit. There was something special about them. As soon as they started talking about Jesus as if they knew Him, I realized this was what made them different. I had always believed in God, but I had never understood that Jesus had taken my sin in His death. Feeling the burden of my sinful life, I asked Jesus for forgiveness, and for Him to change me. As I prayed, I felt Jesus come into the room; a heat engulfed my body and I began to speak in a language I didn't know. All this was completely new and strange to me. Later, when I read the Bible, I saw that I had been filled with the Holy Spirit and was "speaking in tongues", which is one of God's spiritual gifts. From that moment on, I was never the same again!'

Gillian's experience of the Holy Spirit helped her through the problems she had to face during the next eighteen months. She had a very close relationship with her mother, so found it very hard when she died. The following summer, she was rushed into hospital with a burst ovarian cyst, which entailed a full hysterectomy. Complications set in after the operation, so she had to return for further surgery. The ME continued to dog her, the symptoms being worse some weeks than others. Twelve months later she was very ill again; breathing was very difficult and she thought she was going to die. Gillian says, 'During these difficult and testing times, the peace of Jesus never left me. In hospital one day, I had a vision of Him sitting close to me; such was the outpouring of His love, it was beyond description.'

As she was severely disabled, Gillian had to be assessed periodically by a DHSS doctor. This was always a painful and exhausting experience which took her days to recover from. One of these visits was due on 29 June 1990. Her son brought the doctor to her bedroom. After he had written extensive notes, Gillian asked him if he knew of anything at all that could help people like her. Putting down his pad, he looked at her, smiled, and said, 'Yes, Jesus Christ can heal you.' Gillian says, 'A few days previously, totally exhausted, I had prayed to God from my bed, "Jesus, I have nothing left to fight with any more. It's up to you to help me now." Only God could have heard the cry from my heart, and I knew He had sent this man to me. He prayed for me and I was flooded with such peace. I knew from that moment Jesus had touched me, and that I would recover.

'I never again sat in my wheelchair. Within a few weeks, with Christian friends continuing to pray for my complete healing, I was living a normal life. My miracle has been accepted by the medical profession.' In fact, only twelve months later, she was granted a £140,000 life-insurance policy, which would never have been possible in her previous state of health. Since then, she has been working with babies rescued from the streets of a large Philippine city. Now living in a poor country, Gillian's lifestyle is a dramatic change from the one she knew when she was so ill.

In January 1939, Percy Newton, a tram conductor, was being treated for a serious brain tumour in Leeds General Infirmary. Because of the location of the tumour, removal was out of the question, but to relieve the pressure on Percy's brain, it was decided to cut away some of the growth. Percy, however, refused to sign the consent form, so the surgeon, Mr Henderson, asked the curate from the nearest church, Kenneth Harper, who was a hospital chaplain, to talk to him. Percy explained to the curate that he had made his girlfriend pregnant and he wished to marry her. He knew that he was expected to die soon from the severity of the brain tumour, and he wanted to 'do right' by the girl. She would then get a widow's pension when he died, and his savings would also go to her. Revd Harper agreed to make the necessary arrangements for him, since Percy was too ill to do it himself.

The wedding was quickly arranged for 11 January 1939 in St George's church, which was just over the road from the hospital. Even so, an ambulance had to be used to transport Percy, and he was carried into the church on a stretcher, as he could no longer walk. It was snowing that day. The verger, somewhat lacking in tact, had placed the stands normally used to hold coffins ready to receive the stretcher! The curate had to support Percy's wrist to enable him to sign his name in the register, as he was so weak. We have been sent a copy of the marriage certificate of Percy Newton, whose address was given as Leeds Central Infirmary, to Dinah Heavisides of Pogson's Cottages. After the wedding, the ambulance drove the couple through the snow to the girl's home, with instructions for Percy to be brought to the hospital the following Thursday for the surgery to relieve the pressure of the tumour on his brain.

However the following Thursday, Percy *walked* into the Infirmary unaided; the tumour had vanished. Sometime later the couple brought their baby to the Infirmary, so that everyone involved in Percy's case could see her. It was a remarkable healing of a potentially fatal tumour. We do not know of anyone who prayed for actual *healing* for Percy, only that God's will would be done. However Kenneth Harper felt that the healing came as a result of Percy's concern, before he died, to make matters right for Dinah and the baby. Probably a relative or someone on the hospital staff was praying for Percy's healing; we will never know – but there is no doubt that God intervened.

In the New Testament, instances of miraculous healing and the casting out of evil spirits were signs which authenticated the words and works of Jesus. In Acts 2:22 Peter says, 'Men of Israel, listen to this: Jesus of Nazareth was a man accredited by God to you by miracles, wonders and signs, which God did among you through Him, as you yourselves know.' In Luke 5:17–26, Jesus not only healed the paralysed man, but also forgave his sins. Here the miracle reveals the divinity of Jesus and His power to heal not only the body but also the soul.

In the Gospels we read about Jesus healing whole groups of people. 'When the sun was setting, the people brought to Jesus all who had various kinds of sickness, and laying His hands on each one, He healed them' (Luke 4:40). Men, women and children came to Jesus in large numbers. We read 'Jesus went throughout Galilee . . . preaching the good news of the kingdom and healing every disease and sickness among the people' (Matt 4:23).

Jesus' approach to sickness is described in greater detail in individual cases. 'A man with leprosy came and knelt before Him and said, "Lord, if you are willing, you can make me clean." Jesus reached out His hand and touched the man. "I am willing," He said, "Be clean!" Immediately he was cured of his leprosy' (Matt 8:2–4).

Sometimes Jesus healed from a distance, as described in John 4:46–53, where Jesus healed a royal official's son without actually seeing him. The official had travelled a long way to beg Jesus to come to his son's bedside, but Jesus assured him his son would recover. 'The man took Jesus at His word and departed. While he was still on the way, his servants met him with the news that his boy was living. When he inquired as to the time when his son got better, they said to him, "The fever left him yesterday at the seventh hour." Then the father realized that this was the exact time at which Jesus had said to him, "Your son will live." So he and all his household believed.'

A similar thing happened to Ajay Gohil, who was far away from God and in desperate need. He grew up in a Hindu family, working in the family business as a newsagent in Neasden, Greater London. At the age of seventeen, Ajay developed a serious skin disease called erythrodermic psoriasis. By the time he was twenty-one his condition was severe. He lost four stones in weight, and the skin all over his body was badly affected. His raw, red, scaly skin was continuously peeling and very sore. He would not let his arms or legs be seen, as he felt it was such a horrible sight. For nine years he made strenuous efforts to seek treatment and spent the majority of his earnings trying to find a cure. Ajay told us recently that if someone had told him of a doctor who could treat the disease, he would go anywhere. Ajay went for treatment all over England and to Israel, the United

States, Germany and Switzerland, but all in vain. His wife left him, taking their son with her. He lost all his friends because they could not cope with his disease and the depression that went with it. He began to feel desperate at his inability to find a cure.

In September 1987, Ajay was admitted to St Thomas's Hospital in London, where, for seven weeks, doctors tried various kinds of treatment. Nothing had any effect. On 14 October Ajay was lying in bed, wishing he could die. He had never practised any religion; the Hindu gatherings he had been taken to as a child had been only social occasions. He did not know God personally, but, in his desperation, he started to pray for the first time in his life. 'God, if you are watching, please either heal me or take me. I am sorry if I have done something wrong. I can't take this any more.' He immediately felt a 'presence'. He had never read the Bible, but now he felt a desire to do so.

He remembered seeing a Good News Bible in his bedside locker, so he pulled it out and opened it at random. He read: 'O Lord, don't punish me in your anger! You have wounded me with your arrows; you have struck me down. Because of your anger, I am in great pain; my whole body is diseased because of my sins. I am drowning in the flood of my sins; they are a burden too heavy to bear. Because I have been foolish, my sores stink and rot. I am bowed down, I am crushed; I mourn all day long. I am burning with fever and I am near to death. I am worn out and utterly crushed; my heart is troubled and I groan with pain. O Lord, You know what I long for; You hear all my groans. My heart is pounding, my strength is gone, and my eyes have lost their brightness. My friends and neighbours will not come near me, because of my sores; even my family keeps away from me.' (Good News Bible Psalm 38:1–11)

As Ajay read this psalm, the first part of the Bible he had ever read, the words seemed to leap out of the page at him. Every line was about his own situation. Ajay read the Bible until around two in the morning; it had come alive for him. When he fell asleep, he slept peacefully for the first time in many months. The next morning he didn't remember what had happened, but everything felt very new and fresh. Although it was mid-October, there was bright sunshine outdoors, and he felt a great peace inside, as if a huge weight had been taken off him. He went to the bathroom and began the usual lengthy bath-time regime with various ointments. As he lay in the bath, he was aware of something very strange happening. He saw flakes of his damaged skin peeling off and floating to the surface. Soon he was surrounded by a large quantity of these flakes and beneath them new, fresh skin had formed all over his body. He was so excited. His immediate reaction was to say 'Thank God.' It was only then that he remembered all that had happened during the night; his desperate plea, the 'presence' he felt, the words leaping out of the pages of the Bible. He knew it was God who overnight had given him a new skin.

Ajay was thrilled that the healing process had begun that day. However he told us that the healing he received inside was far deeper and more significant. He had been very bitter for years, but now the bitterness gradually melted, as he read the Bible from Genesis to Revelation. In addition his life was becoming better than anything he had known before. God sent Christians to him; first, a ward administrator called Peggy, who said she prayed with a group of Christians in the hospital, so Ajay told her what had happened that night. Ajay did not receive any visitors, so at visiting time he would try and sleep. One evening, from behind the curtains around the opposite bed, he heard a young man talking to the patient he was visiting. The conversation was all about the Christian Gospel. After a while, Ajay went out to sit in the corridor, and when the other patient and his visitor walked past, the visitor put his hand on Ajay's shoulder and said, 'I hope we didn't disturb you.' Ajay just smiled. A day or so later the young man came again, and the patient in the opposite bed introduced his visitor to Ajay as

David, his uncle. The three of them talked together, then David and Ajay continued talking for hours.

Ajay remembered what he had heard David saying on the previous occasion, and asked him more about the Christian faith. That evening David helped Ajay to become a Christian and gave him a booklet called 'What's the Point?' They met up regularly when Ajay was discharged from hospital and have continued firm friends to this day. Ajay is now happily married to our goddaughter, Ruth. They have two lovely daughters, and the reality of their relationship with God is plain to see; it shines out of them. Ajay showed us a verse in Joel 2:25–6 which exactly describes his situation now. God says: 'I will repay you for the years the locusts have eaten . . . you will praise the name of the Lord your God, who has worked wonders for you.' In the Middle East, locusts can wipe out a whole year's crop, destroying it completely. Ajay feels that all those wasted years of bitterness, and seeking in vain for a cure, have been restored tenfold, far more fully and richly than he could ever have imagined possible.

A true understanding of God's care for us is being prepared to accept and use the means provided by Him for healing, including surgery, herbal and modern medicines. Rachel Murray was told in July 1992 by a surgical consultant that the painful swelling on her jaw was a tumour which, untreated, would lead to her death within two or three months. A few days previously, Rachel had had a lovely experience while standing at the bus-stop, which helped her as she now received this bad news. Rachel had just attended yet another hospital appointment, where she had been told that more scans and tests would be needed to find out what was wrong, and she was feeling angry that all the previous tests and treatments had turned out to be a waste of time. Suddenly she saw a shadow which formed a cross and was reminded, 'Take your problems to the cross and leave them there.' Was it just a shadow, or a message from God? She needed time to think, so she decided to walk home. The flowers suddenly

looked especially beautiful, their perfume so strong, the butter-
flies so dainty. Rachel knew that God was in control. In her
mind she took to the cross all the pain she had been experiencing,
and the fear of the diagnosis, and gave it all to Jesus.

Now, although she had been told the worst possible news,
following CAT and MRI scans and a needle biopsy, Rachel felt
incredibly peaceful because of that recent experience. The tumour
was pressing on her brain, situated as it was in the joint where
the jawbone joins the skull. The consultant advised her that two
surgical teams would need to operate on her for twelve hours to
remove the tumour and jaw bone, to take a bone graft from her
hip, and to scrape or replace with bone or titanium plates other
areas of the facial bones and skull. She would be sedated in
intensive care for seven to ten days and would be in hospital for
at least six weeks. As the tumour was on the bone near the main
artery into the cranial cavity, the surgery might cause her death,
or else possible brain damage. She would have temporary and
possibly permanent paralysis of the jaw with no speech or
movement, and she would need speech therapy to see if these
skills could be regained. Feeding would have to take place via a
tube in the side of her neck, for some weeks. After the first
operation there would be radium treatment and then a further
bone graft and brain surgery. Not a cheerful prospect, but God
enabled Rachel to remain amazingly peaceful on hearing this
treatment schedule. The consultant asked Rachel what she would
do until the operation. Rachel replied, 'Pray a bit more and trust
a bit harder.' She remembers his cynical smile as he said, 'If that
is what keeps you happy; we could do with all the help we can
get with this one.'

Surgery was arranged for 20 August, when two of the best
surgical teams would be available. Rachel determined to make
the intervening time as happy as possible for her family, not
knowing if these weeks with them would be her last. Her
husband, not a Christian, was amazed at her calm faith; he felt

very angry about the situation. Her sixteen-year-old son is a Christian, and showed confidence beyond his years. The minister and members of Mitcham Baptist church, which Rachel attends, were wonderfully supportive. God kept reminding her of encouraging Bible promises and a song 'I know Who holds the future and He'll guide me with His hand'. The church minister, Roger Watkins, arranged a prayer rota to cover the time of the operation, and the church members too knew the peace and strength Rachel felt.

When Rachel came round from the operation, she was immediately able to speak normally, to the amazement of all the doctors and nurses. Her jaw should have been immobile. She was able to eat normal food the next day, which was also totally unexpected. There was a tube already in her neck for the liquid feeding which had been considered a matter of course. The surgeon told her the operation had gone brilliantly, better than anyone had hoped. The registrar said her operation was 'unique . . . from the moment we made the first incision, it was beyond our control; nothing can explain it except a miracle . . . God alone did this . . . there is no other reason, it is not medical healing.' She had no pain in her face at all, which was also remarkable. The only slight discomfort was in her hip, from where the bone graft had been taken, but she was able to walk unaided from the first day. Her Christian visitors, including her son, Stuart, were all jubilant at the way God was answering their prayers. However those of her family who did not share her faith were confused, expecting that something was bound to go wrong.

The consultant told Rachel: 'In so severe a case as yours, I felt there was little chance . . . you are cured, please don't ask me how or why, it is beyond my understanding.' Four days after the operation, Rachel was better than could have been expected after months of post-operative therapy. The radiotherapy and follow-up treatments that had been planned, and the second expected operation were not needed at all. A nurse said to Rachel, 'It is wonderful that God has done this. We could do so little; then this happens, and we know God is far greater than any of us.' When the tumour had been tested in the laboratory and was found to be condroblastoma, the most rare and severe kind of jaw tumour, the medical team were even more amazed that Rachel's operation and recovery had gone so successfully.

When she went for a check-up four months later, the consultant said to another doctor in the room, 'Mrs Murray has a deep faith. I never believed in miracles and was very cynical about prayer. Rachel was healed a hundred per cent by the power of prayer. That was four months ago, and I can still remember the wonderful experience. No one left the operating theatre the same person. I feel emotional every time I look at Rachel's notes. She had no pain, almost as if it had never happened – yet it did – I was there. She believed, and her church prayed. Examine her; the scar is hidden now along the hairline. Look at that smile; see, the jaw is perfect. Go and study the notes again; you will never have the opportunity to see the like of this ever again.'

In general, miraculous healings recorded in the Bible are instantaneous, complete and permanent. An example is the healing of the paralysed man in Mark 2:1–12. When someone has been ill for years and doctors have done all they can, there is a sense of hopelessness in the patient, who finds it hard to believe there can be any chance of improvement. It takes something pretty dramatic to give them hope again. Such was the case with David Widgery, who had been treated for years for curvature of the spine, three crumbled discs, and arthritis from the base of his spine to his neck.

David was treated at St Thomas's Hospital, London, where six nerves had been cauterized. He was fitted with a heavy bone corset, which he had to wear at night, and took the strongest pain-killers, but was still in constant pain day and night. In autumn 1987 David sensed God telling him to book into a conference on 'spiritual warfare' in Brighton, in April 1988. David was reluctant, as he knew it would be very painful sitting for hours listening to the talks, and he could afford neither the fifty-five pounds which the conference cost, nor the holiday leave from work, as he only gets fifteen days a year. However within two weeks the money was available and, without asking for it, he had been allocated extra holiday from work. His son, not knowing his father had already heard of the conference, thought his father should go, and gave him the conference fee. David's boss realized that, with the added responsibility he had recently taken on, he deserved a further week's holiday a year, so suddenly there was no obstacle.

It was late evening on the third day of the four-day conference. John Wimber, the leader of the Vineyard Church worldwide, was on the platform. God gave him 'words of knowledge' about different illnesses suffered by various people, unknown to him, in the congregation. If they asked for prayer, they would be healed by God and, as a result, dozens of people were healed that evening. John Wimber asked those with physical ailments to stand. 'That's me', thought David, and stood up. Instantly the Holy Spirit fell on him and God gave him an indescribable glimpse of heaven. It lasted about three-quarters of an hour, and David did not want it to end. When he opened his eyes, David knew he was healed. His friend, standing beside him, said he had seen the bones in David's back moving into their correct position under his shirt. When David got home he told his wife, Marion, about it, and was able to dispense with his corset that night.

When David visited his doctor, he asked him for a new X-ray of his back. The doctor replied, 'David, you know what your back's like.' David said, 'Yes, I do know; God has healed it!' Surprised, the doctor arranged for an X-ray and saw a completely normal back! He was amazed. David discovered that autumn that he urgently needed a heart bypass operation. This was successfully carried out, but would not have been possible had his back been in its former condition.

Even more disabled was Edith Nunn, who was diagnosed as having multiple sclerosis in 1971, although her symptoms had begun the year before. Gradually her condition deteriorated so that she could not walk, and her sight and coordination became so poor that she could no longer read or watch TV. She lived with her mother, brother and sister-in-law and family, but by 1988 it was clear that she could no longer be looked after at home, so she moved into a residential home for the disabled. In August 1991, the MS affected her vocal muscles, so she had to use an amplifier to be heard.

Edith had been prayed for many times over the years but, although she felt peace, she was not healed physically. However on 12 February 1992, a friend offered to take her to a healing service being held locally by a Christian fellowship called Pioneer People. Edith went to this meeting trusting that her voice and throat would be healed. The speaker, Martin Scott, spoke about Jesus healing a man with leprosy, and after the talk he said that the Lord had told him someone with MS would be there whom the Lord wanted to heal. When Martin prayed for Edith, he held her hand, she walked three steps, and the Holy Spirit came on her in power. This made her slide to the floor, as often happens when the Holy Spirit is at work in a person. Edith felt wonderful. Her voice returned as soon as she left the building, and the next day she was able to stand up and walk around her room.

By the end of the week, Edith's balance had improved, so she was able to walk along the corridor and take the lift to the dining-room. After fifteen years of being in a wheelchair, life was not easy at first for Edith, but her sight was fully restored in four weeks, giving her more confidence. Nine weeks after the healing service, Edith went for an assessment to be allowed to drive again. The doctor went through all the necessary tests, and could not believe his eyes, as Edith had no trace of MS. The doctor said that 'no neurological abnormality could be detected'.

Dr John Crossley was Edith's GP from 1978–88, and has

been her doctor again since March 1994. Dr Crossley wrote to us that 'Miss Edith Nunn had proven and severe multiple sclerosis, with extreme weakness in her arms and legs, and visual and speech problems. The original diagnosis was made in 1971, and there was no doubt in the opinion of several neurologists that she had the disease. From 1976 onward, there was slow but steady deterioration in her condition. Her prognosis was poor when I last saw her in 1988, and from her notes it seems that the doctor she was seeing in 1992 felt this was still the situation. When I met her again in March 1994, I was astonished at her recovery, which appears to be full and unexplained.'

Edith moved into a flat of her own, as she no longer qualified to live in a home for disabled people! The following year she was invited to go on a Christian holiday week entitled 'Living Through Change'. During one of the sessions the Lord touched Edith's life again, removing the wall around her emotions that she had built to cope with the pain of all those years, especially the four unhappy years when she was receiving total care. When the Lord gently brought down her defences, she felt vulnerable at first, but He helped her through. She has since been able to use her illness and healing experiences in a greater way to help others, both on an individual level and at speaking engagements. In March 1994 Edith was able to get a flat in Woking, which is the area she considers home. This is a first-floor flat with no lift, which would have been a total impossibility before.

Janet Stenner too was healed of multiple sclerosis. Janet lives in Welwyn Garden City. Her symptoms began in 1957 after the birth of her first child. The vertigo, numbness in her legs and occasional double vision increased with the births of her other two children, but it was not until 1976 that multiple sclerosis was diagnosed at the National Hospital for Neurological Disorders in London. By 1981 she was in a motorized wheelchair and received a mobility allowance. Her husband, Brian, was an elder of the Brethren church they attended, and had invited Tom

Jewett of the London Healing Mission to speak at a local group of about fifty Christians, including Janet, on 10 January 1981.

There was a 'word of knowledge' given from God about MS, and Janet was glad to receive prayer for her condition. Tom prayed for her, and she knew the disease had gone. She was healed instantly, and since that day has not used her elbow crutches or wheelchair again. After three days Janet took a half-mile walk, and later that week she walked two miles into the local town. Two weeks after the healing, Brian bought her a bicycle. Janet has not had any symptoms of MS at all since then; she even goes running. She now leads a busy life as her husband has become a Baptist minister. Her GP was happy to confirm her healing. Two doctors she had not met before could find no residual evidence of MS when they assessed her for the DHSS. She had asked to have mobility allowance discontinued and, as she had been considered permanently disabled, not needing a further assessment until the year 2001, she needed to be examined for the DHSS to prove she was healed.

A 'word of knowledge' also encouraged Maggie Colvin to ask God to heal her. She had suffered with a severe kidney problem for several years. The only effective treatment remaining for her was a kidney transplant. Maggie and her husband Andrew had decided she should ask for prayer at a Full Gospel Businessmen's Evening, but there were many people at the meeting with obvious needs, and she held back. Then someone said into the microphone: 'The Lord tells me there is a young woman in the room with a serious kidney problem, and that He would heal her.' Maggie immediately went forward. She was healed from that moment, as if she had been given a new pair of kidneys. She has been well for fourteen years, has had two children and now works as a journalist, designer and TV presenter.

Out of the thirty-five miracles recorded in the Gospels, twenty-six of them relate to healing or wholeness. These miracles are not secondary to Jesus' message of salvation; they are an integral part of it; demonstrating the kingdom of God coming in people's lives. This is aptly explained by Colin Brown, a British theologian now living in America, who writes in his book *That You May Believe*: 'When Jesus performed miracles, his actions had a significance beyond the immediate act of healing. His actions were signs of the kingdom of God. They were indications of a higher order, breaking into our natural order. His healings were a sign that God is the ultimate healer.'

The first part of Jennifer Rees-Larcombe's story is described in the chapter 'When Miracles Don't Happen'. After years of extreme suffering, Jennifer explains in her own book, *Unexpected Healing*, what happened to her in 1990. She had endured constant pain and increasing disability for eight years, which began suddenly with encephalitis when her youngest child was only four. Over the years she had been prayed for many times and longed to be healed. However she had come to the conclusion that she should concentrate on what she *could* do, since God seemed to want to use her while she was in a wheelchair. She wrote several books on a laptop word processor, propped up in bed, and was sometimes taken by car to speak at groups about such subjects as 'Living with pain' and 'The disabled mother'. In continuous pain, in addition to loss of balance and muscle weakness, and having six children, Jennifer had plenty of experience in both these areas.

On 12 March that year, Jennifer was drinking a cup of tea, about to start work on the book she was currently writing, when suddenly the words, 'I want to heal you' came into her mind. Jen describes how she felt. 'After the surprise had worn off, I decided I must have imagined it, but I could not get those words out of my mind. "This is ridiculous", I thought, "I've got to stop this silly wishful thinking." If healing was not going to happen for me, then I ought to concentrate on the things I could do and not hanker after the rest. "I'm not going to get all unsettled again",

I thought furiously, as I remembered all the months of rising hope and bitter disappointment.

'All that day I wrestled with myself and my faith. The DHSS did not even bother to have me assessed regularly any more. They obviously did not expect me to get better. But all day those words, "I want to heal you" kept disturbing me. Just before I finally turned off the light that night, I whispered, "Please, don't mess with me like this. If it *is* You talking, please give me a sign." When I woke early the following morning, I knew without doubt what the sign would be; I must wait patiently for someone to come out of the blue who would confirm this, pray and lay hands on me and I would be well.'

Jen did not feel she should share this with anyone, especially her husband Tony, as they were so close emotionally. He had suffered as much as she in the troughs of disappointment following the ardent hopes and expectation of healing of the previous years. But over the coming weeks, God gave Jen an indescribable feeling of expectation that He would indeed heal her. She remembered words from the Song of Songs she had learnt as a child:

> Rise up my love . . . for lo, the winter is past,
> the rain is over and gone.
> the flowers appear on the earth;
> the time of the singing of birds is come.
> (Song of Songs 2:10–12, King James Version)

That day came on 13 June, a day Jen had been dreading, as she had been asked to speak at an all-day conference at a church in Haslemere, Surrey, on suffering. Getting her ready to go anywhere seemed to take ages. Two friends were to accompany her on the two-hour journey. She was expected to talk about suffering in the morning *and* afternoon; she felt all she knew about it was how much it hurt! She found she was so apprehensive of the prospect that she nearly pulled out of the engagement the day before. However a special picture Jesus gave her in the early hours of that morning gave Jen the confidence that He would be with her, and would meet the various needs of the people there.

At the end of the morning session, Jen asked if anyone had a question or comment. She explains, 'Right in the front row sat a young woman who must have been in her twenties. "Excuse me", she said quietly, "but what is actually wrong with you?" I simply said, "Oh, I've had five attacks of encephalitis", but she went on talking, and I noticed that she looked acutely embarrassed. She mumbled, "I've never had anything like this happen to me before. I've only been coming to church for a few months, you see. But I feel God is telling me to tell you that you are going to get well." It had happened. I do not know how I knew, but there was never any doubt in my mind that here was the person I had waited to meet for so long. I said, "I've waited three months to hear someone tell me that", and I burst into tears of relief.'

During the lunch break the young woman was nowhere to be seen, and Jen was afraid she had left, but she was in the front row again for the afternoon session. Jen knew this person must pray and lay hands on her, which was part of the promise she had received in March. At the end of the session, Jen drove her wheelchair straight over to her and said breathlessly, 'Please would you mind praying for me?' The young woman looked dismayed. 'All this kind of thing is new to me. I've only been a Christian for a year; I don't have the gift of healing. I wouldn't be able to pray for you properly.' 'Please . . .' Jen said urgently, but just then someone brought her a cup of tea, and when Jen looked round, the young woman was disappearing out of the door. 'She's gone!' Jen said desperately. 'You mean Wendy?' said the lady with the tray of cups, 'she's probably gone home to feed the baby.' But instead Wendy had gone to find one of the church leaders, urgently asking him to come and pray for Jen. Wisely the leader replied, 'You have been given the conviction, so you must pray', and sent Wendy back into the church to find Jen.

Several people were standing around Jen when Wendy returned and she asked what she should do. Someone told her to place her hands on Jen's head adding, 'Just allow God to use your hands as you pray, then His power can flow through them.' Jen says now, 'She was so nervous I could feel her hands shaking, and I really cannot remember the words she used, except that her prayer did not contain any flowery theological phrases. She simply asked Jesus Christ to make me well. I felt no sensations or even any emotion; just the matter-of-fact satisfaction of knowing a job had been done at long last. The moment I moved, I knew something was different. Normally my muscles stiffened when I had been sitting for a while, and it would take a very long time and a great deal of effort to straighten myself out. But that day I simply stood up. Privacy was the first thing I needed, so I walked to the "ladies" and locked myself in so I could move my limbs, jog on the spot, and squeeze the toilet roll!'

Jen's husband Tony and daughter Naomi were waiting as the car bringing Jen home drove up. After a day out Jen would always be exhausted and pain-ridden, and needed helping straight to bed to sleep it off, sometimes for twenty-four hours. Jen says, 'I will never forget their faces as they stood at the front door, watching me pull my own wheelchair up the front steps towards them.' It was harder for Jen to meet all the many disabled friends she had made over the previous eight years. 'Why me? Why not her?' she thought; 'I could list many friends who deserved healing more than I did.' As one such friend, Brenda, who had severe arthritis, had just been strapped into the car seat by her husband, about to go home after a visit, Jen crouched down so her eyes were level with Brenda's. 'I'm sorry,' Jen whispered. 'Why?' Brenda answered gently. Jen could see that the peace she had always admired so much was still intact.

'I feel so guilty,' Jen mumbled. 'But you shouldn't,' Brenda replied. 'You help us to believe that we can all get better when the right time comes. I've given up trying to understand God; it's so much more relaxing just to trust Him.'

Frances Tabbinor had a different but equally disabling illness. Only thirty-one years old, Frances had been critically ill with polyarteritis nodosa, which is an inflammation of the arteries around nerves. This rare disease blocks the vital supply of oxygen, so killing the nerves. Frances managed to live within her limitations, but the emotional strain of the illness, in addition to her husband's long-standing alcohol problem, led to the break-up of their ten-year marriage. She was told there was no housing for the disabled likely to become available, but her prayers were answered and, only one week later, she and her eight-year-old son were allocated a bungalow adapted for a paraplegic.

However complications set in, and the illness became chronic. Frances's left foot and part of her leg, left arm and hand and the top of her right foot were affected. Steroids halted the spread of the disease, but she experienced severe pain. The pain caused by the wasting of her nerves was so harrowing that she was given morphine, and spent long periods of time in Dundee Royal Infirmary and in respite care. She had operations to cut the sympathetic nerves in her foot and leg to reduce the pain, a measure carried out as a last resort when no other pain relief is successful. The situation was compounded by probable osteoporosis and sympathetic dystrophy. Gradually Frances became unable to walk and had to be lifted from her bed to her wheelchair. As Frances's health continued to deteriorate, her relationship with God grew, and she was encouraged by many Bible passages.

On 19 January 1994 the pastor of Frances's church, the assistant pastor and a lady on the pastoral team came to share Communion with Frances at home. They prayed for her, and the foot in which nerves had been cut started to tingle. Then she felt heat in her leg. Within a few minutes the foot straightened up; it was no longer limp, and Frances regained complete use of her legs. She could stand at once and walk at full strength, even up stairs. Her GP had an in-depth conversation with her the following day and did neurological tests. He said, 'I don't know what happened, but I can find no trace of the disease.' He called it 'instant remission'. Frances says, 'I know this complete healing from all the illnesses was miraculous, and shows what our wonderful God can do. I am sure that the future is in His capable hands.' The only problem since then is that Frances keeps forgetting her door key when she goes out; in the past the person pushing her wheelchair took that responsibility! She and her son, John, are now looking forward to a skiiing holiday with a Christian holiday company.

Rex Gardner is a consultant obstetrician and gynaecologist and has been ordained in the United Free Church of Scotland. In the *British Medical Journal* he writes: 'A number of case histories of miraculous healings in the past thirty years have been presented in which independent corroboration is possible. It is noteworthy that, in most cases, members of the British medical profession still in practice actively took part. No attempt has been made to prove that miracles have occurred, such proof probably being impossible. The adjective "miraculous" is, however, permissible as convenient shorthand for an otherwise almost inexplicable healing, which occurs after prayer to God, and brings honour to the Lord Jesus Christ.'

Further to that, in his book, *Healing Miracles*, Rex Gardner says: 'Christian miracles are not wonders to make people gawk, but are congruent and appropriate signs that the creator God has not lost His touch or His concern. If we accept that there is a God, we cannot claim that nature is safe from His intervention. Healing is not an automatic response to an adequate quantity of faith, nor is it withheld if insufficient faith is generated. Nor does it require correct theological understanding. It is in the sovereign will of God. The Christian is entitled to bring all problems, including health, in prayer to God, but is not entitled to lay down what particular answer He should give, or at what time. We can make bold and specific requests, as long as we do so "if it is your will". The conclusion seems inescapable, in the light of the evidence, that we have a living God intimately interested in our affairs, prepared to intervene in a specific practical way in response to prayer.'

Mrs Chen Ti Wen is a schoolteacher in Singapore, who heard Anglican clergyman Trevor Dearing speak at a Christian meeting when he was visiting from England. He said, 'Jesus has taken away our burdens, fears, griefs and sorrows. All you need to do is come to Jesus and receive from Him what He did for you on the cross nearly 2,000 years ago.' At the end of his message, he invited anyone who wanted prayer to come forward. Mrs Chen asked for prayer for the insomnia she had suffered for over three years and which had caused her health to be poor, resulting in a succession of chest infections. That night she slept for nine uninterrupted hours, which for her was unheard of! Since that day, 4 March 1978, Mrs Chen Ti Wen has slept restfully every night and is well and healthy.

Her immediate healing encouraged Mrs Chen and her husband, who is a professor at the National University of Singapore, to take their three sons to another meeting at which Trevor Dearing was speaking. Their third son, Jer Hueih, was then four and a half and in need of healing. He had been a normal healthy baby, but at one year of age he developed a high fever. He was in hospital for ten days, his mother beside him all the time, but the effects of the virus were long-term. Prior to this he had been alert, and could call 'Papa', 'Mama' and 'Chacha' (the maid). Now he lost the ability to talk and seemed quiet and listless, quite different from before. He began to say words again about a year later, but he found it difficult to learn anything. As a teacher, his mother had taught his two elder brothers numbers and letters before they started school. Jer Hueih was a very slow learner; he had a dull look on his face and his speech was limited. At four and a half years he did not recognize a single letter or number, despite the efforts of his parents and brothers.

The whole family went forward for prayer together, the mother telling her sons, 'The pastor will pray for us; you need not be afraid. The Lord is going to bless us.' Jer Hueih stood with his brothers. As Trevor Dearing prayed for them, all three boys fell to the ground as the Holy Spirit came upon them. On the way home in the car, one said to another, 'When I was lying on the floor, it was just like lying on my own bed.' For the next few days, Jer Hueih slept a great deal. A few weeks later his eldest brother told his mother, 'Hueih can do additions!' She knew he could not even recognize numbers, so she just smiled and said, 'Oh, who taught him?' Her son replied, 'I taught him.' He asked her to write out simple sums for Jer Hueih, and for each one, Hueih gave the right answer. His mother was astonished. From then on he learnt easily everything he was taught.

Jer Hueih was transformed from a dull child into a very intelligent one. At O-level, he achieved grade A in all nine subjects, and passed six A-levels, all at grade A. He did well in his studies in electrical engineering at university, has a strong Christian faith, and, like his brothers, leads worship at church. His mother says, 'I know it was God who touched him and made him whole.'

Alec Calver had a routine operation at Lewisham Hospital, London, to remove nasal polyps, on 3 November 1993, but an unsuspected cancer was also discovered. While Alec was under anaesthetic, the surgeon noticed an unusual ulcerated lesion in his throat on the left side of his larynx. The surgeon removed the ulcerated lesion as well as the nasal polyps. When the ulcerated area was examined in the laboratory, it was found to be malignant; it was a neuroendocrine carcinoma. Writing to Alec after a few months for the purpose of this book, the consultant wrote: 'The biggest surprise was when you informed me that the symptoms you had suffered from for years, of pain around the left side of your neck and face, had disappeared. Although initially we had planned some radiotherapy treatment for this carcinoma, it was quite obvious on reviewing your larynx that there was no trace of the original carcinoma. To this date the status quo is maintained, and I am delighted, therefore, to declare this a cure.'

The pain Alec had suffered in his neck for twelve and a half years had been diagnosed as trigeminal neuralgia, yet the pain disappeared the day the cancerous lesion was removed and has not returned sixteen months later. Alec has check-ups every three months, and these have all been clear. When Alec was being measured for a mask to protect his face during the radiotherapy treatment, which ultimately he was found not to need, both consultants were present, the surgeon and the radiologist. None could find any trace whatsoever in his throat of the recent operation. Alec recalls: 'There was no scar, or anything to indicate where the growth had been. The doctors said they had never seen anything like it before and declared it to be a miracle.' Both Alec and his wife Edith believe firmly in the power of God to heal, and their faith and commitment have been attested by their vicar, Revd Michael Kingston, at Plumstead Common.

Maisie Judge now lives in Sussex, and experienced her healing in 1952. As a young girl, Maisie fractured her wrist, and complications had set in. For eighteen months her wrist and arm were in splints and then plaster. Owing to electrical treatments and lack of use, Maisie's hand withered to half its normal size. For the next nineteen years that one hand remained much smaller than the other, and she could neither grip nor lift anything with it. The hand was in constant pain, and it made sleep difficult for Maisie. In 1952 Pentecostal Pastor Howell Harris was holding meetings in Watford and Maisie, with her husband, Frank, decided to attend one Sunday. Maisie felt sure the Lord would heal her.

Maisie asked for prayer, and Pastor Harris raised her useless hand and arm and prayed: 'Jesus, please heal this arm . . .' Maisie says it was as if a surge of electricity ran through her, an awe-inspiring experience that she cannot forget to this day. The pastor told her to move her fingers, which she did freely for the first time in nineteen years. The pain had gone, and she was able to lift a chair with her once useless arm. The packed meeting hall resounded with the praise of those who saw the miracle. 'All Watford knew about it,' Maisie remembers, and from that day her arm and hand began to grow until it was normal size. In a few weeks it was the same size as the other hand, and remained healthy and strong. Maisie was forty-five at the time of her healing.

Kate Reid was only thirteen years old when she was run over in London as she crossed the road to get the bus, in August 1991. She had looked and listened for traffic, but had not seen the car which hit her, turning her over. A wheel ran over her foot, and an X-ray showed that the four bones in the centre of her foot were broken. Kate also had painful gravel grazing on her arms and a chunk of flesh out of her knee, which was very swollen. The following Saturday Kate went with her family to the New Wine Christian camp. She had to use crutches and a wheelchair, and the doctor warned her that she would not be able to walk on her broken foot for twelve weeks. Kate was prayed for at an evening meeting on the Monday of the camp, and her foot and knee began to improve at once. By the Wednesday she could put on both trainers and walk well. She had no pain, and needed none of the expected physiotherapy when she got home.

An increasing number of people suffer from the debilitating condition called myalgic encephalomyelitis, like Gillian Edgar at the beginning of this chapter. It can begin suddenly, and severely disrupts the sufferer's life and family. Barbara Wright, who attends St Andrew's church, Chorleywood, had ME for seven years, after a slight infection. When she was prayed for at church on 9 June 1994, she was suddenly healed of all symptoms and has had no recurrence in the nine months since.

Sozo Ministries, based in Romsey, Hampshire, have also seen many remarkable healing miracles involving all kinds of diseases. Two people who have written to us were healed from severe ME. Becky Penberthy was only in her twenties, but suffered two years of ME making her very weak and lethargic. Sylvia Shakespeare's ME was complicated by multiple allergies, but both Becky and Sylvia, along with another friend who was equally badly affected by ME, were all healed at the same conference run by Sozo Ministries.

Revd Reg East, in his book *Heal the Sick*, states: 'Jesus' own ministry so abounds with physical healings that to eliminate them would change the whole tenor of it. It is no surprise, therefore, that He should say to John the Baptist that these healings, with the preaching of the good news, were the evidence that He was the One who was to come.'

CHAPTER SEVEN
Miracles in Places of Conflict

Men have forgotten God. The failings of human
consciousness, deprived of its divine dimension,
have been a determining factor in all the major crimes.

Alexander Solzhenitsyn

LL OF US face situations of conflict, but it is
how we react to conflict that matters. God
expects us to play our part, for He has 'No
hands but our hands'. We cannot blame God
for the starving in the world when we have
failed to distribute fairly the food He has provided for all.
Conflict began when man chose to go his own way, as described
in Genesis chapters 3 and 4. Adam and Eve disobeyed God, then
their son, Cain, became full of hatred and jealousy and murdered
his own brother, Abel. The three ingredients of conflict are
jealousy, greed and lust for power. We can see this throughout
history. Our own century has seen more wars than any other.
The recent conflicts in the Gulf, Northern Ireland, former
Yugoslavia and Rwanda all have their roots in these three
ingredients, causing much personal tragedy.

It was a cold, blustery day on Sunday 8 November 1987
when the people of Enniskillen gathered at the cenotaph as usual
for the Remembrance Day service. Gordon Wilson, who ran a
draper's shop, stood beside his daughter, Marie, a student nurse.
Before the service began a bomb went off quite close to where
they were standing. The force of the bomb pushed them forward
on to the ground, as Gordon was thinking 'We're in a bomb

blast, but it can't be, not at the cenotaph on Remembrance Sunday!'

The building near where they had been standing, out of the wind and the rain, had collapsed on top of them and the other people nearby. They were lying beneath several feet of masonry rubble. Questions raced through Gordon's mind: 'Where's Marie? Is she hurt? Is she trapped? Is she alive?' Soon after the blast, he felt his hand being squeezed, and heard Marie call out: 'Is that you, Dad?' Gordon shouted, 'How are you, Marie?' Shouting to make herself heard above the din, Marie replied 'I'm fine.' Gordon's heart skipped a beat with relief, but then suddenly, she screamed. Gordon knew she must be suffering badly to scream like that. They continued to call to each other, Marie occasionally screaming out, until she gripped his hand tightly and said, 'Daddy, I love you very much.' Her hand loosened its grip, and those were the last words he ever heard her say.

At that point the rescuers began to dig Gordon out, and he was taken to hospital. After anxious hours of asking everyone for news, Gordon finally learned the extent of Marie's injuries. She was in a critical condition, with profuse bleeding and severe internal injuries. She had suffered a cardiac arrest, and had been given twenty-four pints of blood. By this time Gordon's wife, Joan, and their other children, Peter and Julie Anne, had been called to Gordon's bedside, knowing that Marie was in the operating theatre. Later, Joan and Julie Anne went up to see Marie in intensive care. The specialist, one of the many who had fought for Marie's life in theatre, was standing beside the bed. He looked at Joan sadly and shook his head. Her darling Marie, who had been so full of life, was dying. She kissed her, and saw her eyelids flicker, then her heart stopped beating. Joan remembers, 'I could only utter, "The Lord gave, the Lord has taken away. Blessed be the name of the Lord." I knew I had to lean hard on the Lord now; He was my only strength.' The family cried together for the beloved girl they had lost, and took Gordon home from hospital later that day.

The phone and doorbell were ringing within minutes of the Wilsons' arrival home. They were shocked to hear of the enormity of that morning's disaster — ten others had been killed as well as Marie, and many injured, some very seriously. Friends and neighbours soon thronged to the house to show their sympathy. During the evening, Gordon went outside for a breath of fresh air and met two young men. He recognized one as an Enniskillen man, Charlie Warmington, a producer at the BBC who introduced Gordon to his colleague Mike Gaston, a BBC journalist. They asked if they could interview him for the radio. After explaining the morning's events Gordon said, 'I have lost my daughter, and we shall miss her; but I bear no ill will, I bear no grudge. Dirty sort of talk is not going to bring her back to life. She was a great wee lassie. She's dead. She's in heaven, and we'll meet again. Don't ask me, please, for a purpose. I don't have an answer; but I know there has to be a plan ... It's part of a greater plan, and God is good. And we shall meet again.'

This was not just Gordon's initial reaction, but his firm conviction, which he maintained throughout the following days and weeks when he was frequently interviewed. Gordon said that, after the first interview, 'Some people said, "He's in a state of shock, he can't mean what he says!" Even though I was indeed shocked, and although my voice had broken with emotion once or twice during the broadcast, I knew exactly what I was saying.'

Gordon continues, 'As a family, we were conscious of a deep undercurrent of prayer coming from countless unseen people, which helped us tremendously. I have always believed in prayer, but I was never so conscious of the power of prayer as I was in that week. I commend to everyone who feels they want to help, but maybe cannot do so in a direct way: your prayers for others in trouble can, and do, make all the difference.'

In the ensuing years, Gordon has reflected on his reaction. 'I did not use the word "forgive" in that broadcast, nor in any later one, but people understood that my words were about forgiveness ... It would be wrong for me to give any impression that gunmen and bombers should be allowed to walk the streets freely. But whether or not they are judged here on earth by a court of law, I have no doubt that they will have to face their final judgment before Almighty God. Nevertheless, I still pray for those bombers, and I continue to bear them no ill will. I believe I do my very best to show forgiveness, but the last word rests with God, and those who seek His forgiveness will need to repent. It cannot be easy knowing that, directly or indirectly, you are responsible for the deaths of many people and the maiming of many others, and for the suffering and despair of the relatives ... I wasn't angry at the time, and I'm not angry now. I'll go on praying for all of them, and leave the rest to God.' With these words, Gordon Wilson shows us the miracle of real forgiveness.

There have been many miracles in Northern Ireland during the twenty-five years of the recent troubles. Another concerns a building in Newtownards, which has been owned for many years by a Christian organization called United Christian Broadcasters (UCB). It had been almost impossible to sell buildings of this kind in Northern Ireland during the troubles, but there were tenants in it. Newtownards has suffered more than its fair share of bombings during the violence.

In March 1994, when the troubles were still making life very difficult in Northern Ireland, UCB were considering the purchase of a large, old school near Stoke-on-Trent to use as a prayer house and new recording studios for Christian broadcasts. The school had become available, but UCB needed to find £95,000, which seemed like a fortune. Never in its history had UCB held more than its immediate running costs in hand. The trustees sat around the table considering the opportunity to purchase the school, ideal for their purposes. Where could the money possibly come from? They prayed together that if God wanted them to have this building, He would provide the money for it, but they needed to decide quickly.

Just as they finished praying, a fax was delivered to the room where they were meeting. It brought the news that the building in Northern Ireland had just been sold to the current tenants! After legal fees were paid, the sale realized just over £95,000. Only after the sale had been completed did UCB learn that the building had been fire-bombed in an IRA attack just before the sale was completed. Four other buildings were also targeted, but their own had suffered little damage. The purchasers went ahead with the sale at the agreed price, and the supply of finance was not disrupted.

Michael and Bernadette Power enjoyed a happy family life with their three children. Their Catholic faith had been renewed and strengthened by the Holy Spirit as they came into a fresh awareness of God's love for them. They were involved in their local church in Poleglass, a large housing estate west of Belfast. One Sunday morning the family were driving to church. Eight-year-old Michelle was sitting in the front next to her father. Seven-year-old Gavin and three-month-old Emma were in the back seat with their mother. As they came to a crossroads, another car drew alongside and a gunman opened fire, shooting Michael at close range. The gunman sped away, leaving Michael dying and Michelle nearly blinded by shattered glass. A Protestant terrorist group, the Ulster Freedom Fighters, admitted responsibility for the murder, claiming it was in retaliation for a murder by the IRA the day before.

Soon after the tragedy, Bernadette was praying with the children before school one day, and Gavin asked: 'Mummy, will the man who killed Daddy be in heaven?' Breathing a silent prayer, his mother replied, 'If they are really sorry and ask Jesus to forgive them, then they will be in heaven.' Gavin replied,

'Well if they are going to be there, I don't want to be in heaven with them.' Bernadette replied, 'If Jesus forgives and saves them, setting them free from their terrible sin, He will change them. They will be completely different people.' Gavin paused, then said, 'Mummy, let's pray for those men and ask Jesus to change them.' To be with Bernadette and her children is to experience the amazing grace and forgiving love of God. She radiates the peace of Christ, and joyfully shares with broken and wounded people in a deprived area of Belfast.

David Hamilton joined the Loyalist Terrorists because he and his friends wanted to do what they could for Northern Ireland, believing the fight against the IRA to be a worthy cause. Gradually he became more involved in terrorist activities, including carrying out armed robberies to finance the cause. David had a good job with an engineering firm, and was married, but his wife did not like his being involved in terrorism. In 1973 he was arrested for the first time for armed robbery. While David was on remand, he saw violence inside prison too, when one of the inmates was brutally killed by other prisoners. This made him begin to pray, but like many people he knew, he used God as a 'spare wheel', only turning to Him for help when in trouble, not as a 'steering wheel' to direct his life. He prayed that he would get a short sentence.

Initially David was given a five-year sentence, but the next day he was called back to court. The judge said, 'Last night I was speaking to the manager of the engineering firm where you have been working. He spoke well of you, and said it was a shame you had been sent down for five years, so I have decided to record your sentence and let you out today, on condition that you don't engage in further terrorist activities.' David was overjoyed, but forgot to thank God for the remarkable answer to his prayer. Nor did he stop his terrorist activities. Only one year later, he was arrested again and questioned about bombings, a murder and armed robberies.

After being in prison for one year on remand, he was brought before the same judge. This time the judge gave him a longer sentence because of his broken promise. The day he was sentenced, David's mother was very upset, and on the way home she called to visit David's uncle to tell them the news. His mother-in-law, Mrs Annie Beggs, was there, a fine elderly Christian lady. David's mother was crying and she said, 'David is a hopeless case; he will never change.' Annie Beggs answered, 'If God can change the heart of John Newton, a slave-trader, He can change your David's heart too.' She promised to pray for David every day. Of course, David knew nothing of this at the time, but only fourteen months later, her prayers were dramatically answered.

In Crumlin Road jail, on New Year's Eve 1979, David remembers thinking: 'The new year will be no different from last year.' But he was wrong. Within a month, his life had totally changed. One evening he came into his cell and saw that someone had left a Christian tract on his bed about the second coming of Christ. He glanced at it, then screwed it up and threw it out of the window; he had no time for anything religious. A short time later, he was drinking a cup of tea when the thought came into his mind that he should become a Christian. He was so shocked that he burnt his lip on the tea!

Becoming a Christian was the last thing David wanted, yet he could not get the thought out of his mind. He thought, 'This is crazy – I don't even want to be a Christian. Even if I did, God would say no. God is only interested in good people – not someone like me. All evening he struggled with these thoughts; it seemed as if a light had begun to shine in his mind, showing him what his life was really like. He realized that on several occasions he could easily have been killed in explosions or shootings. He wondered why God had protected him. He tried to go to sleep and forget all about it, but still David's first thought on opening his eyes in the morning was that he should become a Christian. The only Christian he knew was Jacko, a fellow prisoner. Jacko, whose real name was Trevor, had a reputation for being a hard man and was serving twenty years for murder. Two years into his sentence he had decided to commit suicide in the bath. As he was about to cut his wrists with a razor, he heard God say to him, 'Trevor, don't do that – I love you.' He became a Christian that same moment. Each of the prisoners had one pound fifty a week for pocket money, much of which was spent on cigarettes. Jacko spent all of his on Christian tracts, which he gave to anyone he could. David thought he was totally 'over the top'.

The first person David met that morning when he was let out of his cell was Jacko, larger than life, as ever. David said, 'Jacko, I'm thinking of becoming a Christian and I don't know what to do.' Jacko gave him a heartfelt bear-hug, followed by lots of tracts. David couldn't wait to read them, and pored over them at every opportunity during his work in the laundry. The other prisoners mocked him terribly when he went back to his cell at dinner time. It was then he made a decision to ask God into his life. Hungry to read the Bible, he was given a New Testament and read it all in three days in his cell. Just before he finished reading Revelation, the Holy Spirit fell on him in a powerful way. David still had four and a half years to serve, and wished he could be outside so he could do more for the Lord. A year later he was reading Luke 10:2: 'The harvest is plentiful, but the workers are few.' He felt God say: 'You can work for Me in here.' David thought, 'I've just joined the ranks of the prison chaplains. The difference is that they go home in the evenings and I stay to do some overtime!' All over the jail, men started becoming Christians as David talked with them.

In 1981 a succession of prisoners in the Maze prison went on hunger strike. David, along with others, prayed and fasted that the hunger strike would end, and it did. The thirteenth man on hunger strike, Liam McCloskey, stopped on the fifty-fifth day; he was close to death. While recovering in hospital, with the Christian prisoners continuing to pray for him, Liam became a

Christian. More and more men began to read the Bible. There was no segregation in the prison. IRA men and Loyalists, who had been trying to kill each other outside, were all in the same prison. They chose to sit on separate sides of the dining room and to have nothing to do with each other. However one tough terrorist, who had become a Christian, put his chair in the middle of the dining room and called out that anyone could sit with him. New Christians from both sides joined him. One visitor being shown around the prison in the Maze H-blocks saw a group of men studying the Bible together. He could tell by the tattoos on their arms that some were Loyalist and some IRA men. A prison officer told them later that the visitor had said, 'If anyone had told me that Republicans and Loyalists were having Bible studies together, I would never have believed them.'

The greatest test to his Christian faith came when David heard that his wife, Maxine, was living with another man. Not long afterwards, the man lost his temper with David's two-year-old son. He beat up his face so badly that he was unrecognizable and had to be admitted to hospital. David was livid, and thought, 'When I get the chance, I'll kill him.' It was four years later when the man was arrested for another crime and was put in the same prison as David. The first time David saw him, in his hatred he hissed a death threat at him, resolving to kill him at the first opportunity. Alone in his cell a few days later, David twice heard God say, 'Forgive him, David.' Frustrated, he retorted, 'Look what he did to my son.' He heard God reply, 'Look what they did to My Son.' David knew he must forgive him.

Not long afterwards, both men were taken to the waiting room, as they had visitors. One prison officer would lock them in from one door, and another would let them into the visiting room by another door. When they were locked in the waiting room alone together, the other man cowered, believing that David still had every intention of killing him, and could easily do so because of his superior strength. Seeing his fear, David said to him, 'I forgive you, because Jesus has forgiven me everything.' David hoped the other man was not being visited by his own wife, but both their visitors were their mothers. During the visiting time, the other man's mother came up to David saying, 'My son has told me what you said. I want to thank you from the bottom of my heart.' David has now been released. Today he is an ordained minister, and has an international Christian ministry. He travels to different countries, telling of what God has done in his life, how He has worked powerfully, in a person and in a community.

Through the ministry of the Holy Spirit, Christians of all denominations have been meeting together to pray for peace and reconciliation in Northern Ireland. United prayer meetings of this kind have been held in such places as the Christian Renewal Centre in Rostrevor, and in the Corrymeela community in Belfast, and in Ballycastle. There have been various initiatives to encourage unity across the 'divide', such as holidays for both Catholic and Protestant children, and 'All Children Together', which was formed, mainly by parents, in 1974 to promote shared Christian schools. Out of this since 1984 have come Lagan College and other integrated Northern Irish schools, where pupils and staff are Catholic and Protestant in equal numbers. Considered rather extraordinary at the outset, Lagan College has won recognition among the Province's most excellent schools. Since 1972 Sister Anna, an Anglican nun, has lived in Belfast between the sectarian divide, and is equally respected for her reconciliation work by both Catholics and Protestants.

In February 1975 Edmund and Maura Kiely's only son, Gerard, was gunned down in cold blood as he left Mass at St Bride's church, close to the university where he was a student. The only motive to the killing was that he was a Catholic. At first Maura was very bitter: 'To say we were shattered in no way conveys the reality of our feelings. We were so stunned that it was difficult to understand God, or to find that answer to why – why had God allowed such an act to take place on the threshold of His house, and especially as Gerard was performing his religious duties? We did thank God, though, that we were Gerard's parents, and not the parents of the boy who shot him. I don't think one ever completely recovers from the sense of loss. But somehow I received the grace to realize the true value of our Christianity, which has at its very heart the Man of Sorrows. God had sent us a cross for some reason.'

Maura brought something good out of the tragedy by beginning the Cross Group, which symbolically reflects the situation in Northern Ireland. It is a mixed group of Protestants and Catholics who have all lost a loved one through bomb or bullet. They share the same problems, feelings, reactions and difficulties. Maura says, 'If the bereaved from both sides can be reconciled, surely it is not too much to ask for reconciliation in the wider community? I committed myself to work for reconciliation among bereaved families. Thousands of people work quietly together, beneath the noise of war, building bridges. Each community must come to accept the other, not as we want them to be, but as they identify themselves. Forgiveness is imperative in the Christian life, because reconciliation is impossible without it.'

Albert Einstein put it this way: 'The world is a dangerous place to live in – not because of the people who do evil, but because of the people who sit and let it happen.' Throughout the troubles, more and more Christians have been refusing to 'sit and let it happen', and since peace has been declared, we are increasingly seeing examples of their actions.

The most widespread conflict of the past fifty years has been the Second World War. Many people were involved in praying for the situation to be resolved, and national days of prayer were called at the most crucial times. One such occasion was 26 May 1940, when King George VI called the people of Britain and the

Empire to prayer. Millions flocked to churches, queuing to get in, to commit the nation's cause to God. Until that time the British and French armies were in grave danger. The German High Command had boasted that 'The British army is encircled, our troops are proceeding to its annihilation.' The position was serious beyond precedent, but soon the word 'miracle' began to be heard on all sides. The first was Hitler's orders to his tank command to stop only ten miles short of Dunkirk, presumably thinking that the *Luftwaffe* planes could finish off the job. In the event, clouds and rain succeeded in preventing the bombers from moving in.

The weather was also part of the second miracle. A great storm which broke over Flanders on Tuesday 28 May was followed by a great calm on the English Channel for the next nine days. The usually rough waters were like a millpond, allowing the British to send all available shipping over to evacuate British and French troops. Some were just small fishing or pleasure boats, and many made several journeys back and forth. Another miracle was that smoke was effectively used to obscure the Eastern Mole, a makeshift embarkation bridge, thus preventing enemy attack. So dramatic was the rescue of 342,000 British and 123,000 French troops that a national day of thanksgiving was called on Sunday 9 June. C. B. Mortlock reported in the *Daily Telegraph*: 'The prayers of the nation were answered . . . the consciousness of the miraculous deliverance pervades the camps in which the troops are now housed in England . . . it is undoubted that there was such a calmness over the whole of the waters of the English Channel for that vital period of days as has rarely been experienced. Those who are accustomed to the Channel testify to the strangeness of this calm; they are deeply impressed by the phenomenon by which it became possible for tiny craft to go back and forth in safety.'

In July 1940 the Battle of Britain began with attacks on shipping in the Channel. This was followed by attacks on various strategic towns, and bombing of the airfields. By September 1940 the great assault on London had begun, and Hitler threatened to 'erase' the cities of Britain. People all over Britain were praying. For instance, Rees Howells, the principal of the Bible College of Wales, led his staff and students in prayer three times a day during this period. Sometimes they prayed for several hours, interceding for Britain. Rees Howells said: 'We prayed that London would be defended and that the enemy would fail to break through, and God answered prayer.' The situation had been so grave that another national day of prayer was called on 8 September 1940. This had already been organized when, on 7 September, Britain saw the largest aerial assault, when more than a thousand bombers and fighters attacked the nation.

The Battle of Britain reached a crisis one week later, on 15 September, when Winston Churchill, the prime minister, visited the operations room of the RAF. He watched as enemy squadrons poured over, and the British planes went up to meet them. When all the fighters were in combat, Churchill asked the air marshal, 'What other reserves do we have?' and the reply was, 'There are none.' Churchill looked very grave. But as they watched over the next five minutes, the enemy planes started to turn around and go home. There was a continuous movement eastwards, with no fresh attack. There seemed to be no reason why the *Luftwaffe* should have headed for home just when victory was within their grasp. The only explanation can be that there was a great deal of prayer going up about the situation all over the country, not least in the Bible College of Wales.

The national days of prayer certainly made a valuable contribution in focusing the prayers of millions at a particular time. Although some towns and cities had been damaged, it was far less than had been expected, and the threatened invasion of Britain was averted. Air Chief Marshal Sir Hugh Dowding, who was Commander-in-Chief of Fighter Command at the time, said that Britain was not too proud to recognize the need for national days of prayer, and should therefore acknowledge the answers to those prayers before God. In a speech quoted in the *Birmingham Daily Post* on 8 June 1942, he said of the Battle of Britain: 'I pay my homage to those gallant boys who gave their all that our nation might live. I pay my tribute to their leaders and commanders, but I say with absolute conviction that I can trace the intervention of God, not only in the Battle itself, but in the events that led up to it. If it had not been for this intervention, the Battle would have been joined in conditions which, humanly speaking, would have rendered victory impossible.' In another speech, quoted in the *Daily Sketch* on 15 September 1943, he affirmed: 'At the end of the Battle, one had the feeling that there had been some special divine intervention to alter some sequence of events which would otherwise have occurred.'

During 1942 the island of Malta, a vital base for the Allied Forces in the Mediterranean, was under serious attack. All through the spring the island was pounded by mortars without respite. Much prayer went up from the island. General Sir William Dobbie, Governor of Malta during the height of the island's ordeal, wrote in *A Very Present Help*: 'We have found how prone we are to limit the help that God gives . . . He can go on delivering us for as long as He sees we need deliverance. That is one of the lessons He graciously taught us in the siege of Malta . . . Not only had we hardly any fighter aircraft, and a very meagre number of anti-aircraft guns, but the dense population of Malta rendered this form of attack [aerial bombardment] peculiarly dangerous . . . many persons in Malta, both in responsible and other positions, realized our need of His help and were prepared to ask Him to give it to us. By no other means could we be sure of holding this vital outpost.'

A dramatic sign of God's protection was seen in a church in Mosta, a Maltese town of 8,000 inhabitants. It is very near the Ta'Qali airport, and so had its share of bombardment. The people used to go frequently to church for prayer and shelter. One

Thursday, 9 April 1942 at four in the afternoon there was a one-hour service for prayer in the Rotunda church, which boasts the third largest dome in Europe. At 4.05 p.m. a bomb weighing 500 lb crashed through the domed roof, hit a painting on the side of the church and catapulted right through the building. It came to rest on the ground in the middle of the church. The miracle was that it failed to explode: it would have destroyed the whole building. The church was packed with three hundred people, yet not one was injured by the ricocheting bomb, nor even by the slabs falling from the roof. Every year, on 9 April the bells of the Rotunda church ring joyfully, while the people of Malta renew their thanksgiving to God for this miracle.

In Britain, many people told of miraculous escapes during the bombings. Cyril Davey was a London City Missionary, alone at home on 22 August 1944 as his wife, Grace, was on duty at the report centre, where news of all bombings came in. He was about to go out of the front door of their home in Kingston-upon-Thames, when he remembered a newspaper upstairs ready to post to his son who was in the navy. While he was fetching it, there was a terrific explosion and he instinctively dropped to the floor. Doodlebugs normally gave a warning sound before they landed, but this one had gone into a dive and, without warning, hit the road just yards from their house. The blast destroyed the windows at the front of the house, took the roof off and blew the front door right through the house, taking the inner and outer kitchen doors with it. If Cyril had not remembered the newspaper and gone upstairs, he would have been walking down the front path just as the bomb landed. He would certainly have ended up in the back garden along with the three doors. Cyril had not a single injury, yet the turn-ups of his trousers were full of broken glass! He phoned the report centre and told his wife a bomb had landed outside their house. As it had not been a report from official sources, the commander was not sure if he should act upon the information. Embarrassed, Grace phoned her husband back to ask, 'Are you sure?' 'Sure?' Cyril exclaimed, 'I'm standing here holding a piece of the bomb in my hand!'

After the Second World War, stories emerged of extraordinary courage and sacrifice made by men and women who sought to bring God's solution in a situation of conflict. One of these was Father Maximilian Kolbe, a Polish priest who belonged to a Franciscan order. The aim of his work was to combat evil in the world, and he set up friaries in Poland and Japan for this purpose. In 1939 he was in charge of a friary in Poland. After the German invasion he sent all thirty-six brothers to join the Red Cross, or to their homes. He repaired the damaged friary and helped refugees, especially Jews, who were in particular danger. About three thousand refugees passed through his hands, two-thirds of them Jews. For this, Father Maximilian was arrested on 17 February 1941 and taken to Pawiak prison in Warsaw.

Priests were especially badly treated by the SS guards, and Father Maximilian was no exception. One grabbed his crucifix from him and thrust it in his face, shouting contemptuously, 'Do you believe that?' When he replied 'I do', the guard struck his face hard. The guard repeatedly asked him the same question, raining down blows on the priest's head and shoulders when the same reply was given. A fellow prisoner who witnessed this assault later said of Father Maximilian's self-control: 'He behaved as though nothing untoward had happened.'

On 28 May he was moved to the infamous Auschwitz concentration camp, where priests were given the hardest work and cruellest treatment. On one occasion he was beaten and kicked so badly that he became unconscious and was left for dead, but under cover of darkness the other prisoners brought him to the makeshift hospital. His starving, bleeding body, with the flesh on his back hanging like ribbons, gradually began to recover, but all the while he was trying to console the other sick and dying men. He never considered his own needs or hardships, but was always encouraging the others, urging them not to hate. He shared his own meagre ration of bread to give them Communion, and they loved to hear his words of hope and forgiveness. He assured them that God was suffering with them. One survivor remembered, 'Although he wore the same ragged clothes as the rest of us, one forgot his wretched exterior and was conscious only of the charm of his countenance and of his radiant holiness.'

Father Maximilian became a martyr in August 1941. A prisoner had escaped and, as punishment, for every man who escaped, ten prisoners had to die. The men had to stand to attention all day, then, in the evening, the Gestapo chief passed down the rows of men, choosing who would die. As the ninth man was chosen, he uttered an agonized cry: 'My wife, my children – I shall never see them again.' Suddenly a slight man walked towards the Gestapo chief, pointed to the man who had cried out and asked very calmly, in correct German, if he might take his place. The rows of men gasped; it was an unheard-of thing to do. The chief asked, 'Who are you?' and he replied, 'A Catholic priest.' Incredibly, the chief nodded his assent and allowed the reprieved man, Franciszek Gajowniczek, to return to his place in the line.

The condemned men were buried alive in specially con-structed airless underground bunkers and left to die by slow starvation. Usually screams, groans and curses were heard from the bunker, but this time they were replaced by prayers and hymns. Not only had Father Maximilian taken the place of one prisoner, but he also spent the time that remained to him helping the other nine men to die with dignity. An eyewitness later reported: 'It was as though Cell 18 had become a church, as prayers resounded through all the corridors of the bunker.' Feebly but distinctly, prisoners in other cells joined in the praying. Death overtook them one by one, and after two weeks four remained alive, but only Father Maximilian was still conscious. As the cell was needed, it was decided to finish off those remaining with a fatal injection. Still praying, Father Maximilian calmly held out his arm for the injection. The guards had never seen anyone like him. When the guard returned to the cell, Father Maximilian was dead, but his eyes were open and his face was serene and radiant. He brings to mind the words of Jesus: 'Peace I leave with you, my peace I give you' (John 14:27). Father Maximilian's life and death stand out as a miracle of self-sacrifice.

The ten Boom family were watchmakers in Haarlem, Holland, and daughters Corrie and Betsie worked in the shop with their father. As Christians, they showed Christ's love and care to those being persecuted by the Nazi regime. They made a secret room in the upper floor of their home and hid a number of Jewish families there until they were able to get them away to safety. A Nazi raid one day meant the end of that, and the family and the hidden Jews were all taken to prison. The elderly Mr ten Boom survived only a few weeks, but his daughters spent more than a year in Ravensbruck concentration camp, where more than 96,000 women died. Betsie was among those who died, but before that she said to her sister, 'Corrie, your whole life has been a training for the Christian work you are doing here in prison, and what you will do afterwards.'

Corrie recalled: 'God has plans, not problems, for our lives. In the German camp, with all its horror, I found many prisoners who had never heard of Jesus. If God had not used my sister, Betsie, and me to bring them to Him, they would never have heard of Him. Many died or were killed, but they died with the name of Jesus on their lips. They were well worth all our suffering.'

A week after Betsie's death, Corrie was unexpectedly released. She later learnt it was owing to an administrative error, but here she was, at fifty-two, knowing her life had been given back to her for a purpose. In the camp, she had learned how precious life was, and she was thankful to God for everything. In Ravensbruck she and Betsie had even been grateful for the fleas, since the guards avoided searching their beds for fear of being bitten, so the sisters were able to keep their Bible undiscovered. Over the next thirty years, Corrie travelled the world as 'a tramp for the Lord' sharing the message of forgiveness and God's love, especially in prisons. She said, 'Forgiveness is the key which unlocks the door of resentment and the handcuffs of hatred. It breaks the chains of bitterness and the shackles of selfishness. The forgiveness of Jesus not only takes away our sins, it makes them as if they had never been.'

Love must ultimately be the answer to every problem. The following prayer was written by an unknown prisoner in Ravensbruck concentration camp, and left by the body of a dead child:

> 'O Lord, remember not only the men and women of good will, but also those of ill will. But do not remember all the suffering they have inflicted on us; remember the fruits we have brought, thanks to this suffering – our comradeship, our loyalty, our humility, our courage, our generosity, the greatness of heart which has grown out of all this; and when they come to judgment, let all the fruits which we have borne be their forgiveness.'

Man's inhumanity to man has not abated as our century has progressed. In 1975 the Khmer Rouge forces, supported by the Chinese communists, took over Cambodia. The people living in the cities were driven out to work on the land in forced labour camps. Families were deliberately broken up so that they could not collaborate to resist or escape. Millions of Cambodian people were shot or clubbed to death in the process of emptying the cities. Doctors, teachers, leaders of all kinds, plus news reporters or anyone who had contact with the Western world were the first to be annihilated. Dead bodies were everywhere, left to rot. In the labour camps, armed supervisors killed for any petty reason, or for no reason at all. Those who tried to escape were shot, and thousands died from the heavy work and lack of food.

When Vietnamese troops poured into Cambodia on 7

January 1979, many Cambodians welcomed deliverance from the Khmer Rouge, but others were dubious. They remembered the fierce conflicts that had raged for many generations between Vietnam and Cambodia. They also knew the Russian-backed communism of Vietnam was not much better than the Chinese communism which supported the Khmer Rouge. One young man, Sok Em, remembers many times narrowly escaping death. Once, when he was trying to gather a little food from the fields for his wife and himself, he was spotted by Khmer Rouge soldiers. They intended to set fire to the fields, even though it was harvest time. Indiscriminate killers, they began firing on Sok Em with machine-guns and a rocket gun. Bullets showered around him like rain, but miraculously not one of them hit him.

Sok Em and his wife, Savy, were desperate to escape, and when an opportunity arose, they did so. The jungle trails were mined with explosives and patrolled by soldiers, but they survived, though for three days and two nights they had no food or water. Savy was seven months pregnant, so it was particularly difficult for her. As they approached the border with Thailand, they found some other refugees who had made shelters with tree branches and leaves. Savy said, 'I'm having pains, I think I'm going to have the baby now.' Sok Em thought this would be a dreadful place to have a baby, and at seven months it would be too small to live in these primitive conditions. However the birth could not be put off, and Savy was delivered of a daughter, lying on a plastic sheet under a leaf shelter. Amazingly, both Savy and her tiny daughter, whom they named Chap, seemed fine.

Sometimes they were caught in the crossfire between the Khmer Rouge and the Free Khmer soldiers. Savy would hide with the baby in a hollow in the ground. Once, during a lull in the shooting, she came across to where Sok Em was lighting a fire to cook some food. Savy had walked about five metres when a large shell went off in the very hollow where she had been lying. When Sok Em heard the explosion he saw a little pillow fly into the air. He recognized it instantly as the pillow on which the baby slept, and shouted, 'Where is the baby?' 'Here,' she said, showing how she had the baby snuggled close to her. Savy was guided to leave the hollow just in time.

When it was possible, they continued their journey into Thailand and came to the Khao I Dang refugee camp. They built a small bamboo shelter with a mud floor, and got to know the other refugees, including an eighty-year-old man called Taing San and his family. When groups of Christians gathered together in the camp to sing and preach, Sok Em would mock them and disturb them by singing other songs very loudly. Taing San was one of the Christians who patiently bore the ridicule, and was always very kind to Sok Em, Savy and Chap. Taing San came regularly to Sok Em's 'house' and would often help him in practical ways. Sometimes Taing San would tell them about Jesus and explain why they needed to believe in Him. One evening, about two and a half months after meeting him for the first time, Sok Em and Savy went to Taing San's house and made the decision to become Christians. His family clapped their hands and rejoiced with them. Sok Em's parents and brothers had all been killed, as had Savy's father, but now they were part of the worldwide Christian family. It was 14 March 1980.

Sok Em and Savy loved to read the Bible they were given and grew in their faith, enjoying their meetings with the others. One day Sok Em came face to face with a Khmer Rouge soldier who had tied him up years before, back in Cambodia. The soldier had been one of a group that had tormented Sok Em in a terrifying way. It was usual for the soldiers to leave someone firmly tied up and go away for a while to increase their terror, and then return to kill them. On this occasion, for no obvious reason, when the soldiers returned they did not shoot Sok Em, but untied him and let him go. Now Sok Em was face to face with one of his attackers who had also become a refugee, having deserted the armed forces and fled. When they met, the former soldier was frightened as he, too, remembered the incident. However God had freed Sok Em from the bitterness and hatred he once felt, so he said, 'Don't be afraid, I have become a Christian. God has forgiven all my past sins. I am a new man, so I have forgiven the wrongs of the past.' With joy the former soldier told Sok Em, 'I too am a Christian now!' A great reconciliation took place between the men.

In other countries, cruelty and destruction is caused by a desire for revenge. In Bosnia one remarkable village has become a haven of peace in the midst of great conflict. For generations there has been hatred between the different ethnic groups of the region. In 1941 there were brutal massacres in Podbrdo. In the same place, forty years later, the Virgin Mary began to appear to a group of young people at Medjugorje, which is the nearest inhabited village to Podbrdo. She still appears, and frequently Mary gives messages which the visionaries pass on. These include encouragements and expressions of her love for Jesus, but also instructions that people should pray, fast and be reconciled to God. She has continually stressed the need for peace and reconciliation between all people. Her messages were frequently addressed to the people of the former Yugoslavia, before the fighting began, encouraging peace between the different factions. If only her words had been heeded by more.

Before the visions began in June 1981, Medjugorje was a normal community with its usual share of drunkenness, cheating and fighting. Now the church is filled each evening: devotion to God is the main activity of the villagers' lives. Mary once said: 'I have chosen this parish in a special way. I want to protect you and guide you in love.' She directed the community to Matthew 6:24–34 which includes the text 'Seek first His kingdom and His righteousness.'

Medjugorje is only about thirty miles from Mostar which has almost been destroyed. At times Medjugorje itself has been shelled day and night. Serbian pilots trying to bomb Medjugorje from the air have reported being unable to do so because the village was obscured from sight by 'a kind of cloud'. Others have said that 'the village disappeared as a mysterious light hid it from our eyes'. Shells and bombs that have landed in the village have not exploded. No building or person in the village has been damaged, up until the writing of this book, despite the devastation all around it. Yet there have been warnings that the villagers must continue to focus on God in prayer and fasting, and not allow their faith to become dry.

A Christian organization in Bosnia, Novi Most (New Brigade), has set up a centre in Muslim eastern Mostar for humanitarian aid and counselling for those who have been traumatized. They have distributed vast quantities of aid to Serbs, Croats and Muslims, often risking their lives to deliver emergency supplies to those most in need, irrespective of their ethnic status. Many cannot understand the centre's attitude of unconditional concern and some have bitterly opposed it, endangering those who seek to show genuine love.

The majority of people in Bosnia have received no income during the three years of fighting. Yet there have been remarkable stories of provision of food for local people and for the thousands of refugees from other areas who live in camps and are housed with the local residents. One Christian man who was feeding twenty-two refugees in his home had planted ten kilos of potatoes. He expected a yield of between thirty-five and forty-five kilos, but by 22 June when he was interviewed, he had already harvested 530 kilos! It was the same with his bean harvest, and he kept finding he still had money in his pocket after giving it away. What is remarkable is that in Medjugorje people of all three ethnic groups live, eat and worship together. God's love has made a difference. Despite the war, the village remains peaceful, and twenty million people are reported to have visited it since the daily visions began in June 1981 which continued, despite the fighting all around.

Jesus warned us in Matthew 24:6: 'You will hear of wars and rumours of wars, but see to it that you are not alarmed. Such things must happen, but the end is still to come.' Aside from this encouragement, prayer can make a great difference to the outcome in situations of conflict. We have only to look at the recent past and the incredible turn-round in the politics of South Africa for an example. For decades the policy of apartheid controlled the way people thought about others and how they lived their daily lives. Those who spoke out against the injustice of apartheid policies were victimized. Over the past forty years anti-apartheid activists, mostly black, have been beaten, tortured, imprisoned, often without trial, and sometimes killed in the struggle to bring about justice.

We received a letter from the Mother Prioress of an Anglican community in Lesotho, a small independent kingdom completely surrounded by the republic of South Africa. Living in a multi-racial religious community, and in direct contact with many in South Africa who had suffered under the apartheid regime, the nuns were in a good position to pray in an objective way for the situation to change. Mother Josephine wrote: 'I have long been haunted by the look of innocent surprise on the face of a man on television who said in a discussion: "But heaven is for white people only." We have agonized over other "good" people who were quite blinded by prejudice and simply could not accept that black people were their equals.'

Thousands of Christians both inside and outside South Africa have prayed for peace over many years. Michael Cassidy of African Enterprise was one of those who played a part in paving the way for apartheid to end and for a multiracial government to be formed. He says: 'When the final breakthrough came in terms of an election agreement signed by the major players on 19 April 1994, I was one of many who felt profoundly persuaded that we had seen an intervention of God in human history. The odds against a peace settlement, the boiling emotions in the country

which turned almost overnight into feelings of profound reconciliation, the political complexities, the deep stirrings in Kwa-
Zulu-Natal in the direction of civil war between two major
factions, which could have spilled over with disastrous consequences into the townships of the Reef; all of these things added
up to a totally extraordinary set of odds against the breakthrough
which came.'

Michael Cassidy continues: 'Indeed, the very fact that the
secular press used the word "miracle" so much, confirmed this.
One newspaper in KwaZulu-Natal had a headline: "The day God
stepped in to save South Africa". The fact that we in African
Enterprise had a small part in the action, along with many others
who also played their role, brought to us a great sense of
humbling privilege.' As Mother Josephine said, 'Even five years
ago we would have thought it quite impossible that South Africa
could ever have a democratic general election for all its citizens.
But it has happened! The acceptance of black leaders, the
dismantling of the apartheid system, the forgiveness shown by
the black people are tremendous miracles for which we thank
God.' Yet even at the last minute the whole process looked like
being jeopardized. At a 'Jesus Peace rally in Durban on 17 April
it was said: 'We have effectively run out of human solutions, but
this moment of human extremity is God's opportunity.'

After much prayer and last-minute negotiations, Chief
Buthelezi at last agreed to join the elections, avoiding almost
certain civil war in KwaZulu-Natal. On 27 April, Nelson
Mandela was elected as the first black president of South Africa.
Michael Cassidy rejoiced: 'It is an answer to prayer. God has
intervened. But we must not be complacent. God has done an
amazing thing, but there will be inevitable stresses and strains as
this country seeks to break free from its past and step into a
liberated future. The non-racial, democratic society of South
Africa needs to draw on that same God who has been faithful
to us.'

Whatever the cause of the conflict, the purposes of God are greater by far; if we praise God, He will bring good out of the situation.

For four years from 1976 to 1980 we were missionaries in Rwanda, Africa, working on rural development and forestry projects. Rwanda is a beautiful yet poor country; 'the land of a thousand hills', 'the Switzerland of Africa'. The people were dignified, polite, kind and hard-working. We made many friends with whom we have remained in contact during the years since we have been back in England. There was little actual starvation, although some people had very limited diets and suffered nutritional deficiencies as, being a land-locked country, transportation of goods was expensive and Rwanda has few natural resources. Only about ten per cent of the population was in paid employment. The rest grew food on their land and sold crops to realize cash for items such as soap, clothes and blankets, and to pay for schooling and medical treatment. Historically the majority Hutu tribe had been joined about four hundred years ago by a taller tribe from Ethiopia called the Tutsi.

Burundi, on Rwanda's southern border, is very similar geographically, and has the same mix of tribes, both countries having approximately 84 per cent Hutu, 15 per cent Tutsi and 1 per cent Twa. People from the different tribes generally got on well and there were many marriages between the different tribes. Belgium took over both countries in 1919, governing them together as Ruanda-Urundi, ruling indirectly through the Tutsi kings and princes. They found the Tutsi people to be intelligent and quick to learn, so they gave them more education, advantages and opportunities. This differentiation inevitably bred jealousy. After the Second World War the Tutsi king, Rudahigwa, began a campaign of democratic reform, cutting back on Tutsi power and privilege and aiming for independence from Belgium. The Belgians then switched their support from the Tutsi to the Hutu people.

In 1959 the Tutsi king died in suspicious circumstances, and some Tutsi families were killed or their homes burned. The Tutsi retaliated, but the Belgians gave military support to the new revolutionary movement. Thousands of Tutsi were killed and several hundred thousand fled over the borders. In 1962 independence was granted and many dispossessed Tutsi returned to claim their property. This led to further trouble, and more Tutsi were killed. Many Tutsi went to Uganda where they built new lives, but were always considered outsiders. Their intention was to return to claim their land in Rwanda, and the Rwanda Patriotic Front (RPF) was formed. This is largely Tutsi, but has some Hutu members, even among the leadership. From 1990 the RPF began incursions into northern Rwanda, and by February 1993 they had displaced one million people, taking control of a large area. The president began peace talks, aiming at power-sharing with the RPF, but some members of the government wanted none of that.

When the conflict in Rwanda burst on to the television screens and newspapers of the world in April 1994, it was the first time most people had ever heard of Rwanda. The mass murders, the brutal violence, the turning of Hutu neighbours against Tutsi, seemed hard to comprehend. The Hutu people were urged by radio propaganda broadcasts to exterminate the Tutsi. Many were slaughtered in their homes, at the roadside as they fled, or in churches where they sought safety. Millions left their homes, hoping for refuge in camps set up in other areas of the country. Others tried to get out of Rwanda, and vast refugee camps mushroomed just over each border.

Yet we have heard heart-warming accounts of Tutsi who have been hidden and protected by Hutu friends, sometimes for months. Some have been enabled to escape with the help of Hutu who have often risked their own lives to help them. One such person was Bishop Alexis Bilindabagabo, who was Assistant Bishop of Kigeme in the south of Rwanda. A missionary in

Bukavu, Louise Wright, wrote that, at the height of the troubles, 'It was a privilege to have the bishops of Kigeme in my house; one a Hutu, the other a Tutsi. One had risked his life to protect the other. They were both an inspiration to us with their stories of God's miraculous protection.' Bishop Alexis was the Tutsi bishop, so, like all Tutsis at that time, his life was very much in danger. His parents, brothers and most of his other relations had been killed. He had every reason to be bitter, yet he is not, for he believes we are called to show love and forgiveness.

Bishop Alexis was encouraged to leave Kigeme with a group of seven thousand Tutsis who were seeking protection from the police, but he did not go. Those who left were all killed. Later, about 300 who had stayed in Kigeme sheltered together in a big hall at the secondary school, including Bishop Alexis with his wife and their children. One Sunday, around midday, they saw several hundred people approaching carrying weapons. They stopped at the bottom of the hill and sent up three spies, to see if the company had weapons to resist attack. The people had been praying together and repenting of their sins, preparing their hearts for heaven. The three spies said: 'Bishop, we come to tell you that people are coming to kill you.' He replied, 'You tell them that this hill is surrounded by many angels. If these angels allow you, then you will come and destroy us. But if they don't allow you, nobody will approach us. We are ready, we are not afraid.' The mob came nearer, but then stopped. Half an hour later, they disbanded and went away. This happened several times; attack seemed inevitable, yet each time different mobs stood at a distance and did not come any nearer. Bishop Alexis attested that God was protecting His people.

When they did eventually leave Kigeme, it was in the army general's jeep. Another jeep went ahead of them to negotiate the roadblocks, where the bishop and his family could easily have been killed, so the general's jeep was able to drive without stopping. Bishop Alexis had learned how to listen to God and wait for His timing. His wife, Grace, had spoken to him previously about 'a clear road' being a sign for them to leave Rwanda. At the time it had seemed inconceivable, with the many roadblocks and destroyed roads, that there could be a clear road. Alexis realized that God had provided for their release through the general's help.

The Kajuga family lost several members in the first week of the troubles. Marion Kajuga was in Zaire visiting her daughter whose husband had just died of an illness. While she was there, she heard that her husband, their eldest son and his Belgian wife had been killed in Kigali. Another of her sons, Wilberforce, had escorted her to Zaire and in his absence his own wife, Norah, and four children were attacked and believed killed. Several weeks later, grief-stricken Wilberforce received a note written by his nine-year-old daughter, Céline, who he had heard was among the dead. She had seen many people killed, including her mother, brothers and sisters. She too had been attacked and left for dead in a pile of bodies. However she had survived, and was now in a refugee camp inside Rwanda.

Overjoyed, Wilberforce went straightaway to find Céline and bring her back to live with himself and her grandmother, Marion. She surprises Marion with her forgiveness and maturity. Céline has often said to her, 'Let's pray for Rwanda. Let's pray for those who killed other people, that God will have mercy on them.' Céline is now at school and has made friends with a girl whose parents also died in the troubles, and a boy who lost his parents and seven brothers and sisters. Marion writes, 'They all love Jesus, and at mealtimes they pray "for those who do not have enough to eat", as they know what it is like to have no food and only bad water to drink.'

Another miraculous escape concerns Nathan Umazekabiri who was studying at a Christian college in Nairobi when the troubles began in Rwanda. His wife, Helene, and their children were at home in Butare, the second largest town in Rwanda, as they could not afford to house and feed the whole family in Nairobi while Nathan was studying there. As well as their own children, they had also adopted Helene's sister's children when she died several years before. Since April Nathan had not been able to receive news from his family, since all communications with the country had been cut off. Nathan decided to fly to Burundi and then travel by road into Rwanda to look for his family. Every few miles he had to stop at a roadblock. These were sometimes manned by disaffected military, unruly mercenaries or by groups of drunken men ready to rob or kill anyone. At each roadblock any driver or passenger risked being attacked or killed for no reason at all.

Having silently prayed his way through twenty roadblocks, Nathan says: 'Unfortunately I didn't find my family at Butare where I had left them, but I was told they had fled to Kigeme. So I continued my search, having to pass through a further thirty roadblocks to reach Kigeme. I couldn't tell you how I felt when I saw them with my own eyes. I thought I was dreaming or having a vision; I had to touch them to make sure I wasn't. I stayed one night with them in the refugee camp, then I took them with me to Butare and on to Burundi.' The same danger awaited them at each of the fifty roadblocks on the return journey. Nathan testified, 'Only our Father God could keep us safe through all those obstacles, so we praise Him for His love and care.'

A Tutsi couple, John and Vivian Gakwandi, fled their home in Kigali with their four children, when educated Tutsi and their families were being mercilessly sought out and killed. They were taken into the home of a Swiss family they knew and were safe until all Swiss people were evacuated from the country after the Swiss embassy was attacked. The Gakwandi family were allowed to stay on in the house. They then hid in a walk-in cupboard when the house was looted by people who would have killed them had they found them, urged on by the radio propaganda broadcasts, but their hiding-place was not discovered. The noise of looting and violence forced them to stay in the cupboard for a week. John felt something fall on him in the darkness and found it was Swiss chocolate! Reaching up to the shelf above him, he found an ample supply, which he and his family lived on for the first week. When they heard rain falling noisily on to the metal roof, they crept out and collected the water to drink. When the chocolate was finished, the family prayed that God would meet their needs.

During the bombardment a shell hit an avocado tree in the garden which fell right in front of the door. Under cover of darkness John and Vivian crept out and collected the ripe avocados to eat. The supply fed them for another week. When the avocados had all been eaten, they noticed that the lawn was now a carpet of tiny mushrooms, which had not been there before. If they picked more than they could eat in one day, they were bad by the next day. However even if they picked them all on the same day, there was a fresh supply again in the morning. It was just like the provision of manna in the wilderness for Moses and the people of Israel, as recorded in Exodus 16. God continued to supply the family's needs while they remained in hiding for a total of eighty-nine days. They came out when they heard the RPF take over Kigali, meaning their lives were no longer in imminent danger.

The Gakwandi family returned to their own home, which had been ransacked. Speaking to two night guards, they were told which houses all the pieces of furniture had been taken to. Bravely going around these houses, they were able to reclaim all their furniture, bringing it back to set up home again! John and Vivian are now working for aid agencies.

In the Gospel of John, we have a glimpse of the conflict that Jesus said was bound to happen: 'In this world you will have trouble. But take heart! I have overcome the world' (John 16:33). All of us will enter into conflict of some kind or another, whether personal or national. What Jesus tells us is that He is able to help us in the midst of trouble. We are to take heart, for ultimately Christ can weave a pattern of victory through man's conflict.

CHAPTER EIGHT
Miracles in Holy Places

Sing Alleluia and keep on walking.

St Augustine

OLLOWING THE example of Christ, the early Christians laid hands on the sick. By prayer and in faith, healing that came as a result was received as a gift from God. Outstanding Christians, who were later canonized as saints, were thought to be able to continue the working of miracles from heaven, and as a result their burial-places sometimes became sites where God's power was in evidence. Testimonies began to be heard of miracles, healing and deliverance from evil spirits at the tombs of these Christians. The inscription on the tomb of Martin of Tours (c. 335–400), a pioneer of monasticism in Gaul (France), for example, reads: 'Here lies Martin the Bishop of holy memory, whose soul is in the hand of God; but he is fully here, present and made plain in miracles of every kind.'

Since with their physical bodies the saints had performed miracles, it was assumed that the power of God still resided in their earthly remains. For this reason it soon became the custom to place the remains of holy men and women in shrines for veneration and for the working of miracles. In fact the custom of being associated with a saint became so popular that churches without one sought after saintly relics. Gregory of Nyssa (c. 330–395) and Jerome (c. 342–420), two notable scholars, wrote that a Christian could worship 'in spirit and in truth' anywhere; adding that people do not gain anything supernatural by seeing wooden relics of the cross or even Christ's tomb. Nevertheless the practice developed of making holy places for holy relics. To begin with, those who held relics had a real desire to use them to assist those seeking a miracle or a cure. During the Middle Ages, pilgrimage to a holy place was an integral part of the Christian life.

Dr Rex Gardner has combined a career of medicine with the study of theology. He has been a consultant gynaecologist, obstetrician and surgeon. He is also an ordained minister in the United Free Church of Scotland. He writes in his book *Healing Miracles*: 'Healings associated with relics do not figure in our thinking, and with God at our elbow, I do not see why they should. The picture of the Middle Ages when, to many, Christianity *was* relics and pilgrimages . . . our inclination is to spurn the subject . . . but there is biblical precedent for it. "Once while some Israelites were burying a man, suddenly they saw a band of raiders; so they threw the man's body into Elisha's tomb. When the body touched Elisha's bones, the man came to life and stood up on his feet" (2 Kings 13:21). So those who take a high view of scriptural inspiration have got a problem, which is not helped by the New Testament: "God did extraordinary miracles through Paul, so that even handkerchiefs and aprons that had touched him were taken to the sick, and their illnesses were cured and the evil spirits left them" (Acts 19: 11–12).'

The ultimate goal of a pilgrimage was the Holy Land. The Crusaders' zeal to free Palestine from heathen rule was largely due to the importance attached to pilgrimage from the West. Next in line was Rome, because of the claim that the bodies of St Peter and St Paul rested there. In England, Thomas à Becket's shrine at Canterbury attracted people from all over Europe, especially those seeking a cure.

We must remember that simply being alive in the Middle Ages was almost a miracle in itself! The average life expectancy was short by today's standards, and everyone was liable to suffer ill health, pain and disability without effective medicines. Only the wealthy could benefit from the primitive medical help that was available. Childbirth was often fatal and child mortality was common. Disasters in the form of plague, and foot-and-mouth disease in cattle and crop failure due to pests, were part and parcel of daily life. It is not surprising that many of the world's ills were attributed to the devil and the power of evil.

Only the Church, with Christ's power, could intervene to overcome disease, sin, death and everlasting punishment. The prayers of the priest and the faithful, in the name of Jesus, were believed to have supernatural power. It was also thought that water from holy wells had curative powers. Springs had been in use in heathen rites, and were adopted by the Christian Church, bearing the names of saints who would preach the Gospel over them, thereby making the well holy.

In the winter, families often suffered from malnutrition. There was less fresh food and therefore little resistance to disease, in addition to cold, wet weather. A pilgrimage to a holy site in spring or summer gave new hope, renewing the pilgrim's faith that God would act. Prior to a pilgrimage, the pilgrims may have prepared themselves through devotions and fasting. Approaching the holy site, they would kneel and give thanks. An offering would be made in the form of a coin or a candle. Only those who had come for healing would linger round the shrine, other pilgrims departing after hearing Mass.

One such holy site was the burial-place of King Oswald of the Northumbrians, of whom Bede wrote in his *History of the English Speaking Peoples*, completed in 731: 'Oswald's great devotion and faith in God was made evident by the miracles that took place after his death.' Bede continued, 'It would not be right to omit mention of the favours and miracles that were shown when Oswald's bones were discovered and translated into the church where they are now enshrined [Bardney Abbey, Lincolnshire]. There was a little boy in the monastery who had been seriously troubled by ague [a violent fever]. One of the brothers came up to him and said "My boy, shall I tell you how you may be cured of this complaint? Get up and go to Oswald's tomb in the church. Remain there quietly and mind you don't stir from it until the time that your fever is due to leave you." The boy did as the brother advised, and while he sat by the saint's tomb, the fever dared not touch him; furthermore, it was so completely scared that it never recurred, either on the second or the third day, or ever after.'

Before going on a pilgrimage, the sick would have sought a local cure using home-made medicines or herbal treatments. Now their hopes lay at the shrine, waiting for God to intervene. After spending a night or more around the holy place, some would wake to find that healing had taken place. Those who did not experience healing believed they needed to be in closer contact with the saint. There were tombs which possessed niches in the outer stone covering in which a diseased or injured limb could be inserted.

Bede describes Chad of Lichfield's tomb, as a place of pilgrimage, in the following terms: 'St Chad's burial-place is covered by a wooden tomb, made in the form of a little house, with an aperture in the wall through which those who visit it out of devotion may insert their hand and take out some of the dust [near to the dead saint].' Certain sufferers were given treatment in the form of holding stones or any material which had touched the relic.

After a stay of days, weeks or even months, the pilgrims would return to their homes, using monasteries, inns or alms-houses (then called hospitals) for accommodation on the way. Chaucer's company preferred to stay at inns. Healing at the shrines was not expected always to be received instantaneously. Water from a holy well, which pilgrims drank, might be taken away to continue the treatment. If the miracle of healing did not happen, then a second visit to that shrine or to a different one would be considered. Some believers continued to go on pilgrimage until they saw a result. Those whose healing was completed at home after a visit to a shrine usually sent a thank-offering to the keepers of the holy place or even undertook a return pilgrimage to give thanks to God. People throughout Europe embarked on pilgrimages, even taking children where possible. Mostly they travelled in groups, which reduced the risk of attack by bandits.

Thomas à Becket (1118–70) was made Archbishop of Canterbury in 1162. Prior to this, Thomas was friend and chancellor to Henry II, but was not known as an active Christian. As Primate of England, à Becket was transformed from a royal supporter to an ardent champion of the Christian faith and the Church. Owing to the struggle between the authority of the king and the Church, à Becket fled to Europe, returning to England in 1170 where he was murdered in Canterbury Cathedral by four knights, who believed they were carrying out the king's wishes. Europe was outraged at à Becket's martyrdom, and soon the site of his death became a place of pilgrimage, and was adorned with 200 scenes of his life, martyrdom and the miracles performed by God at his hand.

After his murder in 1170, à Becket was laid in the crypt of Canterbury Cathedral in a marble sarcophagus 'before the altar of St John the Baptist and St Augustine'. John of Salisbury wrote a few short weeks after the murder: 'Many mighty wonders are performed, to God's glory: great throngs of people gather to feel in themselves, and witness in others, the power and mercy of Him who always shows His wonder and glory in His saints. In the place where Thomas suffered, and where he lay the night through, awaiting burial, and where he was buried at last, the palsied are cured, the blind see, the deaf hear, the dumb speak, the lame walk, folk suffering from fevers are cured, the lepers are cleansed, those possessed of a devil are freed ... I should not have dreamt to write such words on any account had not my eyes been witness to the certainty of this.'

The news of the miracles God did at Canterbury spread rapidly across France, especially in places where à Becket had lived. Most people believed in the miracles, but there were scoffers too. One of the miracles written about by John of Salisbury in another of his letters concerned an ordinary working man, Peter, who lived at Chartres where John of Salisbury was bishop from 1176–80. One day Peter and other stonecutters, working in the Cathedral of Saint Père, Chartres, were discussing the miracles surrounding à Becket's entombment, while they were eating. Peter burst out laughing, and boldly asserted they were false. Before taking a mouthful of food, he said that if à Becket had any power he was to choke or poison him. Alarmed, his workmates made the sign of the cross to protect themselves from Peter's disbelief. As Peter left to go home he suddenly fell down, speechless and helpless. He was brought back into the cathedral, and his friends begged Bishop John to help him. John dipped a small sealed container of à Becket's blood into some water and gave the water to Peter to drink. He was cured at once, and went on a pilgrimage to Canterbury to give thanks.

While on a family holiday in Norfolk, we visited the Shrine of Our Lady at Walsingham. It was a cold spring day, with a north wind blowing through the village and sunlight straining through black clouds as rain and hail fell upon us. There was a solemn sense of God's presence in the Anglican church bearing the shrine. In medieval times it was the most frequented shrine in the country, even rivalling that of Thomas à Becket at Canterbury. In 1061, during the reign of Edward the Confessor, a woman named Richeldis de Faverches received a vision. The widow of the lord of the manor of Walsingham Parva saw Mary, the mother of Jesus, at the place where the angel Gabriel announced to her that she would give birth to the Son of God.

Richeldis saw the vision three times, during which she was told to take note of the measurements of Mary's house and to build one like it at Walsingham. This she did, and the holy house at Walsingham has been known for generations as 'England's Nazareth'.

At Walsingham, a spring of water gushed up near the holy house which Richeldis built in response to the vision she had received, and the water was found to have healing properties.

Since 1061 Walsingham has had a long record of miraculous cures and answers to prayer. Pilgrims have come from all over Europe, and from all walks of life. Until it was destroyed in 1538, almost every king of England visited the shrine at least once during his reign. Even Henry VIII, who was later responsible for its destruction, made at least three pilgrimages, walking barefoot from the Slipper Chapel at Barsham, about three miles from Walsingham. The shrine was rebuilt and a new chapel dedicated in 1931. Now people travel by car and coach, down country lanes full of charm, with plenty of shops in the village offering afternoon tea and cakes!

The reason we visited the shrine was to try to discover why Christians and non-Christians still come. We met a delightful nun who answered by saying 'I am not "hooked" on shrines, but what is in the heart is what matters.' It was a stunning reply to those who have not looked beyond the physical shrine to the reality of God. God through His Son is able to renew and heal a person anywhere. However for some, a pilgrimage to a holy place lifts the expectation that God will act; because God has intervened in the past on that particular site, He may do so again. The answer to a prayer may not come immediately, but it will come at the right time.

One of the most holy places of pilgrimage for Roman Catholics is Lourdes, a town situated on the Gare de Pau River in south-west France. In 1858 a fourteen-year-old girl, Bernadette Subirous, experienced eighteen visions of the Virgin Mary between 11 February and 16 July. After the first vision, crowds of people accompanied her to Massabielle near the riverside. Here only Bernadette saw the visions, but the spectators were convinced by the effect they had on her. During one vision, she was prompted to dig for water, and a spring was found exactly where she dug. This spring still flows at a rate of 32,000 gallons of water a day, and is used by pilgrims for sacramental bathing.

In another vision Bernadette was instructed to build a chapel in honour of the Virgin Mary, encouraging pilgrims to visit Lourdes. A Gothic-type church was built, and later the magnificent Rosary Basilica was completed in 1901. The number of pilgrims increased until they came from all over the world. A staggering six million pilgrims visited Lourdes in 1958, the centenary year. Even now an annual average of two million pilgrims visit the shrine, seeking spiritual renewal, cures and miracles. Thousands of cures have been confirmed by doctors actually at Lourdes, and the Medical Commission in Paris has scrutinized some of the cases and verified sixty-five of them as miracles.

One of these miracles happened to Evasio Ganora, who was cured of Hodgkin's disease on 2 June 1950 at the age of 37. He had been ill for six months and had failed to respond to the best treatment available. He was given blood transfusions and two courses of deep X-ray therapy to his axilla and spleen, but he continued to deteriorate and was thought to have only a short time to live. He was brought to Lourdes and went to bathe in the spring water. On immersion in the water he felt a great warmth surge through his body. He was immediately able to walk back to the hospital and help others as a stretcher-bearer. When members of the medical bureau at Lourdes examined him, they found that his fever had gone and his liver, spleen and glands were no longer enlarged. He returned to work as a farm labourer, his own doctor testifying to his good health. Four years later the Lourdes medical bureau fully examined him again and found no abnormality.

Win Faulkner of Market Drayton told us about her brother, Joseph Sylvester. In 1967 Win received an urgent call to visit Joe at his home in Brampton, in the Lake District. He had been suffering from cancer of the liver for nine months, but was now expected to have only a few days to live. He was very thin and, with no hope of recovery, had been sent home from hospital, as he wished to die at home. Win suggested to her sister-in-law that they pray, which they did. Win also asked Joe if he thought it would be a good idea to go to Lourdes. He was not a great believer at the time, but was willing to try anything. From the day they prayed, Joe began to improve. Slowly he regained strength and after three months, Joe and his wife Hilda went to Lourdes. The healing he was already experiencing continued and he became well, with no trace of illness. He led a full life, but nine years later he developed cancer of the stomach. He was ill for five months and died in March 1976 at the age of fifty-nine. A post-mortem was performed, and in the liver no trace of cancer was found at all. In fact, there was a cross on the liver, as if it had been engraved into it!

An English girl, Alison Davis, who was born with spina bifida, wrote of her visit to Lourdes in her book *From Where I Sit*. 'Love must eventually be the answer to every problem, large or small. It was demonstrated to me in a gentle yet powerful way when I visited Lourdes. It is the only place in the world ever where I have *not* been stared at, ignored or talked down to by shopkeepers and passers-by, or made to feel a curiosity. In Lourdes, for five days, I became in the eyes of other people what I am in my own eyes – an ordinary person who happens to have a disability which shows.'

Like Lourdes, there are other places where springs and wells have been found to contain water that has healing properties.

This phenomenon should not be confused with medicinal water, as found at Bath and other spas; nor is it holy water which has been blessed by a minister of Christ for baptism or spiritual cleansing. In some places, the well has been known for centuries as a holy well, and on recent analysis, has also been found to have medical qualities. One such place is Gumfreston, near Tenby in South Wales, which we visited in July 1994.

Gumfreston has been known as a holy place since Celtic times because of its springs, of which there are three in close proximity. The significance of three, symbolizing the Trinity, was special for the Celtic Christians, and a church was built near by, so that people could worship God when they came to ask Him for healing. In the thirteenth century the present church, dedicated to St Laurence, replaced an older building. The fact that, in the Middle Ages, many people made pilgrimages to the springs at Gumfreston has been noted in the church records. In the seventeenth century there was a traditional Easter Sunday pilgrimage. Bent pins were thrown into the water, the pins symbolizing the nails in Christ's hands and feet. This was known as 'throwing Lent away'. The spring waters were analysed by Dr Davis, a physician to William IV, who found their medicinal qualities rich in chalybeate and sulphur and as rich in iron as the famous Tunbridge Wells. A later analyst, Dr Golding Bird, stated that the water resembled that of Malvern in its purity and that of Tunbridge Wells in its quality. When we visited Gumfreston, we were impressed by how clear the water was. It bubbled up constantly from the three springs, and a lovely feeling of peace surrounded the place.

In North Wales we visited a holy well which became so popular that the whole town is called Holywell. The well is connected with St Winifred, who lived in the seventh century. She was the daughter of noble parents and was taught by her uncle, a monk called Beuno. One Sunday, alone at home, she was visited by Prince Caradog, who attempted to rape her. She fled towards Beuno's church, but Prince Caradog caught up with her just before she reached safety and severed her head. When Beuno replaced the girl's head and prayed over her, she was restored to life. Legend claims that on the spot where her head fell, a spring of clear water gushed forth. Beuno prayed that anyone seeking help at that spot 'might receive an answer to their request'.

Winifred became a nun and was eventually Abbess at Gwytherin, where she died in about AD 650. Since then there has been an unbroken tradition of pilgrimages to the well, and pilgrims bathe in it and drink its waters. Many people have received miraculous healing. The well archives contain hundreds of letters testifying to the power of God. From the middle of the last century, accounts of healing at the well survive in quite astonishing numbers, and they were frequently published in the newspapers of the day. Many crutches and calipers were left at the well, no longer needed by the cured pilgrims. St Winifred's well came to be known as the 'Lourdes of Wales' in the 1890s, when as many as five thousand pilgrims visited each day. It is probable that, like many Celtic holy wells, there was initially no structure around the spring itself. The present well chapel was begun around 1500 by the mother of Henry VII who, it is said, benefited from answered prayer here when the infant Henry's life was in danger.

More recently, Tristan Gray Hulse made his first visit to St Winifred's well out of curiosity when he was about fifteen years old. A Catholic, he was interested in the history and beauty of the place. In 1979, when in his thirties, while stacking hay-bales on to a slow-moving cart, Tristan slipped and twisted awkwardly, sustaining a painful knee injury. Despite strong painkillers, physiotherapy and osteopathy, he was never able to walk properly, even with the use of sticks. Osteoarthritis set in and, by 1982, it had spread to other joints, especially his elbows, hands, one shoulder and the other knee. At the end of the October of that year, Tristan suffered the indignity of falling over in a shop in Chester, and was unable to stand up again until he was helped. The fall galvanized his resolve to seek God's healing. The thought occurred to him that 3 November was the feast of St Winifred, and he decided to get the bus to Holywell that day. The one-mile walk from the bus-stop took him about one and a half hours.

Tristan prayed before going into the water, not specifically for healing, but that God's will would be done. He prayed that if he was to have this disease for the rest of his life, he would be given the grace to accept it, and make some positive use of his life in spite of it. While bathing, he was conscious only of the stingingly cold water, and afterwards he said a final prayer, lit a candle and walked back to the bus. He remembers: 'I felt great pleasure that I had managed to get through my Holywell visit, and had done something to "confront" the osteoarthritis. I also had an extreme feeling of the nearness of God and of St Winifred, a feeling of love towards them, and, inexplicably, a great sense of gratitude. The pain continued, but lessened imperceptibly until about two or three weeks later when I suddenly recognized that, though I was still stiff and wobbly (from two years of lack of exercise), I was free of pain. This gave me new confidence; I stopped using my sticks. Since that time, I have had no recurrence of the arthritic pains, my joints and muscles have grown strong again, and I can walk and run as fast and for as long as most people of my age. My GP, while admitting that the speed of my recovery was surprising, suggested that the osteoarthritis had gone into remission, and warned me that it might eventually return. Twelve years later, it still hasn't.'

Tristan reflects, 'Twelve years of renewed health and the certain personal experience that this renewal – humanly inexplicable – was directly gifted by God at the prayers of St Winifred, make it almost inevitable that my trust and love for Him should be strengthened and constantly sustained. I suppose the crunch would come if the arthritis were to return; but these twelve years have given me so much to be grateful for, that I could not otherwise have achieved, that I feel confident that such a reverse would make no real difference now.'

Desmond Seward in his well-researched book *The Dancing Sun, Journeys to Miracle Shrines* writes from his Catholic background of how miracles of faith have occurred in oases of peace often surrounded by conflict. Setting out on a pilgrimage of doubt, Desmond Seward surprised himself by rediscovering his Christian roots. Struggling with the changes in the Catholic Church, he comes to the conclusion: 'Regardless of whether one sees the sun dance or not, the shrines heal, both physically and spiritually. I think that after my pilgrimages, I began to find it easier to accept the changes in my religion.'

He has based the book of personal insights gained through visiting places where, in recent years, the sun has done extraordinary things, often in conjunction with visions of the Virgin Mary who gives messages of warning. This phenomenon was first seen this century at Fatima, in Portugal, in 1917. After three young shepherds had seen Mary at monthly intervals from 13 May 1917, 70,000 people gathered for the promised appearance on 13 October. They included the devout, the curious and unbelievers, as well as journalists who had come with the express purpose of 'unmasking the hoax'. Everyone was soaked by the rain which fell continuously right up to the moment of the apparition. At midday, Lucia, the eldest of the young shepherds, cried out: 'Our Lady is coming!' Lucia presented to Mary the requests of a great number of people. Mary replied, 'Some yes, but not others. They must amend their lives and ask for forgiveness for their sins. Do not offend the Lord our God any more, because He is already so much offended.'

As Mary ascended, she shone more brightly than the sun. Then Lucia suddenly cried out: 'Look at the sun!' The astonished crowd saw what was afterwards called the 'miracle of the sun', which was described by reporters of the newspaper *O Dia*: 'The sun began to spin, turning on itself like a giant Catherine wheel, hurling itself at the earth in zigzag fashion. Then it went back to its orbit, only to start the process of descending twice more, appearing to come so close to people's heads that they feared the end of the world had come.' A reporter in *O Seculo* wrote: 'It was possible to look at the sun without the least discomfort; it neither burned nor blinded the eyes. The sun trembled and made sharp unheard-of movements in defiance of all cosmic laws; "the sun danced", in the peasants' characteristic expression.'

Some people were so terrified that they confessed their sins out loud. Everyone who had been drenched by the rain suddenly found themselves inexplicably completely dry. The miracle of the sun lasted for twelve minutes, and was visible over a distance of fifty kilometres. Pilgrims continue to visit Fatima in their thousands, and many have experienced miracle cures there.

The Virgin Mary is reported to have given a similar message to a peasant in 1958 who had never heard of Fatima. He was working in a forest near Turzovka in Slovakia when he saw Mary. As a result, hundreds of pilgrims visited the site, and were enveloped in a cone of prismatic light. She appeared again at Garabandal, a mountain hamlet in Spain in 1961, among blinding flashes. There have been reports of similar phenomena down the centuries at Czestochowa in Poland. Mary was also seen by half a million witnesses at Hriushiw in the Ukraine in 1987, in flaming robes, floating within a bright orb which rested on a beam of silver light 200 metres high.

Similar visions of Mary giving advice and messages have been seen regularly since 24 June 1981 at Medjugorje in Bosnia Herzegovina. Two local teenagers, Vicka, a girl aged fifteen, and Ivan, a boy of sixteen, were walking near Podbro with Ivanka, a girl of fifteen from Mostar, and Mirjana, a sixteen-year-old girl from Sarajevo, who were staying in Medjugorje with their grandparents. As they were chatting, all four suddenly saw a strange light on the mountainside, and then, within the light, a young woman holding a child. She called to them, but, terrified, they ran back to the village. Next day they returned, despite the mockery of their parents, with two others, Marija, aged sixteen, and Jakov, a boy of ten. Climbing the mountainside, they found themselves confronted by an apparently impenetrable wall of light, and again they fled. Turning to look back, they saw a young woman of amazing beauty emerge from the light, in a glow so dazzling that she seemed to be 'clothed with the sun'. Once more she called to them, but, panic-stricken, they ran off, and did not stop until they reached home.

On 26 June, the six came to the mountain again, this time accompanied by about five thousand intrigued people. They prayed, and, just after 6 p.m., many in the crowd saw three great rays of light pass overhead. They realized that the six young people were seeing something even more unusual. They had dropped to their knees, seeing again the young woman they now knew to be the Virgin Mary, and she gave them a message. Since then, Mary has appeared every day at about the same time. Thousands of people have been there and experienced blessing, conversion to Jesus, healings and a profound peace they had never known before.

In her messages on the subject of prayer, Mary has said: 'Today, as never before, I call upon you to pray for peace; peace in your hearts, peace in your families, peace in the whole world.' About conversion to Jesus she has spoken urgently: 'To the whole world I am saying this to you, to tell everybody. Be converted. Give up everything that goes against conversion.' Her message on 25 January 1994 was: 'In these days, Satan wants to create disorder in your hearts and in your families. You must not allow him to control you, nor your life.' Visions of Jesus have often been seen. On one occasion a Protestant doctor who was visiting Medjugorje to find out if it was all true, heard Jesus say to him, on two consecutive days, 'I have asked my mother to come here. She draws people here and brings them to Me. All generations shall call her blessed.' A priest once asked the visionary young people to ask Mary if people should pray to her or to Jesus. Her answer was emphatic: 'Please pray to Jesus; all prayer goes to Jesus. I will help, I will pray, but everything does not depend on me. It depends also on the strength of those who pray.'

Many people have been healed at Medjugorje, both local people and visitors from other countries. When asked about healing, Mary replied: 'I cannot heal – only God can.' Some of the comments of those who have visited Medjugorje include: 'What is happening in Medjugorje is authentic . . . it is truly a unique experience . . . it's just a little village that is now a very holy place . . . it's almost indescribable.' As well as the visions of Jesus, Mary and angels, other signs have been seen too. There is a huge fourteen-ton cross, ten metres high, which was built on the mountain as long ago as 1933 as a great act of dedication and sacrifice by the villagers. They had carried thousands of bucketloads of cement and water up the mountain to build the cross, to mark the 1900th anniversary of the death and resurrection of Jesus. Visitors to Medjugorje, since the visions began, have sometimes seen this huge concrete cross glow and shine, as though it were covered in light, although there is no electricity on the mountain. It seems impossible, but thousands have seen it happen on many occasions. However what is really important is the depth of love now experienced in that ethnically diverse community.

Although Geoff came to the Christian faith in the Protestant Church, on his mother's side of the family there are Catholic connections. His mother boarded at a Catholic school for the deaf in Yorkshire, his grandmother having come from Lithuania with her parents in 1898. His great-grandmother, who was from Krakow in Poland, married a man from Lithuania who was also from a Catholic family. Back in the fourteenth century, Poland joined with Lithuania to form a mighty realm which included the entire Ukraine.

From a Protestant viewpoint, it may be difficult to understand the veneration of Mary. Most Catholics nowadays do not worship Mary, but look upon her as 'God-bearer' with an awesome role in history. 'Be it unto me according to your word', she said in obedience to God, her heavenly Father. God is not limited to the doctrines of men. Geoff's Lithuanian grandmother, who had a great influence on his life, once said in response to his Protestant evangelical zeal: 'Don't be too hard on Mary.'

In 1976 when, along with our baby son Luke, we were living in Belgium, we travelled through Europe on a 'grand tour', visiting as many countries as time allowed. One visit we made was to the 'Mary Sisters' near Darmstadt, a Lutheran community which now has members in many countries. In May 1949, God moved Basilea Schlink to build a community of Protestant sisters. The land was provided by the father of one of the sisters.

Throughout the building project, Basilea Schlink discovered that the granting of requests does not usually happen automatically. To experience miracles means getting in touch with a holy living God. From the initial vision the sisters learnt that God's glorious interventions were preceded by lessons they needed to learn, through such trials as the endless trips to the authorities to obtain planning permission (does this sound familiar?). Darmstadt had been severely damaged in the Second World War, and everyone was clamouring for permission to put up new buildings. One sister, Eulalia, felt that she must repent of her frustration at seeking her own timing of events; which did not allow God to intervene. She began to plead with God for help. She trusted that He would enter into a hopeless situation, since, despite many attempts, the sisters had not even been allowed to begin the process of application, which in itself was expected to take many months.

Later that same day, on 25 July 1950, Sister Eulalia again

went to the office of the Building Department, and experienced the same refusal as before. 'It does not go so fast. Six months is the minimum time to process a building petition; indeed, it often requires a whole year.' Just then, the supervisor opened the door of his inner office to hand out some papers, and remarked: 'What does the sister want?' On hearing that she wanted to build, he invited her into his office and listened to the plan God had put in their hearts. A few telephone calls were made and, before she knew it, Sister Eulalia had the building permit in her hand. It was absolutely incomprehensible. On returning to the other sisters, there was much joy and praise for the God who works miracles. Later they heard it was said among the building officials: 'Such a thing has never happened in Darmstadt as long as the Building Department has existed, that a building permit has been issued without the completed plans being inspected — and so fast!'

Time and again the sisters saw God intervene with miracles enabling them to build. In Basilea Schlink's book *Realities – The Miracles of God Experienced Today* she states: 'We experienced not only positive miracles but also some seemingly negative ones. The sisters who worked on the construction of the chapel told this story: "We had a heavy dump cart which ran on a small track. One day it started jumping off the track, and as it weighed several hundred pounds it was a troublesome and time-consuming task for the sisters to get it back on the track each time. This continued to happen, interrupting the work and sapping the energy of the sisters, until finally the sister in charge said, "We can't go on like this; all of you come into the prayer tent."

'"We asked God why He had taken away His blessing from us that day, and then it came out: one was harbouring something in her heart against another sister . . . another had got angry with a fellow sister because she worked too slowly or hadn't cleaned the machinery properly . . . the sisters had allowed angry judgements and condemnations to creep in and tension had built up between us. We begged forgiveness of one another. We came as poor sinners to God and received afresh His gracious forgiveness. We went back to work and the dump cart never once jumped the track again!"'

The Lee Abbey community in North Devon began when a young curate on holiday from Cheltenham was walking through the Valley of Rocks in 1932 with his sister. Roger De Pemberton reached a large Victorian mansion that was being used as a hotel, and which commanded a breathtaking view. 'One thing is certain – you and I will never stay there,' said the young man to his sister, continuing their walk down to the bay. Ten years later, Roger, who had a zeal for bringing people to a personal faith in Jesus Christ, was back at the same spot. A vision was born to use the house and grounds for a twentieth-century style Christian community, so plans were made to purchase the building when the war ended. It had been used meanwhile as a boys' school, and by 1945 it was in a sorry state. Windows and basins were broken, the house had been left completely void of furniture, it needed rewiring and the grounds were overgrown.

Jack Winslow, one of the founders, wrote of its beginnings in *The Eyelids of the Dawn*: 'It was a venture of pure faith. Some £28,000 had to be paid for the house and estate. Many thousands more were needed to furnish it and bring the whole place into repair and order. There was not a penny in the bank. One of the trustees received a legacy of some £6,000 which was given as a loan. On the security of this, and the estate itself, a mortgage for the needed amount was obtained. From a worldly standpoint, it might well have been considered a reckless gamble. But we acted on the conviction that "where God guides, He provides". We were confident that the inspiration to take over Lee Abbey was God-given. We were prepared to trust Him for the needed supply of funds ... Our financial needs have been wonderfully met.'

Jack Winslow served on the commission that compiled 'Towards the Conversion of England', a report published by the Church of England in 1946, at which he gave the opening talk. The report did not merely analyse problems; it contained many practical suggestions. Training in evangelism was needed, and Lee Abbey was very much part of that vision. Here was a great opportunity to launch out into something new in the Church of England – a permanent centre for evangelism and wholeness.

Richard More in his book *Growing in Faith* writes: 'In the same way as Nehemiah rebuilt the walls of Jerusalem, or the Lord called on St Francis to rebuild the church of San Damiano, the physical work needed to restore the Lee Abbey building and estate was a visual parable of the work of God through the community in rebuilding His Church.' Lee Abbey is not an abbey in the strict sense, though it stands on old abbey lands which possibly belonged many years ago to the Cistercians. The name Lee Abbey was given to the house and estate when the mansion was built over 160 years ago. Prior to this it was known as Lee Manor, as readers of *Lorna Doone* will remember. The house commands a stunning view of the North Devon coast at the far end of the Valley of Rocks, to the west of Lynton.

At the heart of Lee Abbey is the community of men and women whom God brought together to fulfil the vision of the place. Working as a member of the community for nearly three years from 1969–72, Geoff came to realize that for thousands of people from the UK and abroad, Lee Abbey has become a place of pilgrimage where they have found healing and wholeness, a renewal of body, mind and spirit. As a community member, he saw countless people changed by the power of God's love, 'the rough corners of our lives being knocked off as we lived alongside each other. The miraculous change in those who worked in the community and with guests was very often sublime and profound. Moving from our own agenda to seeing more of Christ in each other, and knowing the desire for Christ to change us, was at times a real struggle, but so worth while.'

During Geoff's time in community, he witnessed new life flowing from God into people who arrived bewildered and seeking a renewal of purpose. There was one memorable instance which occurred in the chapel during a service of healing and wholeness, when a man crippled with arthritis struggled forward. He said to those who gathered round him that his son had been most cruelly tortured in a Japanese prisoner of war camp during the Second World War, leaving him with permanent disabilities. The father had become increasingly bitter and deeply resentful against his son's torturers. He now wanted release from his inner torment. Knowing forgiveness was the key to wholeness, once he had accepted Christ's forgiveness for what others had inflicted on his son, he visibly changed, and the pain of resentment which was binding him was withdrawn. Not only did he accept the longed-for inner healing, but the arthritis also eased considerably. He looked remarkably better as God healed his joints, and he walked unaided back to his seat.

We have enjoyed a long connection with another abbey, this time a parish church called Waltham Abbey on the Hertfordshire–Essex border. Soon after we returned from Rwanda, Revd Ken Pillar invited Geoff to work in a daughter church on a housing estate in the parish. One hot June day in 1994, with Hope's parents, we retraced our steps to this historical church. While looking round the crypt, it dawned on us that Waltham Abbey had become such an important holy site because of a miracle!

Tovi, the standard-bearer to King Canute, began to build a church in the forest at Waltham where he had a hunting lodge. He was led by God to bring to this church a cross which had been found in the ground in Somerset. The Holy Cross became known as a place of pilgrimage where God showed His mighty power.

Harold, the future King of England, was taken ill during

the 1050s with paralysis. He prayed before the Holy Cross of Waltham and the paralysis was miraculously healed. As a thank-offering, Harold founded a collegiate church which was dedicated on 3 May 1060. As King, Harold endowed the Abbey, so it was well provided for and ably administered. Waltham Abbey remained a significant place of pilgrimage throughout the Middle Ages, and was the last abbey to be dissolved by Henry VIII in 1540.

God has created all things through which He reveals Himself to us. Some hold strong convictions that God is particularly at work in certain places which remain holy sites where God still works special miracles.

CHAPTER NINE

Miracles in History

The mission of the Church is to discover the source of lost joy.

Bernanus

N ORDER TO understand the present, we need to read about the past. Much of our current understanding of God and His power throughout history is only truly grasped when we discover how He has laid His imprint on past generations. From history we learn that our way of thinking and believing (especially in the twentieth century) are not the only ways. Looking at the rich tapestry of our Christian heritage should humble us and equip us for today's world.

The Early Fathers, or 'Fathers of the Church', were popular titles given to important Christian writers who defended the Gospel against heresy and misunderstanding. As the New Testament period came to a close in the first century AD, the Early Fathers picked up the baton of the Christian faith from the Apostles, and expounded quite eloquently the life, ministry and miracles of Jesus.

Justin, an Early Father and Christian philosopher martyred in Rome between 163-7, states in his writings about Jesus: 'He raised the dead and gave them life, and by His actions challenged the men of His time to recognize Him.' Origen (c. 185-254), one of the greatest early Christian apologists, wrote: 'Without miracles and wonders the Apostles would not have persuaded those who heard new doctrines and new teachings to leave their traditional religion.' Origen went on to speak of healings and exorcisms performed by Christians in his own day, during the third century, through the same Spirit of God which empowered Jesus Himself.

Athanasius (296–373), an Egyptian by birth but a Greek by education, and another recognized Early Father, wrote concerning the person and character of Jesus: 'He who can do these things is not man, but the power and word of God.' Gregory of Nyssa (c. 330–95), another outstanding Christian thinker, gives us a portrait of Christ in the words: 'His very miracles have convinced us of His deity.'

Today we tend to assume that our society is far removed from that of the ancient world; that somehow people living centuries ago were more accepting of the Christian faith and the miraculous than we are. Nothing could be further from the truth. Fierce persecution and ridicule surrounded those who made a profession of the Christian faith, and, like the twentieth century, the ancient world had its share of sceptics, atheists, Satan-worshippers and pagans.

In 361 Martin of Tours decided to live as a hermit, near Poitiers in France, but he was soon joined by other monks, and they formed a community. One young man came to them, wishing to be taught about the Christian faith. However he became ill with a violent fever and died. This happened while Martin was away from the community, and when he returned three days later, he was distressed to hear of the young man's sudden death and that he had not even been baptized. Martin stretched himself full length on the young man and began to pray that he would come back to life, just as Elijah had done when a dead boy was raised to life (I Kings 17:17–24). After about two hours, Martin saw the dead man's eyes flicker and he began to move. When Martin shouted out with joy, the other brothers rushed in and were amazed to see the man alive. The man was baptized immediately and lived for many years afterwards.

Perhaps the greatest of the Early Fathers was Augustine (354–430), the Bishop of Hippo, a province on the coast of North Africa. After a dramatic conversion to Christ, he rose quickly to be the most brilliant theologian of his age. While reading the Bible, Augustine wrote: 'It was as though the light of faith flooded into my heart and all the darkness of doubt was dispelled.' A key phrase of Augustine's was: 'Believe, in order to understand.'

Augustine stressed the fact that the wonders of nature are no less miraculous than the spectacular intervention of God, and that God wants our response to Him not to be based solely on the extraordinary. For Augustine, the Biblical miracles had a tangible purpose; they were not specifically designed to impress, but to meet a human need. In the working of a miracle the true character of God was revealed. He was seen to be merciful, just, loving and forgiving.

This outstanding scholar saw that there was no fundamental difference between what we call miracles and the daily heartbeat of creation. Augustine understood that by looking deeper into the person of Jesus we would discover a profound message: 'It is more important that He healed the faults of our souls than that He healed the weaknesses of mortal bodies.'

When, in the fourth century, the emperor Constantine decided that Christianity should become the state religion of the Roman Empire, the miraculous became less evident. God's Spirit began to be quenched and overshadowed by Church-State bureaucracy. However Britain was far from pagan. Like other parts of the Roman Empire, England gained converts to Christianity through the Romans. St Alban was the first known British martyr during the late third century.

One of the most influential Christians of the fourth century was St Patrick, the patron saint of Ireland. Towards the end of the fourth century, Irish pirates raided Wales to capture slaves, and one of those caught was Patrick, who was then about sixteen.

In Ireland he was bought by an Irish chieftain, Milchu, and was used as a slave in East Antrim. His conversion dates from this period, when, as he said, 'The Lord opened to me the sense of my unbelief that I might remember my sins and that I might return with my whole heart to the Lord my God.' In his later writings we learn that Patrick's father and grandfather were Christians, but it was not until he was sold into slavery that his own faith became alive.

After about six years Patrick either escaped or was freed from captivity, and in a night vision he was told to go to the sea where a ship would be waiting. He walked for two hundred miles across unknown territory until he reached the sea and found the ship. It is believed that the ship was ready to sail with a cargo of Irish wolfhounds, but the fierce creatures had broken loose from their cages and were roaming the deck. Patrick offered to look after them in return for his passage, which the captain welcomed. To the surprise of everyone, when Patrick spoke, the fierce dogs licked his hand and went meekly back to their cages.

The ship sailed to France, and there Patrick received theological training in a monastery in Gaul. Eventually he returned home to Britain where he was warmly received by his family. However after a while, in about 432, in another night vision God called him to return to Ireland. For many years Patrick travelled throughout Ireland preaching the Gospel. He had considerable influence on the Irish chieftains of his day, and was responsible for breaking the power of heathen superstition in Ireland. It is recorded that Patrick was once present at a Druids' spring feast, held by the king of Ireland. The king listened while Patrick told the story of Jesus, then he challenged his own Druid priests to reply. They worked all kinds of spells and magic, but whatever they did by their powers, Patrick was able to undo.

According to the story, the next day the Druids gave Patrick a cup of poisoned wine. Making the sign of the cross over the wine, he drank it; the Druids were amazed to see him unharmed, so they decided on one last test. A lad called Benignus, who was with Patrick, was wrapped in a Druid's cloak and bound to a bundle of dry wood. A Druid was wrapped in Patrick's cloak and tied to a bundle of wet green wood. They set fire to both bundles, but the wet wood blazed up fiercely, while the dry wood refused to burn. Suddenly a flame caught and the Druid's cloak was burned to ashes, while Benignus, the lad wrapped in it, was unharmed. As the king was convinced by this miracle, Patrick was given freedom to preach the message of Jesus to the people of Ireland. He founded churches throughout the country and many people became Christians during his lifetime. Patrick had a significant effect not only on the people of his own time, but on subsequent generations.

It is only when we turn back the pages of the history of the British Isles that we see afresh an age of emerging Christian faith. Bede (673–735), a monk from Jarrow and the 'father of English history', wrote of a Celtic Britain of forests, fens and scattered communities. Miracles were often seen at the hands of Celtic monks. They believed God could heal, and accepted the idea that He would use them to cure illnesses and cast out evil spirits as part of their calling.

Celtic Christians left an indelible mark both on Britain and on other parts of Europe. They broke the strongholds of paganism through their dynamic ministry of the supernatural, pointing to miracles as evidence that God was with them. After Patrick came Columba, an Irish scholar who sailed from Ireland and arrived on the island of Iona on the west coast of Scotland in 563. Columba founded an abbey community which was so spiritually dynamic and attractive that much of Scotland became Christian through his influence.

Aidan, sent by Columba, began a mission to the English in Northumbria, reproducing the vision of Iona on Lindisfarne, an island off the north-east coast of England. Aidan trained two brothers at Lindisfarne, Cedd and Chad. Cedd went to Bradwell on the Essex coast, while Chad became the first Bishop of Lichfield in the Midlands. St David (c. 520–89), the patron saint of Wales, was also a Celtic Christian and the charismatic founder of monasteries in Wales. In word and deed, the power of God's Holy Spirit was upon him, and he became Primate of Wales.

God's Spirit was also at work in a missionary capacity during the sixth and seventh centuries. Columbanus (543–615), an Irishman, had tremendous zeal to evangelize. With the power of God he went to Switzerland and Italy, where many people became Christians. Boniface, born at Crediton in Devon in 680, went as a missionary to Germany. He built up a strong Christian following in the Frankish Empire and became the 'Apostle of Germany'. He challenged the worship of pagan gods, and once came across people offering sacrifices to the god Thor at a large oak tree he was supposed to inhabit. Boniface took an axe and struck the tree. As soon as he had made a V-shaped cut, a great wind suddenly sprung up and dashed the tree to the ground, splitting the trunk into the shape of a cross. When the people saw that Thor did no harm to Boniface for this action, they lost faith in their old gods. The wood from the oak tree was then used by Boniface to build a Christian chapel.

Leo Sherley-Price in his book *Bede (A History of the English Church and People)* writes: 'We realize even more clearly that the past is not dead and done with, but a force to be reckoned with, silently moulding the present and the future.' Bede wrote of a God who was acknowledged as the Source of all life, and that he was recognizable in everyday living. The writings of Bede give us insight into how storms, healings, comets in the sky and victories on the battlefield were regarded as signs from God for men. Miraculous signs and wonders were reported to Bede by those who claimed to have had a personal acquaintance either with the persons 'performing' the miracles or from those who benefited from them. In writing this book, we feel a real affinity with Bede who, in a sense, pioneered the work of 'true stories of how God acts'!

Bede wrote: 'About this time [the seventh century] a man already dead returned to bodily life and related many notable things that he had seen, some of which I have thought it valuable to mention here in brief. There was a head of a family living in a place in the country of the Northumbrians known as Cunningham, who led a devout life with all his household. He fell ill and grew steadily worse until the crisis came, and in the early hours of one night he died. However at daybreak he returned to life and suddenly sat up, to the great consternation of those weeping around the body, who ran away; only his wife, who loved him more dearly, remained with him, though trembling and fearful. The man reassured her and said, "Do not be frightened; for I have truly risen from the grasp of death, and I am allowed to live among men again. But henceforward I must not live as I used to, and must adopt a very different way of life." Then he rose and went off to the village church, where he continued in prayer.'

In the past, men and women were perhaps less critical of the miraculous. However Bede was not gullible, accepting every account that he heard. In many respects he was more careful and circumspect in his recording of miracles than some later historians. The Celtic Church was, in a sense, a 'freelance' Church (free from centralization and institutionalism), having a refreshing reliance on God's Holy Spirit to act, removing obstacles which were in the way of Christian faith. Miracles, signs and wonders were part of their spiritual diet.

The Roman mission to Britain began with the arrival of Augustine, who was sent by Pope Gregory I to found a church base at Canterbury in 597, the year in which Columba died. There ensued a struggle between the Roman and Celtic Churches, which came to a head at the Council of Whitby in 664. It was at this point that the decision was made that the Church in Britain should follow the style of Christianity of the Roman Church.

The Roman bishop, coming from the mission of St Augustine, had more administrative affairs to deal with, whereas a Celtic bishop received a strong spiritual charge to preach the Gospel, heal the sick and cast out demons. The Celtic emphasis on the apostolic ministry of bishops surely has relevance for us in the twentieth century. Bishops today are frequently distracted by countless administrative tasks, committee work and financial budgets, and their true function is increasingly obscured. Bishops who exercise a missionary ministry accompanied by spiritual signs and wonders would more truly be following in the footsteps of their great Celtic predecessors. Thankfully some bishops in Britain have courageously taken God at His word, and exercised a more dynamic, spiritual ministry.

In the later Middle Ages, great emphasis was laid upon the miracle of the Eucharist. Here the priest would invite God to perform the miracle of transubstantiation, or the belief that the blood and wine literally became the body and blood of Jesus. Miracles became the exclusive province of the Church, and spiritual life was more directed than spontaneous. The ideal of the Galilean ministry of Jesus on the grassy hillside, with life and movement, was being replaced by vast ecclesiastical buildings, and the Gospel of Jesus was becoming rigid and controlled.

However there were still signs of supernatural intervention. *The Life of Aildred of Rievaulx*, written by one of his monks, Walter Daniel, included many miracles. Aildred was Abbot of Revesby in Lincolnshire from 1143–7, and Abbot of Rievaulx from 1147–67.

Walter Daniel wrote: 'The sub-prior of the house, a God-fearing man, had long been the victim of very sharp attacks of fever. His vital force was so sapped . . . that he could scarce retain the panting breath in his body. His frame was so wretchedly wasted that it looked like the hollowed woodwork of a lute:

eyes, face, hands, arms, feet, shins, blotched and misshapen, proclaimed that the death agony was drawing nearer. Only his voice, begging God for a longer lease of life, prevailed over matter in the man. So the sick man lay upon his bed, his limbs scarcely holding together, for the contraction and loosening of his joints and nerves made them leap from the sockets of his bones and only the thin layer of fragile skin kept his body together. But see! the holy father [Aildred] comes into the infirmary and visits the sick-beds one by one, and looking upon him, utterly refuses to allow such a loss to the house, and such a distressing state of body. He says to him as he lies there, "Tomorrow, in the name of the Lord, make your way to the church, take your place in the choir, sing with them and pray to God and through Him, I believe, you will be well." When morning came the brother did as he had been bidden, and to his joy everything happened as Aildred had promised. Health triumphed over the long wastage of the fever. He suddenly became a strong cheerful man. He lived henceforth as he had been wont to live long ago.'

Francis of Assisi, an Italian, lived a free and spontaneous Christian life which challenged the rigid structures of the Roman Church. In the year 1224, while in prayer on Mount Alverna, he received a vision of the cross of Christ. This was followed by the miraculous 'stigmata', the imprinting of the five wounds of Jesus on his hands, feet and side. Francis was the first person recorded to have received the stigmata, but they have appeared upon others over the centuries, including Padre Pio in Italy in 1918, and Sister Anna Hadija Ali, currently living in Rome, and Christina Gallagher, who lives in Ireland.

St Clare was also born in Assisi, and became a nun. When her sister Agnes also joined her, St Francis established a convent at St Damian in 1215, with Clare as abbess. Once the Pope visited the convent in order to speak with Clare, who was renowned for her devotion to Christ. She asked him to bless some loaves of bread, but the Pope insisted that Clare do it. Reluctantly

St Francis preaching to the birds by Giotto da Bondone,
courtesy e.t.archive

she obeyed, and made the sign of the cross above the loaves.
Immediately a beautiful cross appeared, imprinted on the loaves,
and remained on them, visible for all to see. Everyone including
the Pope was filled with wonder at the miraculous sign. Some of
the loaves were eaten with great devotion, while others were kept
as a record of the miracle.

The greatest medieval theologian was the Italian Thomas
Aquinas (1224–74), who was strongly influenced by the fourth–

century Early Father Augustine. In his work *Summa Theologica*, he defends Augustine's statement that 'God does on occasion do something against the usual pattern of nature.' Aquinas further adds: 'Thus the works of God that surpassing any cause known to us are called miracles.' He then declares that the further God departs from the known path of nature, the greater the miracle is said to be, and thus Aquinas indicates degrees of miracles. Thomas Aquinas realized the need for reform to take place within the Church of Rome. Like Francis of Assisi, Thomas Aquinas was also prepared to challenge the medieval Church.

John Wycliffe, the 'morning star of the Reformation', was born in Yorkshire around 1330. He yearned for a Church 'shorn of its complexities', and the blasts of his criticism swept across medieval England like a gale-force wind, attacking the shortcomings of the Church. He longed for clarity, and that the Gospel of Jesus and His supernatural power be available to ordinary men and women.

During the fourteenth century, the miraculous was generally tied up with the superstitious, which thrived because there was no clear understanding of how God acted in the Bible. The ordinary people of Europe could not read the Bible for themselves, as it was only available in Latin. Thomas à Kempis (1380–1471) was a German spiritual leader who probably wrote the classic Christian work *The Imitation of Christ*. He illustrated the miracle of a transformed life through an intimate relationship with God, showing to his readers that God was close at hand.

The founder of the Reformation in Germany, which was greatly to influence England, was Martin Luther (1483–1546). In common with earlier theologians, he stated that the miracles of Jesus were divine works wrought by the power of God. Referring to John 14:11 where Jesus says, 'Believe me when I say that I am in the Father and the Father is in Me; or at least believe on the evidence of the miracles themselves', Luther wrote: 'These [miracles] are not only divine works, but they are also witnesses of God the Father. Therefore He who sees and hears these, sees God the Father in them; and He is not only persuaded that God is in Christ and that Christ is in God; but from them he can also be comforted with the assurance of God's fatherly love and grace towards us.'

As far as Luther was concerned, miracles of nature paled into insignificance when compared with the miracle of a transformed life through conversion to Christ. For Luther, the ultimate display of God's power was the victory of Jesus on the cross. Luther saw this act of self-giving by God's Son, in obedience to His Father, as victory over evil, and the very source of the changed life. Luther also laid great emphasis on the miracle of the resurrection of Jesus, where God raised His Son from death.

William Tyndale (1494–1536), an Englishman, wrote: 'It was impossible to establish the lay people in any truth except the Scriptures were plainly laid before their eyes in their mother tongue.' As a young man, William Tyndale promised a priest: 'If God spares my life, before many years pass, I will cause a boy that drives a plough to know more of the Scriptures than thou dost.' This he achieved (despite severe persecution from the ecclesiastical hierarchy), and the ordinary people of Britain came to learn of Jesus' miracles.

John Calvin (1509–64) was a French Reformer who spent a large part of his life in Geneva. He was a prodigious writer, and in his 'Prefatory Address to King Francis', he stresses the fact that the miracles of Jesus confirm His divine Sonship. Later Calvin developed the theology of miracles in his great work *Institutes of the Christian Religion* concerning the action of the Apostles, whose preaching of the kingdom of God was 'illumined and magnified by unheard of and extraordinary miracles'.

Calvin was aware of false prophets who could deceive by performing signs using power from a source other than God. The distinguishing factor was the power claim made by the worker of the miracle. If the miracle focused attention away from God, it was to be rejected. 'At that time if anyone says to you, "Look, here is the Christ!" or, "There He is!" do not believe it. For false Christs and false prophets will appear and perform great signs and miracles to deceive even the elect [those chosen by God] – if that were possible' (Matthew 24:23–4).

Calvin taught that evil has the power to lead people astray when they have not understood the person of Jesus Christ as the Way, the Truth and the Life. 'The coming of the lawless one will be in accordance with the work of Satan displayed in all kinds of counterfeit miracles, signs and wonders.' (2 Thessalonians 2:9.)

George Fox (1624–91) was the founder of the Society of Friends, who were soon known as the Quakers because of the way in which the Holy Spirit came powerfully upon them. George Fox's ministry was remarkably powerful, taking him all around Britain, to Holland and Germany and to America. Unfortunately, Fox's *Book of Miracles* has not survived; however in the late 1940s, the scholar Henry J. Cadbury attempted to reconstruct it, drawing on papers he discovered in Quaker archives and in Fox's *Journal*. The book, Cadbury discovered, had described 150 notable miracles, with those of healing being vouched for by their recipients and frequently confirmed by a physician.

In 1649 George Fox went to the village of Mansfield Woodhouse in Nottinghamshire where he saw a woman, bound hand and foot, about to be 'bled' by the local doctor. Bleeding was a practice often employed in an attempt to draw out illness and evil spirits. Fox wrote in his *Journal*, 'I desired to loose her . . . for they could not touch the spirit in her, by which she was tormented. In the name of the Lord, I bade her to be quiet . . . and she was so. The Lord's power settled her mind, and she mended. Afterwards she received the truth and continued in it all her life.'

In 1672 Fox went to America, his reputation as a powerful preacher and healer having gone before him. In New Jersey he healed, by God's power, a man who had suffered a broken neck in a fall from a horse that he was trying to break in. It is probable that the young man, John Jay, was already dead when Fox ministered to him, thus making the miracle even more remarkable.

John Bunyan (1628–88), the author of *Pilgrim's Progress*, the book that epitomizes the Puritan movement, writes of a God who intervenes, speaks and works out His purposes in every aspect of our lives. He sees the miraculous as being part of the warp and woof of everyday life.

For Blaise Pascal (1623–62) born in France, miracles were revelations of the true God, serving to identify Jesus. Pascal was a Christian thinker, literary stylist and inventor of the calculating machine. His niece, Marguerite Perrier, was healed by God of an eye complaint, a miracle which was supported by medical evidence and authenticated by the diocesan authorities. Pascal became a Christian following a miraculous vision. Pascal described this experience on a piece of parchment that was sewn into his clothing and was discovered on his death at only thirty-nine years of age. It includes the words:

> Certainty, certainty, heartfelt joy and peace
> God of Jesus Christ. My God and your God.
> The world forgotten and everything except God.

As for the Church of England in the eighteenth century, miracles seemed to be a thing of the past. As a result, it was powerless to meet the real needs of the new urban population created by the Industrial Revolution. Small of stature, John Wesley became the man of the hour. On 24 May 1738 at a meeting in Aldersgate Street in London, while listening to a reading of Martin Luther's introduction to the book of Romans in the New Testament, he felt his 'heart strangely warmed'. This was the point of his conversion to new life in Christ, as he experienced his sins truly forgiven and knew that he was on his way to heaven. He travelled all over the country, preaching simply and directly that all should believe in Jesus Christ and receive the power of the Holy Spirit to bring new life. God acted through Wesley miraculously to change the hearts and lives of literally thousands of people of his age. The worldwide Methodist Church grew out of the Wesleyan revival.

A man called Samuel from Tiverton wrote to John Wesley protesting that God does not work instantaneously. Rejecting his argument, Wesley replied: 'I have seen very many persons changed in a moment from the spirit of horror, fear and despair, to the spirit of hope; and from sinful desires, till then reigning over them, to a pure desire of doing the will of God . . . Him that was a drunkard, but now exemplarily sober . . . These are matters of fact, whereof I almost daily am eyewitness.' John Wesley himself wrote in his journal on 8 September 1784 of his ministry at Coleford: 'When I began to pray, the flame broke out. Many cried aloud, many sank to the ground, many trembled exceedingly.'

America saw the 'great awakening', beginning in 1734 with the powerful preaching of Jonathan Edwards, particularly in New England. It became more extensive geographically in 1740–41, when an English preacher, George Whitefield, toured large areas of America. Different church denominations were touched, with healings and transformed lives resulting from conversion to Christ in thousands.

America saw a second Great Awakening at the beginning of the nineteenth century, primarily in Kentucky. This was followed by the revival of 1857 which swept the land like a spiritual tornado, once again resulting in changed hearts and transformed lives, building on America's great Christian roots.

There were two significant revivals of this kind in Wales, the effects of each being notable throughout the whole population, but especially on the men. The first revival began in 1859 near Aberystwyth, and the second in 1904, a year that stands out in the history of Wales as one that will not be forgotten.

Dr Campbell Morgan declared: 'There is no organization, yet it moves from county to county with the order of an attacking force. There are no song-books, yet I nearly wept tonight over the singing. There is no advertising – think of that. Here is revival that comes from heaven.' The effects were amazing. Dr Martin Lloyd-Jones, a Methodist leader, reported: 'Thousands . . . were converted in the sense that their whole lives were changed and remained changed, and they joined the Christian Church with no pressure on them to do so. This was the power of the Spirit.'

As a result, Eifon Evans recorded: 'The coalmines were transformed by the sound of praise in the place of blasphemous oaths. The pit-ponies could no longer understand the miners' instructions because of the absence of curses. The workmen on the next shift went down the mine half an hour earlier than usual, so as not to interfere with the operations of the pit, in order to be able to meet to read the Bible and pray. At Llanfair in Anglesey all the public houses except one were closed. Convictions for drunkenness in Glamorgan were halved.' The revival did more to sober up the country in three months than anti-drinking campaigns had achieved in forty years. In some communities crime disappeared; magistrates were presented with a blank sheet – there were no cases to be tried. Family feuds were healed. Even rugby took a back seat! In more than one place, the post office's supply of money orders were exhausted as people sought to pay their debts.

Among the writings on the subject of miracles in this century, none has enjoyed greater popularity than C. S. Lewis's book *Miracles*. His writing is clear and challenging, putting forward theological argument in everyday language. His belief in miracles past and present is succinctly stated in his Epilogue: 'A miracle is emphatically not an event without cause or without results. Its cause is the activity of God; its results follow according to natural law . . . I contend that in all these miracles alike, the incarnate God (Jesus) does suddenly and locally something that God has done or will do in general.'

Christian men and women throughout the ages have shaped the nations in which they performed mighty works of God. Over the last century, Christians have begun to return to a New Testament understanding of the miraculous. Christians have formed communities of hope within society. This is what Jesus intended: 'You are the salt of the earth . . . You are the light of the world' (Matthew 5:13–14). There will always be outstanding individuals who will challenge the impoverished view of those who refuse to believe in a God who is alive and active. And He will continue to surprise us with miracles, as He has so vividly in the past.

CHAPTER TEN

Miracles in Relationships

How wonderful to be in the centre of God's will

Corrie ten Boom

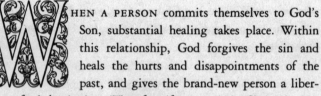HEN A PERSON commits themselves to God's Son, substantial healing takes place. Within this relationship, God forgives the sin and heals the hurts and disappointments of the past, and gives the brand-new person a liberating, fresh beginning. 'Therefore if anyone is in Christ, he is a new creation; the old has gone, the new has come!' (2 Corinthians 5:17).

In Genesis 1:27 we read that God created mankind in His own perfect image. God's purpose is for us to be whole people, with good relationships being enjoyed at every stage of our lives. Once we are 'in Christ', God is able to say yes to us, accepted and loved beyond our imagination.

God wants to rebuild broken lives. The basic fabric of every society is made up of good relationships between parents and children and the extended family, but if we are honest, all of us are broken in some way. St Paul tells us that: 'For all have sinned and fall short of the glory of God' (Romans 3:23). God is ready and waiting to intervene and restore the broken image.

There may be unresolved tension or distress in our lives, owing to unhealthy family bonds. Dr Kenneth McAll has written in a most enlightening way on the whole area of healing within the family. Born in China in 1910, Dr McAll studied Medicine at Edinburgh University. He returned to China as a missionary surgeon, and was interned by the Japanese, with his wife and child, for four years during the Second World War. His experiences in China led him to work as a Christian psychiatrist for many years.

In his book *Healing the Family Tree*, Dr McAll quotes an instance where the past behaviour of a mother deeply affected her son. He writes: 'Cliff, a schoolmaster in his thirties, was a homosexual. He lived under his mother's protection and feared any relationship, not only with women, but also with chaplains and he refused to attend the school morning assemblies. After treatment with various drugs and many sessions with psychiatrists, none of which helped his problem at all, I approached Cliff's mother and asked her for information about her son's early life. She was a good woman, and had been a nurse before she married. After much heart-searching, she brought herself to tell me about her own life and her own pregnancy. At that time she had been working in a large hospital and was already pregnant. On several occasions, when on night duty, she had allowed sexual intercourse to take place with one of the patients who was an army chaplain. Seemingly the mother's behaviour had produced some sort of inexplicable reaction in the unborn child which influenced his whole life and thinking in regard to women and chaplains. It is a fact that when the mother made her confession with true repentance, now shared with the son whom she had damaged so badly before he was born, he forgave her just as Jesus Christ had been waiting to forgive her, and he immediately felt freed. The total forgiveness of the person who was responsible by the one who has been hurt had broken the controlling bond of fear, anger and aversion. Cliff is now happily married and living a very full, normal life.'

The key to healing in the area of relationships is often forgiveness, made through Jesus, who has the power to bring release from bondage. The Lord's Prayer includes the words 'Forgive us our sins, for we also forgive everyone who sins against us' (Luke 11:4). Often there are fears within a family that are linked with the past. Since 'Jesus Christ is the same yesterday and today and for ever' (Hebrews 13:8), past failings within the family that affect the present generation can be taken to Jesus for healing.

When someone has been badly hurt or let down, they may look for love and security in the wrong places. Such was the case with Mandy, who had been through two broken marriages. Both husbands had been domineering and violent, and had left her when she became unable to cope. Then she had a relationship with a man she thought was kind. Mandy found she was expecting a baby, and thought, when she told him, that he would decide to marry her, but his only comment was: 'Invite me to the christening.' He was not prepared to take any responsibility for Mandy or the baby.

Mandy already had a small son, and was finding it difficult to cope with him, her finances and life in general. She knew there was no way she could cope with another baby on her own. She was in her thirties, but had no family or real friends to support her. The only people she could confide in were her doctor and health visitor, and they were both adamant that she must have an abortion. She agreed to go through with it, although she knew it was wrong. She felt the decision had been taken out of her hands, and she was powerless to stop it. Lying in the corridor of the abortion clinic, she remembered the stillborn twins she had given birth to several years before, and she felt desperately sad.

The guilt of the abortion stayed with Mandy, and did not ease as the years went by. We became friends with her some fifteen years later. Soon after she had become a Christian, we were the first people with whom she shared this dark secret. We offered to pray with her for Jesus to bring healing into those areas of hurt in her past. When we prayed about the day of the abortion, Mandy saw herself lying on the trolley in that corridor.

She cried, and asked the Lord's forgiveness for the sin of taking the life of her unborn child. We invited Jesus into the situation and, as she pictured herself at that painful time, she could see Jesus there with her. Her face lit up as she described what she could see happening. Jesus came up to her, and His smile showed that He understood her dilemma and still loved her. He gave her a hug. It changed her memory of the situation and took away her guilt. At the time she had felt so alone, but now she could not think of it without remembering Jesus with her.

We got to know Vicky in a different parish, when Geoff took the funeral of her baby, Lucy, who lived for only three and a half hours. Over the following weeks, her grieving for Lucy continued to be intense. One day she shared with us her belief that Lucy's death was a punishment from God for an abortion she had had several years previously, and her fear that she would never have a live child. Vicky told us that she had become pregnant before she married. Although the baby's father was now her husband, he was not ready for marriage at that time, and had insisted that Vicky have an abortion. Since then she had never forgiven herself and, although she had prayed to God for forgiveness, she had never felt it forthcoming. She did not feel she deserved to be forgiven, since she had taken the life of her unborn child.

We explained to Vicky that God did love and forgive her, and we read a booklet with her explaining how she could accept Jesus into her life. She was keen to do this and afterwards Geoff prayed, absolving her from her past sins through Jesus who had paid the penalty for them on the cross. Then we asked her to remember the time several years before when she was in hospital having the abortion, and we prayed that Vicky would know Jesus had been there at the time. She saw Him standing there, and Jesus held the unborn baby. Vicky was glad for Him to have the baby.

Next, we asked her to think back to when she was in hospital only two months ago, when the medical staff decided to remove the tubes keeping Lucy alive as nothing further could be done to save her. We prayed for Jesus to be seen in that situation too. Vicky saw herself beside the cot, then she saw Jesus standing there too. Vicky saw herself pick up Lucy and give her to Jesus. Lucy looked beautiful and well, complete and safe. Afterwards Vicky felt peaceful and secure. She knew she was forgiven and felt free for the first time. Since then, she has been blessed with two other children.

These two women had felt much guilt because of a wrong decision to have an abortion. Equally destructive can be an addictive craving for love, the result of a lack of love in childhood. Suzy's parents had divorced, and her mother had often said to her that it was only since her birth that the marriage had begun to go wrong. Suzy's mother had been very young when her own mother had died, and consequently seemed unable to show love to her two daughters. Suzy had never been hugged or told she was loved by either of her parents, and had always felt rejected by them both. Throughout her childhood, the atmosphere at home was very tense, and she always felt it was her fault. When her parents eventually divorced when she was seventeen, she felt she was to blame. Suzy lived with her mother after her parents split up, but always found her demanding and bitter. When she saw her father, she always felt very angry, and that she could not trust him. She kept trying to win her father's affection, but he saw her very seldom and was always too preoccupied with himself.

When she left school, Suzy went to Europe as an au pair, but when the job ended she became desperate in her search for love. She even became a prostitute for a few months. She buried these experiences deep inside her and, until she got married, did not think about them. It became apparent that she had a problem coming to terms with how she had allowed her body to be used. She had expected lovemaking within marriage to be better, without the guilt, but it had been strained and fraught, especially on the honeymoon. She and her husband were now Christians, so he advised her to come for counselling.

Having learned of Suzy's experiences, we prayed that Jesus would heal the hurtful memories of her childhood. We asked her to remember a specific occasion. Her parents were in the garage and were arguing furiously, and Suzy had tried to stop them, causing their anger to be turned against her. When we prayed that Jesus would show Himself in the situation, Suzy saw Him walk up to them and tell them they were being silly. They stopped arguing and had a normal relaxed conversation with Jesus and Suzy. On another occasion, her father was drunk and standing beside the drinks cabinet, with her mother taunting and provoking him. We prayed that Suzy would see Jesus in that room too. Jesus opened the door so that Suzy could see her father was behaving like this because he was hurt. Jesus walked over to him and comforted him. Then his wife hugged him too. These two changed memories brought healing to Suzy so that she no longer remembered those occasions without also remembering that Jesus was there, making it all right. By inviting Jesus into two specific incidents like this, it changed Suzy's perception of all the hurtful years of her childhood.

We then asked Suzy to remember one of the times she was a prostitute, memories of which were haunting her. She recalled an occasion when she had gone to a man's flat with him. When we prayed for Jesus to come into the situation, Suzy saw Him sitting at a supper table with wine and food. Another man, a Christian she knows well, was also there. Jesus invited Suzy and the man she was with to join them. The four of them shared a lovely conversation together over the meal. It was an incredible experience for Suzy. She felt whole, healed deep within, and, for the first time ever, felt she was forgiven. She now has a beautiful, loving personality and is able to give love and care to many other people, as well as to her own family, including both parents. In recent years her father has become a Christian and they now have a healthy, trusting father-daughter relationship.

When Jesus is invited into situations like this, to change the damaging memories of the past, only the person being prayed for sees the memory, which they describe. Then, when He is invited, they see Jesus come into the picture, and He always does something which alters that memory for ever. The person leading them in prayer does not see Jesus, nor do they need to. It is most rewarding to see the relief and joy on the face of the person who has been hurt, when Jesus changes the situation. The inner healing which results is complete and beautiful – something which cannot have been achieved by hours of ordinary counselling.

Helen was brought up in a family that was, to all intents and purposes, respectable and middle-class. Unfortunately her mother contracted leukaemia, and began to spend long periods of time in hospital, leaving Helen to be looked after by relatives. It was during these times that some of the relatives took advantage of her vulnerability. Frequently she was mentally, sexually and emotionally abused during her mother's absence; but when Helen tried to tell her mother, she would not – or could not – believe it, and appeared to brush Helen's allegations aside. Trapped and isolated, Helen began to feel imprisoned by her pain and fear. The abuse culminated in a brutal rape when Helen was sixteen.

Over the following years, fear and pain were Helen's constant companions. She began to suspect that it was this that seemed to be attractive, in a perverse way, to the most unsavoury of men, and at the age of thirty, she was raped again. After the rapist was arrested, he was diagnosed as a psychopath. She had tried to fight him off as strongly as she could, but he inflicted serious injuries on her, resulting in a broken nose and ribs, multiple bruising and an injury to her eye. Helen had become a Christian a few months before, which had not protected her from this awful experience, but God gave her the strength to cope with the turmoil of pain and fear it produced.

After six months Helen realized she might be pregnant, but could hardly believe it possible as she had resisted the attack with all her strength. Eventually she went to London, where she did not know anyone, for a pregnancy test. When told the test was positive, Helen wandered the streets aimlessly for hours, shocked and in panic, not knowing what to do. She went into a rather gloomy church, which was dismal and depressing. With no one else to turn to, she sat there crying out to God for His help.

Helen recalls: 'Suddenly I felt this tremendous warmth on my head. I looked up to find a single ray of sunlight had come through a little window high up in the church, and was shining only on me. With that, an amazing thing happened – I found I was feeling tremendously excited and joyful. I started to praise God, and to thank Jesus for this little life that He had entrusted into my care. A great love for the child welled up from deep inside me. I made a promise that, whatever this child turned out to be, I would love it, and bring it up to God's praise and glory. When I looked down at my stomach, I realized that the ray of sunlight had moved from my head to my stomach, and was now encircling the baby I was carrying. At that moment I knew that the man who had raped me could no longer have any hold over me, my baby or our lives: no physical or mental hold, no spiritual influence. Over the years it has proven to be so.'

Helen continues: 'I gave birth to a daughter, Joy, who is beautiful, and has been a real treasure and blessing to me. When I look at her, it never ceases to amaze me how God has brought something so lovely out of something so terrible. She knows God as her Father. We are very happy together and count all the blessings that God gives us.' Helen and Joy have both received healing over the years through prayer ministry, which has allowed them to become more free and whole as each year passes.

Helen explains, 'Eighteen years have now gone by, and I have surrendered all my deepest feelings – the fear, pain, anger, uncleanness, rejection, injustice, guilt and shame of the past – to God. I now feel able to face up to life with a freedom and a joy in my step that I had never thought possible.'

An emphasis on Christian values and worshipping God is now no longer a part of the bringing up of children in Britain, for the majority, and we feel it is this situation that has led to the disintegration of family life in our nation. As an Anglican minister Geoff is called upon to baptize children into the Christian faith, with suitable preparation for the parents. However it is one thing to bring a child for baptism; it is of much greater importance for parents to carry out their baptismal promises. These are to help the child first, to turn to Christ, second, to repent of sin, and thirdly, to renounce evil.

For wholeness of mind, body, and spirit it is important to establish sensible rhythms of sleeping, eating, work and relaxation. Many people expect to get the most out of life while abusing their bodies by smoking heavily or by eating all the wrong foods. In the same way many people look for emotional and physical well-being in life without looking at their lifestyle. God expects us to take care of ourselves. We may need to implement a more balanced way of life with exercise, enough rest, a sensible diet and time alone with God. If we are not prepared to acknowledge the One who has created us, we can expect to make some wrong decisions in our lives.

Whilst living in Dorset we knew a teenage girl who was diagnosed as having anorexia nervosa. A confusing and complex disease, anorexia affects an increasing number of young people in our image-conscious world. Our friend Sarah was a pathetic sight, with her bony frame showing through her clothes. Often an anorexic cannot see his or her real self, and the frightening loss of weight goes completely unheeded by the sufferer.

In May 1992 we agreed to pray for Sarah, who was already a

Christian, and one Monday we prepared ourselves by fasting. That afternoon we met with her and her brother, who was also a Christian, for a Holy Communion service and prayer for healing at our church. First, bread and wine were placed on the Lord's table in preparation for Holy Communion. We prayed for all known, and unknown, connections with eating problems in Sarah's family tree, cutting her free from their continuing effects in her life. Then we all said the Lord's Prayer together. As soon as we reached the words 'Give us this day our daily bread', Sarah began to cry, with tears streaming down her face, since the prayer addressed the matter of food. Her stomach began to heave in involuntary spasms, as if in waves, from her abdomen up to her throat. We immediately prayed that whatever was unwelcome inside her would be removed. As we did so, she made more pronounced heaving movements and then slumped gently to the floor.

We then prayed that God's Holy Spirit would fill Sarah. Her face became radiant, and looked beautiful, with her hair cascading around it. She lay there for several minutes, her eyelids flickering, and a great sense of God's presence surrounding her. It was a very peaceful and special time. When she opened her eyes Sarah said, 'It's gone! It's gone!' 'What has gone?' we asked. Sarah replied, 'Something which has been inside me, holding me, for months. I don't know what it was, but now it has gone.'

After she stood up, we continued with the Communion service, giving thanks that God had intervened in response to prayer at Sarah's point of need, and that healing had taken place. Afterwards Sarah asked, 'What shall I tell my friends has happened?' Geoff replied, 'You can tell them that whatever it was that was troubling you has gone. You are now at peace with God and with your body; your recovery from anorexia has begun.' From that day onwards Sarah made a definite recovery, having previously lost weight continually. To this day, she has had no recurrence of the disease and lives a full life as a Christian.

Anorexia nervosa takes different forms and begins for different reasons. Chantalle Rowland's father is a minister at an Elim Pentecostal church, and the anorexia she experienced seemed to be a spiritual attack on the family. Chantalle has a twin sister, Heidi, and a younger sister, and they were a close family. At the beginning of 1993 Chantalle was thirteen years old, and started dieting. She was not at all overweight, but she saw herself as fat. She remembers, 'At first I was hungry, but I quickly enjoyed the feeling of being in control. It seemed a great achievement to be able to refuse food.' Chantalle's parents began to notice the problem, but any discussion about it only made matters worse, and ended with Chantalle storming out of the room.

Chantalle became clever at hiding food, giving the impression that she had eaten it. Sometimes, when encouraged to eat, she would react by throwing food across the room or walking out in a temper. Her mother, Janice, recalls: 'Mealtimes were a nightmare, so the problem was playing havoc with our family.' The doctor diagnosed anorexia nervosa and referred her to a psychiatrist, who saw the whole family in group sessions. Chantalle now says, 'Looking back on those sessions, I feel really sorry for the poor man because I refused to speak to him. I did not think I had a problem. I was being made to go, but nobody could make me talk.' The teachers at school tried to help, but she would throw half her lunch away, saying she had already eaten it, and would make herself vomit after she had been made to eat something. She continued to lose a great deal of weight, to her delight and everyone else's consternation.

The strain of the situation at home meant it was difficult for her father, Roger, to preach and lead worship at times, but the church elders were very helpful and supportive. Members of the church were praying for them, and the family was determined to keep trusting God although at times it was hard to feel able to. Chantalle's own faith was at a low ebb, and everyone else except her could see she had a serious health problem. The psychiatrist decided she should spend time in a special hospital unit. The nearest one was a long way from home, and Chantalle could not understand why everyone hated her so much that they wanted to send her away to make her fat and ugly. During her time in the special unit she met other anorexic girls, and learnt new tricks for hiding and disposing of food.

By April 1994 Chantalle was very thin, but went with her family to Bognor Bible Week, an Elim Pentecostal family conference, where she and Heidi helped with the worship. Chantalle plays saxophone, oboe and piano and enjoys music. On the Tuesday, Janice went to a lunch meeting for ministers' wives. The speaker could see a picture of Janice's daughter in a hospital bed with a 'spirit of death seeking to take her life'. Janice sobbed as she was prayed for and she felt the bondage of the problem being broken in that prayer.

Chantalle remembers: 'Mum came and told me afterwards, but I would not believe a word of it, because I still did not think I had a problem.' The next evening she was in the teenagers' group and one of the leaders asked Chantalle if he could pray for her, as he believed it was God's time for her to be set free. Chantalle remembers: 'I was about to say "No, I don't need prayer," when I remembered a verse Heidi had given me months before. "For I know the plans I have for you," declares the Lord, "plans to prosper you and not to harm you, plans to give you hope and a future" (Jeremiah 29:11). I agreed he could pray for me and, as he did so, it felt as if something inside broke, and I began to cry. I began to see myself in my true likeness again, and realized that I needed to eat to live. In that prayer I was totally healed by Jesus. People had tried everything to cure me of anorexia, but only Jesus was the answer. He rose from the dead so that our burdens could be taken away.'

Janice describes her daughter's transformation as 'dramatic'. From that moment Chantalle enjoyed, rather than rejected, food, and ate normally. In just a few days her weight returned to normal – the transformation was amazing. Looking back, nearly a year later, Chantalle remembers all the feelings of self-loathing and fear, but she is glad that Jesus has brought her through. She is now using her painful experience and the insight she has gained to help others with the same problems.

Lisa was older than Chantalle when she became overwhelmed by the associated condition of bulimia nervosa. The problem got out of hand at university, after she'd lost a lot of weight through illness and gradually became neurotic about keeping the weight off. She says, 'It was partly the pressure of my final exams, and partly the media image that you have thrust at you to be slim, that led to the illness. I'd make frantic calorie counts when I ate a biscuit, then binge and make myself sick, then get depressed about it and eat some more to comfort myself, then go on a crazy diet because I felt so guilty, then binge again. It was a vicious circle. My dad put a lock on the kitchen door, but nothing my friends or family tried helped me, and I gradually alienated them. I'd become a Christian at college, but got fed up with it, so I thought it would be weak to turn back to God just because I needed Him. Instead I tried counselling, fasting, positive thinking, without success.

Lisa continues: 'One evening I was walking home from a counselling session feeling sick and guilty as usual, when suddenly I heard a voice say, "You don't really *want* to get better. You're just using this problem to get attention." I knew it was God, and I was furious! I got home, yelled, shouted, threw things at the wall and finally got down on my knees and said, "I'm sorry, God, you're right. I don't want to change, but I *want* to want to change. Will you take over please?' From that day I was completely healed of bulimia. More than that, I had the most overwhelming peace.

'The next day I felt as though I had been tightly bound up for months and that someone was undoing the bonds one by one. Instead of seeking attention, I found I was giving attention to other people's needs. I even stopped counting calories in my head, and found I could eat a little of what I liked, then stop, which is very difficult for a bulimic. That evening when I opened the Bible my eyes fell on Leviticus 26:13: "I have broken your chains and will make you walk with dignity" [Living Bible]. The word dignity had special significance because during the bulimia I felt embarrassed, worth nothing, and could not hold my head up. I knew God was speaking especially to me through His word, and I believe God did what no amount of counselling could achieve – He gave me the power to change as well as the will. I couldn't see the solution until I gave in to God and let Him help.'

Restoring the broken image cannot be fully achieved with the help of psychiatrists or drugs. We can't become the whole person God intended us to be without His intervention. 'But thanks be to God! He gives us the victory through our Lord Jesus Christ' (I Corinthians 15:57).

After a person has been released in prayer from the past, there is a strong temptation to revert to old habits. Some will feel that they can recover from conditions such as alcoholism solely by their own will-power. Any lasting reform, however, needs to include a willingness to allow God to intervene. Ideally those who have received healing need to continue to lean on God through prayer and through support from other Christians, and to establish a regular pattern of worship. It is like learning to ride a bike. We have to keep moving forwards; if we stop still, we fall over. As St Paul said, 'I press on towards the goal to win the prize for which God has called me heavenwards in Christ Jesus' (Philippians 3:14).

The need to rely on God is demonstrated in Patrick's case. He had a serious alcohol problem and found it increasingly difficult to take responsibility. His wife, Sally, tried to hold the family together, but for about four years Patrick's daily drinking caused him to become aggressive and violent, and Sally was quite frightened of his unpredictable temper. He spent all his money on drink, leaving the family penniless, and had several affairs. Eventually, in 1985, Sally felt she had no option but to take the three children and leave him, hoping that this action would shake Patrick into reforming.

However it failed to have the desired effect. Patrick's drink problem worsened, and he became heavily in debt, losing his flat and eventually his job. For several years he wandered from place to place, in and out of different relationships, and several times considered suicide. Meanwhile Sally and her children had become Christians, and they kept praying that God would change him. Even on the occasions when there was contact between them, Patrick was unable to help in any way with the upbringing of the children or with the finances.

About eight years after the separation, Patrick phoned Sally to say he had been touched by God. At first she was sceptical, but apparently he had heard someone preaching the Gospel in the street and had felt compelled to stop and listen. Afterwards he approached the preacher, who took him back to his church and talked to him about the reality of Jesus, who could change his life. With help and prayer, Patrick committed his life to Jesus and became a new person. He no longer drinks, swears or smokes; he isn't violent or bad-tempered and is learning to take his responsibilities seriously. He spends much of his spare time helping homeless people, organizing a 'soup run' every evening for those on the streets. He is also active in persuading local firms and large shops to provide food and accommodation for the homeless. In fact, his life has turned around completely.

Relationships take on a new challenge when God is allowed to enter at the point of need. We have seen evidence of this in the lives of two childless couples in particular. Kim and Chris McKenna had been trying to have a baby for seven years. Numerous fertility treatments had failed to help Kim conceive, and she was feeling very despondent. During a break in the treatment, which she was told was not working, Kim was offered a trip to Israel through her job as manager of a travel agency. She was able to visit all the sites of Biblical interest in Jerusalem, and at the place where Jesus is said to have been crucified, she spent some time alone with God. Kim prayed especially for the gift of a child. Just one month later, in December 1985, she found that her prayers had been answered and she was expecting a baby. She later gave birth to Sean, and the couple were thrilled.

Anxious to have another baby, so Sean would not be an only child, Kim once again embarked on the fertility treatment. Three years passed with no sign of the longed-for second child. She decided to go away for a few days' break, and ceased all medication at that point. She found that having given birth to one child, delighted as she was with him, did not take away the pain she felt at being unable to conceive again. While she was reading I Samuel, where Hannah prayed to God for the gift of a child, Kim prayed again that God would grant her this gift. The following month she went to the hospital to resume the fertility treatment, and the consultant was as amazed as she was to discover she had conceived. Her daughter Freyja was the second miracle, reminding Kim and Chris that God is responsible for the creation of their beautiful children.

Janine Belmudes' situation was different in that she was single, and did not feel the need of a child for her own benefit, but wanted to share her life with a child. She prayed, and was prepared to wait for the child she felt God had planned to come and live in her home. Janine sent a letter to the Children's Welfare Authority, which in France, where she lives, is the first step in the adoption process. The night after she sent the letter, she had a vivid dream in which she was giving birth to a child. Her mother and sister were with her, telling her everything would be all right, in response to the fears she was expressing that she felt 'unqualified'. She dreamt that while she was in labour, a child of about four or five years old was near by, and that she said to him, 'Wait for me, I am coming.'

Janine went through all the required stages for the adoption of a child, and exactly nine months after having the dream, she received a letter from the lady in charge who said, 'We have a little boy of five ready for adoption; if you want him, he may arrive very quickly.' She said 'Yes' immediately, and Simon arrived from Ethiopia on 14 January 1987. Janine says, 'Since then, we have gone a long way together, and I've never regretted his adoption. I'm deeply moved when I think of this miracle of a child born so far away who has come to think of me as his mother, and to identify with my father and family.' Simon's mother, before she died, had become deranged, and had burnt him all over his body. Simon once said to Janine: 'It was not her fault, she was very ill in her head.' Janine was moved by Simon's compassion.

A few months after his arrival, Simon asked Janine if he could have a brother. She said she would try to adopt again when he was six. In May 1988 Janine began the adoption process once again, and this time she felt she would be able to accept a child with a physical disability. On 30 June the lady at the adoption agency phoned to say: 'I've just had a telex from Ethiopia; they have found a child in the streets. He is very poorly. He is blind in one eye, and has been sold to a man who makes him beg in the streets. Are you ready for this sort of challenge?' Janine's response was, 'Is this really going to be a problem. My father lost one eye during the war, so for me it is quite normal. Of course I'll adopt this child.'

André, aged four, arrived on 22 July. At first he was so frightened he would not let people touch him. He was especially wary of adults, which was understandable, in view of his past experiences. Janine took the two boys to visit her parents. At their first meeting, her father took André to the bathroom, took out his own glass eye and put it in André's hand. André then realized that here was someone like him, who had also lost his left eye. He is now a very happy child who loves football, and his grandfather is very important to him. In 1990, a little girl, Josephine, joined the family when she was three and a half years old. Janine says, 'I often think that our family in itself is a bunch of miracles!'

It is significant that, in the Gospels, Jesus is often found engaging with people who are hurt, diseased and bewildered. He said, 'I have come that they may have life, and have it to the full' (John 10.10).

Problems in our own nature are often buried deep. There are inherent flaws in every person. There is also the influence of the family tree, for better or worse, according to the goodness or otherwise of our ancestors. Inevitably, hurts manifest themselves in our lives because people are not perfect, and we in turn unintentionally hurt others.

Every child has a right to its parents' love and to be accepted as a full member of a family, without favouritism. The lack of such a welcome can cause an enormous amount of harm. Emotional and physical love are needed from both mother and father. In this generation, so many fathers have walked away from their families, and are absent for long periods of their children's lives, or do not make themselves available to their children even when they are at home. We heard Mary Pytches, a Christian counsellor, quote this poignant prayer by one young boy which expresses the hurt felt by many children at this neglect: 'O God, please make my face like a TV set, and then maybe my daddy will look at me.' The anger and sadness caused to children will affect them in the coming years if God is not invited to intervene with His healing power.

On a more positive note, family life can be a great blessing, and a strengthening experience for all of its members. We have received a number of letters telling of the good side of being part of a family. One was from David Vincent, who was raised in

India by his missionary parents, Alan and Eileen, and returned to England with his family when he was four years old. David was partially deaf, which Eileen feels could have been the result of a bout of amoebic dysentery that she suffered in the early days of her pregnancy, and which was treated with strong antibiotics. David was a demanding, hyperactive child, who was often disobedient, probably because no one at that stage realized the extent of his deafness. When they returned to England, extensive hearing tests were performed and David was found to be 'profoundly deaf' in the left ear and 'very deaf' in the right. Hearing aids were ordered for him, which would take seven weeks to be made.

During those seven weeks the family and the church the Vincents attended prayed for David's healing, which they believed God had the power to bring about. David was five by this time, and his father went back to India for a short working visit. One Sunday there was a service at church during which adults were baptized by immersion, and that evening at bedtime David asked his mother if he could be baptized in water. She said he was too young yet, but there was no reason why he couldn't be baptized in the Holy Spirit. She prayed with him there and then, and he was immediately filled with the Spirit of God. He spoke and sang 'in tongues', laughing and crying at the same time. Eileen then put a finger in each of David's ears and in Jesus' name prayed for his hearing to be healed. Immediately his ears were opened, and David knew he was healed. Mother and son were united in great joy and they praised God.

The next time David had an appointment at the hospital, the extensive hearing tests were repeated. The doctor accused Eileen of bringing a different child to be tested! He could not believe that David's hearing could have improved to above the normal range, and he could not understand it. Eileen explained that they had asked Jesus to heal him and He had. If the two hearing tests had not been done in the same hospital, the doctor would have thought one was a mistake. Seven months later hearing tests were done at the school David attended. The school nurse called David's mother to question her, since his records indicated profound deafness, yet his response to the tests was 'way above normal'.

Beat Muller's mother also played a crucial part in his healing. This was at their home in a village in Switzerland, on Beat's third birthday, 28 March 1950. Beat's mother was seven months pregnant and needed to wax the floor, so she asked Beat's father to keep an eye on him. Just as she was finishing the floor, she heard a noise and looked out of the door. Her son was staggering around as if drunk. She picked him up and his breath smelt of petrol. Apparently he had found a green bottle and taken a drink because he was thirsty. At once Beat's mother cried aloud, 'Jesus, have mercy on him,' and she heard a voice saying, 'If he drinks any deadly thing it shall not hurt him.' His grandfather gave him black coffee to drink, while his mother telephoned a doctor. He advised her to feed him with baby food containing fruit and to keep him away from the fire for three days. She was grateful for the advice, because she cooked on a solid fuel stove. A year later, Beat's mother read a newspaper article about a three-year-old who had drunk petrol, been taken to hospital and had died. This inspired her to give God thanks again for His protection of Beat.

At her home in Wales, Megan Watkins was helping her physically disabled granddaughter, Bethan, up six stairs to the bathroom. Bethan is ten and a half, and nearly as big as her grandmother. Bethan was struggling to get her foot on the sixth step, so Megan gave her leg a push with her knee. Bethan, not realizing her foot was against the top step, also pushed, and her grandmother toppled backwards. Megan recalls: 'When I found I was overbalancing, I just held Bethan tight in my arms, so I would take the fall. I remember my left heel on the step and then both my heels were on the floor of the room downstairs, with my back to the stairs. Bethan and her younger brother, Paul, were laughing, and Bethan was standing on her own by my side. Normally she cannot stand on her own at all. I know this miracle saved us both from falling.'

God wants to use loving relationships to enable His work of intervention to overflow into every human experience. Many people have been changed because of the way Christians have introduced Jesus into the heart of hurting, broken lives.

Sometimes a Christian may pray for an unbelieving friend or relative for years before seeing a result to their prayers. Danny Vicary, who lives in Liverpool, had always been terrified of the dark, even though he was a tough man. He was an atheist, although his wife, Linda, had a deep Christian faith. He wrote: 'Even as a married man with three children I always had the house lit up like Blackpool illuminations. If my wife went to bed before me, I would turn the lights off one by one as I went to the bedroom, then undress as quickly as possible, turn off the last light, then dive into bed, burying my head in my wife's back. She thought I was just giving her a hug (which I was) but really I was trying to get away from the dark.'

Linda prayed constantly for her husband, that he would become aware of a 'God-shaped gap' in his life and find God to be real. One night Danny was doing the usual routine of turning off the lights, and when he got to the last one he heard a voice: 'As you walk through the valley of the shadow of death, you shall fear no evil, for Jesus is with you.' Danny wrote to us, 'For the first time in my life, I turned off the last light without being afraid of the dark, and I have never been afraid since that moment. I changed from being an atheist into a Christian. It still amazes me today how God could do such a wonderful thing for someone who for years had denied His very existence; but then, that is the power of prayer.'

A family at a Baptist church in Essex were going through a time of great friction caused by petty squabbles, and they had drifted apart. One day in 1993 John, aged 51, and his wife, Linda, returned from a hospital out-patient appointment with the news that John had cancer. His sister, Dorothy, felt they should meet together as a family to pray for John's healing, so she contacted her brothers and sisters to invite them to her home.

The first time they met together, God spoke to them using the gifts of tongues and interpretation of tongues, starting with the words 'Jesus said, "If any man thirst, let him come unto Me and drink".' Dorothy had been on holiday the previous week, just after hearing John's news. She had been given that same verse on two separate occasions, when praying for John, and had felt encouraged to believe that God would heal John. The family prayed a great deal for John, and those who could manage it met together weekly.

Dorothy writes: 'When John did not make the progress we had hoped for, we found it very difficult to understand. We knew God had the power to heal, and we knew from past experience that He does heal today – even cancer – and could not understand it. Not only this, loving John so deeply we could not help but absorb his suffering, and we felt so helpless. Yet God did answer in that He gave John the strength to teach the Scriptures at church throughout the months of his chemotherapy treatment. God used him as a channel, despite the weakness of his body.' When healing did not come, God spoke to John's brother, Colin, about the need for reconciliation in the family. Colin led the way in healing the rift which had been evident between certain family members. Those in dispute talked and prayed together and, following the re-establishment of family unity, Colin felt that God was saying to him 'It is done', which he shared with them all.

A week later the family joined together for a Communion service at John and Linda's home. John was deeply moved and blessed by the family service, at which fourteen members of the family were present. Dorothy continues: 'Still John did not get well; in fact his condition deteriorated, and we were puzzled.

John was increasingly tired, but said he wanted us to come and pray again. Four of us met on 19 March, planning to stay only twenty minutes, as we knew how ill John was. He was exhausted, but we prayed for him and anointed him with oil. We prayed for Linda who was under a lot of strain. Then the Holy Spirit came on John and he began to pray for us and for other members of the family, his voice growing stronger all the time.

'Then John said, "You can sing if you like." We sang "Set my spirit free that I might worship Thee", and John not only joined in, but started the chorus again. Then, again following his lead, we sang "When I feel the touch of Your hand upon my life". John's voice was strong as he sang, his hands were raised and his face was shining. It was a miracle to hear John, whose body was riddled with cancer, singing "You are my God, you are my King and I love you Lord".

'John went to be with the Lord five days later. His son, Kevin, picked up John's Bible just after he had died, and it fell open at Revelation 21:6: "He said to me: It is done . . . To him who is thirsty I will give to drink without cost from the spring of the water of life." God was reminding us that He is sovereign, our times are in His hand, and that John was now with Him. How amazing that God should say to us a second time "It is done", and a fourth time, that He alone can satisfy our thirsty souls.'

God brought healing and wholeness to a family, even though a loved one died. In terms of miracles in relationships, one could pray:

Lord Jesus,
You have no body on earth but ours,
No hands but ours
No feet but ours,
Ours are the eyes showing
Your compassion to the world;

Ours are the feet with which
You go about doing good;
Ours are the hands with which
You are to bless others now.
Lord Jesus, take us and use us
In Your service. Amen.

CHAPTER ELEVEN
Miracles in the Local Church

> Where can I go from your Spirit?
> Where can I flee from your presence?
> If I go up to the heavens, you are there;
> if I make my bed in the depths, you are there.
> If I rise on the wings of the dawn,
> if I settle on the far side of the sea,
> even there your hand will guide me,
> your right hand will hold me fast.
>
> Psalm 139:7–10

T WAS IN the scattered communities of Palestine that most of Jesus' miracles occurred, affecting ordinary men and women. However important big Christian events held in cathedrals, conference centres and outdoor rallies appear to be, the local church and the community around it is where God's Spirit wants to be in action on a daily basis. Ronald Blythe writes in his book *Divine Landscapes*: 'One's own parish can be so rewarding that one doesn't need to go much further. But it will offer a thousand leads to more distant versions or origins of the historic sanctity which is bound up in every native place.'

It is at the grass-roots level of the local church where Jesus continues to be as real as He was in the village of Bethany or in the town of Nazareth. John Keble, a nineteenth-century professor of poetry at Oxford, could have reached great ecclesiastical heights, but preferred to work in a country parish where he believed that the best of God could be seen.

> The trivial round, the common task,
> would furnish all we ought to ask;
> room to deny ourselves a road
> to bring us daily nearer God.

Here again the golden thread of this book is emphasized: God is interested in the common things of life. We would suggest that God is more ready to show His power right where we live. He wants us to bloom where we are planted. The great resources of God's Spirit are with us in our own locality.

A strong, Cornish tenant farmer named Vivian Champion was working on the family farm. One day in September 1986 his hip gave out, and the doctor suspected spondylitis of the lower spine, or premature wearing of the vertebrae. X-rays confirmed the diagnosis, and Vivian was sent for physiotherapy. Both the doctor and the physiotherapist told him not to lift anything or bend, which are not easy to avoid on a farm.

Vivian had to carry on with his usual work, but with increasing pain in the lower back and hips. By May 1990 he had pain in the upper arms and neck, and spondylitis of the upper spine was diagnosed. He had to continue working to maintain the tenancy, since the family home as well as their income was dependent on it. He had to employ extra help for the tractor-driving and heavy tasks he could no longer manage, and the landlord allowed him to sublet some of the land. The physiotherapist told Vivian he could do no more for him. He was also seeing a chiropractor, an osteopath and a homoeopathic doctor who all agreed there was nothing they could do as his spine was badly damaged.

George, a retired farmer, invited Vivian to a service of Christian healing at the Trelowarren Fellowship near Helston, on 5 November 1991. Vivian had agreed to go, but was very tired and discouraged when the evening came, having just been to see the fifth consultant within a period of about fifteen months.

Vivian had been told by the consultant that he was in such a bad state, hips as well as spine, that even if he found the lightest possible work, he would not be able to carry it out. Before leaving, his daughter Rebecca, aged sixteen, asked him, 'Dad, do you believe Jesus can heal you?' Vivian had been brought up to go to church, but had not looked to God for healing. Now in answer to Rebecca's question, he said, 'Yes; I think I always have done, but I have not been able to speak it out loud.' Rebecca replied, 'That's all that matters, Dad.'

Entering the healing service and seeing people truly worshipping God, Vivian was able to praise God as he had never done before. He remembers: 'We were encouraged to follow the summary of the first commandment as Jesus said in Matthew 22: 37, "Love the Lord your God with all your heart and with all your soul and with all your mind." I knew I had not done that – I had never put God first. The man speaking at the front said, 'God is God of love.' When he said that, it was as if a barrier had been removed for me. There were five or six pairs of men and women praying for people at the front, and I went forward to two men. They prayed for me, and I knew I was in God's presence. I felt smaller than a grain of sand in comparison to Him, but I knew that He still loved me. More surely than I could see my own hands stretched out in front of me, I knew for certain that He could heal me.'

Vivian arrived home very tired, and went straight to bed. When he awoke next morning, he thought he must still be dreaming. He felt no pain at all – in his back, his neck, his hips or his arms. He had forgotten what it was like to be without pain. When his children woke up, they were delighted. His wife, Jill, had already gone to work with the Home Help service. When she returned home in the afternoon, there was a trailer in the farmyard piled high with firewood. It was not easy for her to accept that Vivian had cut all this wood himself, loaded it, and was springing in and out of the tractor like a kitten! Most days she arrived home to find him lying out flat with a hot-water bottle under his spine to ease the pain. That day he worked until after dark, like a new man.

Three weeks later Vivian went to his doctor, who could not find a thing wrong with him. He says, 'I also went to be examined by the physiotherapist, who remembered vividly twenty months previously having to tell me he could not help me any more, and he did not know what I could do.' Now he said Vivian's body was 'just like a new one'. Vivian recalls: 'At first I was afraid that, as time passed, I would be less thankful to God, but it has been the opposite. To live another day is yet more glorious. All glory to God, who loves us so much through Jesus Christ our Lord, and the power of the Holy Spirit.'

In contrast to the big farmer, Elizabeth Murray was just a tiny baby, in need of God's healing. She was born on 3 March 1991 an apparently healthy baby, but when she was just two months old, her mother, Sharon, found a small lump under her skin near her shoulder. The GP assured her it was a harmless cyst, but by the beginning of July, Elizabeth refused feeds for several days. She was referred to the Birmingham Children's Hospital, where tests showed she was in an advanced state of neuroblastoma, a cancer occurring mainly in children. She had four primary tumour sites and more than twenty secondary sites. The consultant paediatric oncologist's report stated that 'this extended above and below the diaphragm, and involved the pleura, the extra-dural space, the skin, the subcutaneous tissues, the liver and three ribs'. Elizabeth's lungs were about to collapse under the pressure of the growths, and chemotherapy was begun immediately.

Her parents, Jim and Sharon, were not practising Christians, but arranged for Elizabeth to be baptized, as they were warned she had only a few months to live. After that they went regularly to church in their home town of Rugeley, Staffordshire, finding comfort and support. The treatment progressed causing much physical pain for Elizabeth, and emotional pain for her parents. In early October the medication was increased and she was seriously ill again, but three weeks later a full body scan showed the cancer was under control. However she still weighed only the amount she had been at three months of age, and her immunity was very low. This led to a severe episode of pneumonia in November 1991, and her condition became critical. In intensive care she was put on a ventilator, and one night her chances of surviving the next twenty-four hours looked very slim.

That night Sharon prayed in the name of Jesus Christ for Elizabeth's suffering to end, and she was filled with warmth and well-being. Christians at the church they attended were praying regularly for the family. The next day the vicar, Robin Charles, came to pray with Jim and Sharon for Elizabeth. He anointed her with oil and holy water praying, 'God bless this child and keep her safe.' For the first time, Sharon felt a peace and certainty deep inside that she was now a Christian, and she felt prepared if Elizabeth was to die. Jim too now shared Sharon's new-found faith in Christ, and it has since become an important part of their lives. Two hours after the vicar prayed with them Elizabeth began to improve, and the oxygen level she required dropped from 90 per cent to 65 per cent, the first hopeful sign. Within three days she was free of the pneumonia, and Jim and Sharon were sure that God had saved her, with the help of the skill and care of the medical team.

Two months later Jim and Sharon were confirmed into the Anglican Church. By the time she was one year old Elizabeth was clear of cancer, with no apparent lasting side-effects from the disease or the treatment. Two years later the consultant reported: 'Elizabeth is well, with no recurrence of her tumour and, I hope, an excellent outlook.' Her parents describe her at just over three years old as 'full of life and love; she seems to shine. She is a bright, forward little girl who reads, counts, draws, adores music and never stops talking.' They are convinced that God saved her life.

God has been showing Himself powerfully at work in many places around the world. In Seoul, Korea, there has been an incredible church growth at the Yoido Full Gospel Church under the leadership of David Yonggi Cho. Hundreds of thousands of people have become Christians and now reach out to others to share the Gospel. The key to the miracles they have seen in Korea, and the amazing church growth they have experienced, is the emphasis on prayer in the local church. Korean Christians, led by the example of their leaders, regularly spend about an hour in prayer in the morning, at midday and in the evening, privately or together in prayer meetings. They are just as busy as we are in the West, but they have found prayer to be a vital element in their lives, and the key to revival.

Pastor Yonggi Cho writes: 'I have been a pastor for twenty-six years, but I still need the Holy Spirit every day to cleanse my life because there are many temptations that creep in. When you become the pastor of half a million people, you are in the centre of temptation. If I don't tap the resources of God through prayer, I cannot meet the challenge of my daily work. If I don't spend long enough with the Holy Spirit, I soon know I have a dry well. To be filled each day with the resources of heavenly power, I've got to pray each day.'

Prayer precedes and saturates the services at the Yoido Full Gospel Church. Members spend the entire night in prayer every Friday, and at any time people can go to the Prayer Mountain. This was land originally set aside for a church cemetery but, during the building of their church on Yoido Island, when they were facing difficulties, people started going to this land to fast and pray. Now there is an auditorium that seats 10,000, as well as several smaller prayer chapels and 'prayer grottos', which are dug right into the side of the hill so that individuals can find complete solitude for prayer. Thousands go there each day; the larger prayer gatherings have seen as many as twenty thousand people praying and fasting at any one time. Thousands of people are healed of all manner of diseases, and many miracles of all kinds are seen every week. But the most important miracle is the transformation of a person's life, in coming to know the love and power of Jesus. Pastor Yonggi Cho writes of 'the extreme importance of prayer': 'In 1983 alone we had a total of 120,000 new converts. Why are so many people being saved within a single church? We have seen the importance of developing and maintaining a prayer life. If we stop praying, the revival will wane. The answer is prayer.'

Recently in the vast nation of China, there has been greater freedom to preach the Gospel and people are becoming Christians in their thousands. God's power is clearly at work, with signs and wonders accompanying the preaching. In one district, as Christians were preaching outdoors, a miraculous visual presentation appeared of the birth, life, death and resurrection of Jesus, portraying as if on film exactly what the preachers were saying. However there was no video or film equipment there at all. This went on for four hours and over one thousand people saw it with their own eyes. As a result of the miracle, almost everyone there repented and believed saying, 'God is real and alive in our midst. What can we say, but to thank Him and believe Him.'

In another district of China, some Christian women were preaching outdoors during the Chinese new year festival. A group of police arrived and one stretched out his hand towards the Christian women shouting, 'Arrest them.' His arm immediately became rigid, and he was not able to put it down. He went back to the police station in that condition and, in desperation, asked, 'What can I do?' Someone said, 'You must find a Christian to pray for you.' They invited the Christian women to the police station to pray for him, and he was immediately healed. When they preached there, many of the police became Christians. The

Christians later discovered a very similar incident described in the Bible, in I Kings 13:1–7, where King Jeroboam rejected God's word to him from a man of God and pointed at the man saying, 'Seize him!' His hand became stiff and shrivelled; only when he implored the man of God to pray for him was his hand restored to normal.

A special outreach called Gospel Month was held in China, during which every believer was encouraged to bring one other person to Jesus. One Christian, who had received the gift of healing, saw in that month twenty-six deaf people gain their hearing. He also prayed for a man born with a severe mental deficiency; the man had no speech or general ability. Immediately the man was healed, and received a brilliant mind, excellent speech and new talents. Eighty-three people who had known him were so amazed at the change in him that they responded to the power of God and became Christians. Many new churches are springing up in every available meeting-place, as a result of these widespread conversions.

Asian Outreach International reports that North Vietnam is also seeing more Christian growth than ever before, after communist control of nearly forty years. Many people of all ages in the nation are addicted to opium, and a drug rehabilitation centre in Ho Chi Minh city has been trying since 1975 to help addicts. The aim of the centre is to cure the addicts and to train them to do productive work and lead a normal life, but results have been only limited. However in recent years, the authorities have been astonished at the changes in people who have become Christians. Whole villages have been miraculously delivered from addiction and have begun a new life in Jesus. Many have given up drugs, smoking and drinking and become model citizens. There has been much superstition and demonic influence in the past in Vietnam. Those converted to Christianity have burned their charms, realizing the danger of their power. In one village, after a witch-doctor burned her charms, she fell down dead with blood oozing from her nose and mouth. Evangelists prayed over her and she was raised from the dead. Now she is a committed Christian worker.

All over South America there are vast numbers of new Christians, reports of miracles and the planting of many new churches. One such place is Santiago, Chile. Alfredo Cooper has been involved in evangelism and church-planting there (with the South American Missionary Society) for several years. He wrote to us: 'I have experienced so many miracles over the years of my ministry, that I have difficulty in selection.' He quotes one instance: 'Lucho is a doctor who was new to our church, and had come to our church weekend at a house near the beach. He was having difficulty in reconciling his "scientific world view" with what we were experiencing – a God who intervenes in the mechanistic universe of cause and effect.

'Towards the end of our time together, as we gathered for Communion, I found him tugging my sleeve. "Pastor, I won't say I have faith yet, but I need you to pray for my son." His one-year-old son had been diagnosed as having a cancerous brain tumour. As a doctor, Lucho had seen it himself on the scanner prints. We prayed for his child, who was a strange grey colour and had an odd look in his eye. Hardly a week had passed before Lucho came to church with his family. "I can't tell you I'm fully a believer yet, but something strange is happening that science cannot explain," he said, smiling. In new scanner readings, his son's tumour had simply vanished, and the boy had recovered remarkably well in every way. Today, five years later, the boy is still whole, and Lucho is now a believer and practising as a Christian doctor.'

Christ for all Nations is an organization begun in 1972 by the missionary Reinhard Bonnke, who was then ministering in southern Africa. He was given a vision by God to reach out to all of Africa. The Lord told him to hire a sports stadium in Botswana and preach the Gospel there. In one meeting alone, a thousand people came forward to receive God's gift of salvation. As the ministry grew, they bought a tent suitable for the thousands who were coming to the meetings in South Africa, Zambia and Zimbabwe. In 1984 they commissioned a cathedral-sized tent which could seat 34,000. At its dedication, more than 5,000 people received Jesus as their saviour.

In 1986 Christ for all Nations was planning a large Christian crusade in Blantyre in Malawi. As the organizers prayed, the Lord gave them a promise that He would do wonders in this nation that He had never done before, turning the nation to Himself. Over the next couple of months, there was a great prayer revival among all the Christians, and a unity between all the local churches that they had not experienced before. Then Gordon and Rachel Hickson, who were organizing the crusade on behalf of Christ for all Nations, were informed by the Inspector General of Police that their permission to stay in the country was cancelled, that they must leave within a week, and that the crusade could not go ahead. They were suspected of being CIA agents as they had had such an influence on the town in such a short time. All the local Christians prayed fervently and within three days, Gordon had an appointment with the secretary to the president of Malawi, to share the vision of Christ for all Nations. He promised to arrange an interview with the Inspector General of Police.

The day before they were due to leave the country, Gordon and the crusade chairman met the Inspector General together with other chiefs of staff. They were told that they were prohibited immigrants, and that nothing like this would ever be allowed in their country again. But the prayers of the people of the town turned the situation around. The two of them were taken into the Inspector General's private office, so he could ask them alone why they were so persistent about having a crusade in Malawi. The Holy Spirit enabled them to speak about God's plan for the nation, and the Inspector General was so influenced by God's presence in the room that he knelt down and asked them to pray for God's blessing on his life. Then he opened the door and told the chiefs of staff that the missionaries were free to remain in the country and must receive all the advice and support they needed because 'these people have a message from God for our nation'. Gordon remembers: 'It was a remarkable and miraculous breakthrough. The state house protocol officer was assigned to us to organize a national banquet the night before the crusade. The chief minister and several other top dignitaries gave their lives to the Lord that night.

'Within a week up to 200,000 people crammed on to the field where the mission was being held, and the Spirit of God moved powerfully; tens of thousands gave their lives to Jesus. At every single meeting cripples were healed, deaf people heard, dumb people spoke, blind eyes were opened and people were delivered from demons. It seemed as if we had arrived in Blantyre at just the time God intended. People were walking for five days or coming by bus from every corner of Malawi, saying that they had heard Jesus was in Blantyre. God had indeed turned the nation of Malawi to Himself, and everybody was aware that there was a living God who saved, healed and delivered.' Shortly afterwards, the Hicksons learnt that they had come to Malawi exactly one hundred years after the founding of Livingstone's mission in Blantyre. In his diary David Livingstone wrote that they were sowing the Gospel in tears and with their own blood, and that only a few people were being saved. He wrote prophetically that in years to come, God would come in glory to that city and men would reap a spiritual harvest of thousands.

In Eastern Europe and Russia recently there have been evangelistic events both large and small. Eurovision a Christian organization working in Eastern Europe, reported that in Russia a team of four hundred Christians led crusades in Belorussia, Siberia and the Ukraine. In four and a half months they saw 100,000 people become Christians: as many converts as in the first six months of the 1904 Welsh revival. There were also 1,300 documented healings during those crusades. Other missions working in Eastern Europe are seeing similar results.

In all continents and in every denomination of the Christian Church, God shows His power when His people are faithful in prayer and are open to His intervention. More recently, a new wave of refreshing by the Holy Spirit, bringing a renewal of faith in Jesus, has spread to many countries, including Great Britain.

From the beginning of 1994 God started visiting churches across Britain in a more powerful way than they had known before, through what has become known as the Toronto Blessing, a new outpouring of spiritual renewal from God that first blossomed in a church called the Airport Vineyard in Toronto. This renewing of faith in Jesus has had the effect of giving people a greater desire to read the Bible, to pray more fervently and have a greater concern to reach out to those who do not know him.

In June 1994, God's power was shown at St James's Church, Bream, in the Forest of Dean. One of the church members, Helen Terry, writes of her own experience: 'During my teens, life revolved around my local Methodist church, attending all the services, drama group, choir, young people's fellowship, and so on. However no one acknowledged the presence of the living God among us. It was as if He was simply an historical figure. Oh yes, we said "Christ is risen", and "Come close to God and He will come close to you", but I went away as confused and heartsick as when I arrived. Inevitably my reaction was to damp down these feelings. At all costs I had to keep a "stiff upper lip" in church. Whatever inner turmoil I felt, it wasn't to be shown. From then until now (twenty years on) I have suppressed my emotions through fear of what others might think. The unwritten rule is that you can't trust emotions; don't let your heart rule your head. As a result, I was wrapped in a shroud of years of protective intellectual cynicism and scepticism, along with all the hurts I've dished out to other people and they've returned to me.'

Helen remembers the day her life began to change: 'At church one Sunday in June 1994, an invitation was given to stand if you wanted to receive the Holy Spirit. I stood, not because I believed it would happen, but because the three people with me in the music team immediately sprang up, as if tied by some invisible cord. So I thought, "There's safety in numbers; if they're brave enough, I can be too." The vicar then announced he would pray for the three elders, Simon, Stuart and Greta, and they would go amongst the congregation and pray for those standing up. From my vantage point in the music team, I exchanged glances with my atheist husband. The unspoken message from him was, "Well, you've burnt your bridges now", and mine to him was, "Do you think anyone will notice if I sit down?"

'I watched with trepidation as our vicar prayed for Simon and Stuart, but when he prayed for Greta, I heard a thump and Greta fell to the floor. That shook me! Mid-fifties and not given to flights of fancy, she was smiling angelically and occasionally twitching. Stuart prayed for Mike and Fiona to my right in the music team. What a relief – they might have been carved in stone – not a wobble between them! As Stuart prayed for me, I asked God to fill me with His Holy Spirit and make me a living sacrifice. I joined Greta on the carpet. I didn't feel anything as I landed, but I was crying uncontrollably. Me, the mistress of self-control, crying in front of 150 others. My overriding thought was to "get up and get out". It was a struggle, but I did it. I rushed through the vestry, flung open the door and ran out into the graveyard.

'As I sat blubbering among the dead, the door opened; Fiona and Mike, they of the stone feet, came to find me. They comforted me and talked about what had happened. They accepted it as perfectly normal that God should reach out and that, in doing so, His presence might knock you off your feet.'

Helen continues: 'The weeks that followed found me in the grip of what were, for me, unusual compulsions. I read the Bible avidly, including passages about the gifts of the Spirit; I prayed as I'd never prayed before. I've tried to explain it away – "I was under stress", "It was auto-suggestion". But however much I try to wriggle, I know God has touched me. He is the Living God. Why should I want to be filled with the Holy Spirit? Because by filling me, I can become a channel of His love. Already I am becoming less self-conscious in admitting my Christian faith to others, which I was terrified to do before, and in sharing my beliefs and about how I've changed. I listen to other people now, trying not to be intolerant and judgemental, but reflecting on what Jesus would have said or done in any given situation. I will stand up for the truth, but I won't thrust it down people's throats.'

Analysing the experience, Helen asks herself, 'Do I feel more holy? Most emphatically not. Each day I battle with impatience, selfishness, anger, pride. Just when I think I've slain one giant, another rises to take its place. What I am slowly learning to do is ask God to be with me in those moments when self gets in the way of His love. If anything, I've been more aware of my failings. In coming closer to His love, He is pouring healing into me. He digs deep and brings old hurts to the surface, shouldering the burden Himself.

'Letting go is hard; old hurts have been constant companions for so long, that I want to hold on to them, and I can't believe they can be taken away. Yet in giving my burdens to Him, I am free to become a channel of His love, so that He can reach out to others through me and release them from the chains that bind them too. I will not be immune to future pain, but I'll not be the ultimate pain-bearer; Christ will. Also, I thought that once God revealed Himself, I would believe, no two ways about it. Instead I clear away one area of doubt to reveal another. Questions still pile up, clamouring for an answer. But it would be a poor God who could not stand questioning. Consciously I seek the answers and move on to a deeper level of faith. Asking these questions forces me to focus on what is important. Falling down when you're prayed for isn't, although it is often the way God chooses to do His work of healing. It's just an external sign of what He is doing on the inside. The point is that I've been seeking God, and He's revealed Himself to me in a very tangible way.'

Reflecting on the situation nine months later, Helen writes: 'I now preach sometimes and write for a national Christian women's magazine; things I would never have contemplated before. Either you give God permission to tear out your heart and give you a new one, in the assurance that you will be raised into new life, or you turn your back on Him. The Holy Spirit will come in power anywhere people are open to receive.' Her 'atheist husband', Robert, has become a Christian and has been confirmed into the Church of England. He has enjoyed two discipleship courses at church, and now regularly prays and reads the Bible. He too is gradually being set free from the hurts that he has suffered in the past, and shares his faith at work.

The vicar of St James's Church, Bream, Revd Alastair Kendall, reflects on the current developments: 'From day one of experiencing as a church the present outpouring of the Holy Spirit, we have focused on the "fruit" of the spirit rather than the "manifestations". When testimony has been given, it has been of what God is accomplishing in people's lives. Numerous people say: "My love for Jesus has grown deeper", and we are encouraging members to see the blessing as an equipping for service and evangelism. Healing has remained in those who have received it. We have seen 42 per cent growth in our morning congregation, and 67 per cent growth in the evening, requiring the establishment of a "church plant" to accommodate the larger numbers. We are reaching out in new ways to others with a bikers' group, a parent and toddler group and a luncheon club for the elderly.'

Another man in the same church who has received God's touch wrote: 'We like to think we're good, don't we? But the nearer we get to God, the more grotty we realize we are . . . It has changed me. I've matured in a very short space of time.'

A doctor in the congregation relates: 'God appears to be

dealing with the old hurts and pain that people have borne for years, almost in one fell swoop. Psychologically He's making a clean sweep, which might usually have been expected to take years of counselling.' This does not minimize the real anguish that some people are suffering. All over the world, God is healing those in His Church who are willing to let Him, making them ready to reach out to those outside the Church who are hurting. Another man at St James's says: 'God's sweeping the stage; the play hasn't begun yet. He's clearing away the rubbish, putting the props in place and getting the actors ready. The Church has to go out into the world.'

When Christians do reach out to others, it can have a powerful effect. Gillian Ross in Cumbria started going to church because she wanted her son, Graham, to go to Sunday School. Her marriage was pretty rocky. Her husband, John, could turn the air blue with his language, and was often found drunk and disorderly by the police. Gillian found the peace she lacked by attending church, and enjoyed the friendship she found there. John was not interested in church in the slightest and wanted nothing to do with it. In 1988 Gillian had to go into hospital unexpectedly as her liver had been damaged by prescribed drugs. After two weeks in the local hospital she was transferred to the intensive care unit in Manchester, seriously ill. The friends Gillian had met at church helped John by cooking meals for himself and Graham and by giving them lifts to visit Gillian in hospital in Manchester. None of his own friends offered any help at all, so John was very impressed that people he hadn't known should show such care.

When Gillian was allowed home and wanted to go to church, John said he would come with her. It was a turning-point for him. He started to ask questions about the Christian faith and attended a 'Christian Basics' course. The family are now committed Christians, fully involved in church life, as a result of the care Christians showed to a non-Christian husband.

The opportunity for prayer may come through a person's first contact with church, just when it is needed. In King Williamstown, South Africa, Norma de la Rosa and her husband Clarence were unable to have a child, to their great sadness. Prior to marriage, Norma had suffered much abdominal pain for eleven years, and had undergone tests and surgery. Crohn's disease was diagnosed, and fifteen centimetres of her colon, her appendix and left Fallopian tube had to be removed as they were adhered together.

A year after she married Clarence, severe pain in her right side was diagnosed as a blocked Fallopian tube. With delicate surgery this was cleared, but there remained only a slight chance that Norma would ever become pregnant. Norma heard that the leaders at Holy Trinity Church, King Williamstown, prayed for healing, so on 26 October 1992 they went along. She says: 'Our lives changed dramatically that day.' When Philip Leonard-Johnson, the rector, and his wife, Mary, prayed for Norma, an amazing calm came over her. She cried because she knew that inside she was healed. That day Norma and Clarence both made a significant step on their Christian journey. On 1 July 1993 baby Franco was born, and he has brought them great joy.

In Guyana, Revd John Dorman met with an unusual situation, just after taking evensong at an isolated parish in the Upper Mazaruni River area. It was 123 miles from his base, along a forest road, so he did not get there very often. On this occasion he was told that a middle-aged lady, Irene Joseph, who, together with her husband, had been confirmed into the church the previous month, was now gravely ill. She was the victim of a 'Kanaima'. This is a man who has developed an obsession to kill, as a result of demon possession. The person killed is usually alone and defenceless, sometimes asleep, and the method may be violent or by poison.

John and his catechist assistant, Charles, crossed the river to the small island where Irene and her family lived. Irene was in her hammock, rigid, unable to speak or to recognize anyone. Her husband, Bernstein, said she had scarcely been able to paddle the canoe home after she had been attacked and compelled to swallow a poisonous plant. Family and friends gathered in sorrow and fear. John and the church members prayed around her hammock and sang some hymns. John went back to Charles's home for the night, but others promised to stay and pray round the hammock all night. Charles felt sure she would die.

The next morning they celebrated Holy Communion in the church, and then took some bread and wine across the river to Irene's home. The singing could be heard before they landed on the shore. The little 'post, bark and leaf' house was filled with singing people. Irene was sitting up in her hammock, and gladly received Communion. They all praised God that He had healed her. The people were astonished, saying it had never been known for the victim of a Kanaima to recover. The people were in no doubt that this was a miraculous answer to the Christians' prayers.

Terence and Jane Coulter from Halifax, Yorkshire, had no church connections before responding at an open-air service in 1992 organized by members of the Church of the Holy Nativity in Mixenden. Terence, a former builder, has diabetes and serious heart disease. On 6 June 1993, at the age of forty-three, he suffered a severe angina attack and was admitted to the coronary care unit. An hour later, Jane was told he had gone into cardiac failure, and was not expected to survive the next hour. She immediately began to pray, asking for healing for Terence and strength for herself. Ten minutes later a doctor came to tell Jane that Terence had gone into renal failure and his veins had collapsed. His blood pressure was too low even to be measured on the electronic monitoring equipment. The unit sister phoned Jane's relatives, and when her brother arrived, he contacted Jane and Terence's vicar, Richard Bradnum. Jane was taken in to see Terence who looked waxen, and had difficulty breathing.

When Richard Bradnum arrived, he and Jane prayed in the waiting room for Terence. At 3 a.m., since nothing further could be done medically, they were allowed to go and sit at his bedside. They held his hands and prayed. Terence was unable to move and did not know who was holding his hands. He could hear, but did not have the energy to speak. He says: 'Suddenly a tremendous light appeared at the back of me. I felt it spread forward and engulf my body. Simultaneously, a terrific breeze blew on my face, and I began to gulp great breaths of this wonderful air. I felt my body pushed forward, with light and breeze all around me. I could now breathe with ease. I assumed that dawn had broken and there was a fan working, but it was neither.'

Jane and Richard noticed Terence's irregular breathing, but suddenly he bolted forward, his eyes wide open, and began gulping at the air. The readings on the machines immediately began to improve, and, having been in renal failure, he now started producing urine into the catheter. The dramatic improvement was welcomed by the doctors, and a nurse on duty at the time told Terence later that she felt it an honour to have witnessed this miracle. She assured him that his recovery could not be accounted for by medication, since no drugs had been administered that night as his veins had collapsed.

After that, Terence went home and recovered sufficiently to undergo a triple heart bypass operation that September. He experienced the feeling of the wonderful breeze several times between June and September, especially when he received Communion or when Christians laid hands on him and prayed. A prayer chain was set up at church in the form of a telephone link, keeping members fully informed so they could pray regularly for Terence. He made an excellent recovery from the operation, but suffered another setback in late March 1994. The diabetes went out of control and he had fluid retention, and was in hospital for three weeks. Richard, the vicar, and several church members went together to the hospital. They laid hands on Terence and prayed for his healing.

Terence recalls: 'Suddenly I felt a great heat on me, and the breeze came again. Then I experienced the most peaceful sensation I have ever felt and now understand with my heart the terrific words, "the peace that passes understanding".' Those gathered around saw Terence immediately go to sleep, and he slept for five hours. Previously he had only taken catnaps. When he awoke he was able to pass urine, which he had been unable to do for days. He was now able to stand, walk and bend his legs, which had previously been impossible. The doctors were amazed at the sudden improvement, one saying, 'Prayer is the most powerful medicine.' Terence and Jane have been greatly supported by their fellow Christians and are grateful to the Lord for His strength and peace.

Another man who made a miraculous recovery from a heart condition is Leslie Rice of Hampshire. On 21 April 1991, Leslie and his wife Rhoda set out earlier than usual for the Anglican church they attend in Hythe. There was to be a confirmation service, with refreshments afterwards, so they helped to set out the tables in the church hall. When they took their seats in church for the service, that was the last thing Leslie remembered. He collapsed with a very severe heart attack and slumped in the pew. Fortunately a nurse and doctor were in church, who rushed to Leslie's aid, and the rest of the congregation prayed and provided sympathetic care for Rhoda.

An ambulance took Leslie to a Southampton hospital twelve miles away where he received the necessary medical assistance. Before the delayed confirmation service got under way, Bishop John Perry led the congregation in earnest prayer for Leslie's recovery. At the hospital, Rhoda was warned that he was unlikely to survive the night. After being at his bedside all day, she and her son were sent home in the evening to await the outcome. During the night, one nurse was individually caring for him. In the early hours of the morning, he made such a sudden and decisive turn for the better that she rushed down the ward saying excitedly, 'My patient has awakened!' At this point the combination of medical care and God answering the prayers of His people came together. Leslie made a definite recovery from that moment, instead of dying as expected. The doctors said Leslie was their miracle of the year.

A fourteen-year-old girl, Rachel Maylor, lives with her family in Greenford, outer London. Rachel had been almost completely deaf in her left ear for a year, since an infection had left the inner ear irreversibly damaged. She had been referred from one hospital to another, each of which specialized in hearing problems, and then on to St Mary's Hospital, Paddington. The diagnosis was confirmed and it was explained to Rachel that no hearing-aid would help as the damage was at the back of the ear, and that she would be deaf in that ear for the rest of her life.

As a Christian family, the Maylors started to attend Holy Trinity Brompton, in London, after hearing that God was blessing His people there in a special way. When Rachel went forward at a church service to be prayed for, she asked God to show her the reason why the deafness had happened. A lady called Victoria on the ministry team prayed for her, and she felt peaceful and happy. Then Rachel started to experience a great deal of pain in her left ear, which had not happened before. She was screaming with pain and shaking all over. Victoria continued to pray for the love of God to be with her. Then her father, Stephen, bent over her, put his finger in her good ear and whispered in her deaf ear, 'Can you hear me?' Rachel exclaimed, 'Yes, I can hear you.'

Rachel was so thrilled, she leapt up and started jumping around. 'I could hear him with my left ear. It was such a wonderful feeling, I just can't explain it. My relationship with God has got so much stronger. The next Sunday I went forward in church because I was so thankful for what God had done for me.' When Stephen took Rachel to the hospital to confirm the healing, the tests showed normal hearing in both ears. Stephen told the lady who carried out the test that they believed God had healed her. The lady replied, 'Well, praise God, I'm a Christian too.' The Hindu specialist was rather more surprised: 'I didn't know God was an ear, nose and throat surgeon!'

Another teenager urgently in need of God's help at his local church was fifteen-year-old Bob Gillies. He was to serve at the altar for Christmas midnight Mass. The parish priest had given him the church key, so he could arrive early and prepare in good time. It was a cold, still night. Alone in the church, Bob heard the door open and saw his own father walk in, very much the worse for drink. Bob went down to the church to speak to him. He was very talkative, unsteady on his feet, and the air around him smelt of alcohol.

Bob recalls, 'People were going to be arriving soon, and my embarrassment could not be measured. As I went back to the sacristy (a place in the church where the vessels for Holy Communion are kept), my father was talking aloud to an empty church. I stood and prayed to God for help. The church suddenly went very quiet; my father had stopped talking. I carried on setting up at the altar, noticing as I did so that my father had sat down. When I went back down the church to find the readings at the lectern, I went to speak to him again. He was rational, calm and lucid. He showed no sign of being affected by drink and – what is most significant – the air no longer smelt of alcohol!'

In the many cases of accident or serious illness that have been reported to us, healing is far quicker and more remarkable than could medically have been expected. The following are two examples of how God has answered the prayers of many Christians in local churches and further afield.

The first began on Ash Wednesday 1981, when Liesl James was walking home from school. She was waiting at a crossing-point on a grassy central reservation when a speeding car mounted the spot where she stood. Liesl was hit and three cars were written off by a speeding motorist who was trying out a new car. Thirty minutes later Liesl's life was hanging in the balance in Leicester Royal Infirmary's accident and emergency resuscitation room. Her father, Hugh, was a consultant anaesthetist in the same hospital and her mother, Vivien, a qualified nurse. They phoned their vicar with the news.

Their local church, Holy Trinity Leicester, was due to meet for prayer, and there the news was broken to the congregation. The decision was taken to pray for Liesl every night. Through the contacts of family and friends, news of the accident spread with incredible rapidity. A huge unofficial prayer chain began. Over the next few months, Hugh and Vivien were to meet people they had not known before, who would say: 'Our church was praying for your daughter.'

Liesl's injuries were serious: both legs were broken, one above and below the knee, she had a fractured pelvis, a chipped neck vertebra and a cut right across her forehead; but by far the most serious was the brushing of the brain. If that healed quickly, there was hope. If it increased, the pressure of the bruising would cut off the blood supply to the brain and she would be 'brain-dead'. Liesl was being ventilated artificially on a life support machine and was heavily sedated. On the third day, the intensive care consultant told her father that the retinae of her eyes were showing that her brain was becoming more swollen. Hope drained from Hugh. He and Vivien went to the vicarage in tears, where the vicar and his wife prayed with them and comforted them.

That night at a special prayer meeting for Liesl, someone had the conviction that Jesus would heal her, as He had healed Jairus's daughter, who had died before Jesus reached her (Mark 5:22–24, 38–42). Until then, prayers for Liesl had been very much of the 'May Your will be done' type. Now there was an assurance that God would heal her. News of the prayer meeting was relayed to Hugh and Vivien, who had been at Liesl's bedside.

Later the doctors took the decision to stop the sedatives, to see what the response would be. The next day several relatives and the church's curate, who were at Liesl's bedside, were asked to wait outside while the nurses attended to her. Someone said: 'We're all Christians here; let's pray.' An uncle prayed for a specific sign that God would heal Liesl. When they returned to the intensive care unit, the nurse greeted them with, 'When we turned her over, she coughed!' Brain-dead people cannot cough. Prayer had been answered. Within three days Liesl was conscious. Although she had to spend three months in hospital for all the fractures to heal, from that cough onwards she got progressively better. Today Liesl is very fit and active. She is a nursery nurse, working with primary school children.

A more recent example of God performing a miracle in answer to the prayers of a local church is that of a family who belong to a church in Normanton, West Yorkshire. On Saturday 3 September 1994, David and Barbara Teece returned to their car after shopping with their sons, Daniel and Simon. Suddenly, Simon was struck to the ground by a three-foot length of scaffolding which had been thrown from the top floor of the multi-storey car park. He was rushed to hospital with a severe depressed compound fracture of the skull. The only positive aspect of the injury was that the fracture was at the thickest part of the skull, and that had prevented instant death. However Simon was not expected to survive the night, or, if he did, he would certainly be severely brain-damaged. David recalls: 'Where was God now? We had only been Christians for a year, and our lives were brimming over with the newness of our conversion. We asked, "Lord, why us?" and wondered where to turn.'

Simon's CT scan revealed that his brain was badly swollen. The consultant confirmed everyone's worst fears. David phoned a Christian friend, asking her to pray for them, but she did much more. She phoned the vicar, Jeff, and curate, Tim, then spent the rest of the evening phoning dozens of others, mobilizing the prayer-force of the church family. Groups of people gathered together where they could and some individuals prayed for hours.

David remembers: 'Jeff and Tim were with us at the hospital in a flash. We faced a critical seventy-two-hour period in which the brain would continue to swell and maximum secondary damage was likely to occur. Simon was on full "life support", heavily sedated. Both Jeff and Tim wonderfully gave us the support we needed at that moment. They prayed over Simon, anointing him with oil. The next day he was still in a critical condition, facing death, but he was alive. Jeff and Tim returned, with news of a seventy-two-hour prayer vigil. The church family had organized themselves into groups, following an hourly rota to pray around the clock, covering the critical period with prayer. Some contacted family and friends around the country, so that Christians in dozens of churches were praying for Simon. This lifted our spirits and renewed our faith in God. We prayed so much ourselves that, at one point, we couldn't pray any more, but were carried on the wave of prayer and love by others sharing this difficulty with us.'

Simon's condition stabilized during the seventy-two hours but was still critical. His face was swollen like a football. He was heavily sedated, and had been given a drug to paralyse him, restricting his movements. Some of those praying received assurances that God would heal Simon. One had a picture of one of God's angels standing at Simon's head, waiting patiently for God to tell him what to do next. After ten days the doctors felt Simon was sufficiently stable to start reducing the drugs he was being given. David and Barbara were warned that he might be violent and disturbed as the drugs were withdrawn, as if he were experiencing 'cold turkey'. This turned out to be an understate-ment. David was very upset to see Simon so disturbed, and prayed that the decision would be taken to sedate him again. His prayer was answered. Observations and tests revealed that Simon was making a good recovery. The consultant, with a very wide smile, told Simon's parents: 'I don't know how, but Simon has made an incredible recovery. We gave him the same standard of treatment that we would have given to anyone on intensive care but, in spite of the odds being very much against him, he has made an almost complete recovery.'

The decision had been taken to reduce the sedation the following Monday, but two days before, exactly two weeks after the accident, God decided that it was time for Simon to wake up. David and Barbara returned from visiting their elder son, Daniel, to be greeted by a smiling nurse saying, 'I've got a surprise for you.' Simon was propped up slightly on a pillow, watching television! Within days of waking, he was fit enough to go home, but the medical staff were so amazed at the speed of his recovery that they kept him in hospital for a few more days. He had gone from near-death to full recovery in four weeks. The neurosurgeon said there was a slight chance of epilepsy developing from brain scarring, but as yet that hasn't happened. His external scars were soon covered by a full head of hair. His parents say, 'Simon is completely back to normal; but we will never be the same again. We believe that God used Simon to show us the way forward in prayer. As a result our church, and other Christians locally, have drawn closer. We feel that we have a direction in which to go, and a purpose to follow.'

Linda Cooper's back pain was diagnosed by the doctor as curvature of the spine, for which she was told there was no medical treatment. Not long after that, the minister at Buckhurst Hill Baptist church, which she attends, was preaching about healing. Anyone seeking healing was encouraged to go through to one of the rooms at the back of the church to be prayed for. Linda felt challenged to offer her back problem to the Lord. Two or three people laid hands on her and prayed for God to heal her. As she was walking home, she suddenly felt the pain pass right out of her body. Linda found she had much greater freedom of movement, and was able to join a keep-fit class, which she could not have considered previously. In the years since, the pain has not returned.

In October 1992, Alison Reid was part of a church home group near Wimborne, that was studying the healing miracles of Jesus. At the end of the study there was an opportunity to pray for anyone in need. Alison said that about ten years previously, her mother had noticed that Alison's left leg was markedly shorter than her right. She was sixteen and applying for nursing at the time, so her GP was concerned about the strain the difference in the length of her legs would put on her spine. He was unable to suggest any treatment, so Alison saw a chiropractor, who took X-rays and measured the leg difference. She said that the femur bone in that leg was shorter than the other. The only remedy was for Alison to wear a false heel in her shoe. Alison was embarrassed at having a 'wonky body', but, more importantly, once she had got used to the false heel, she found that she developed backache and very painful toes if she forgot to wear it.

At the home group, everyone gathered round to pray for Alison's leg. She sat upright on the floor, with her shoes off and her legs stretched out in front. Cath, who is a radiologist, made sure her hips were equally placed and then measured the leg difference with a ruler. It was nearly one and a half centimetres. Then they placed their hands on her and Hope prayed, 'Lord, please make Ali's legs equal in length, either by lengthening one or shortening the other.' In her head Alison added the prayer: 'Oh Lord, please make it longer.' She had always wanted to be taller, rather than shorter. Her eyes were closed, and she felt a sensation of numbness in her upper left thigh. Everyone else had their eyes open and Cath, who had never witnessed an answered prayer before, was so excited: 'It's grown! I saw it grow!' The legs were measured again and everyone could see it had grown. Alison stopped wearing the false heel immediately, but keeps it as a reminder of God's healing. She hasn't had any problem with her back or leg since then.

Jesus said, 'For where two or three come together in my name, there am I with them' (Matthew 18:20), and 'I will do whatever you ask in my name, so that the Son may bring glory to the Father' (John 14:13).

CHAPTER TWELVE

Miracles in Business

The people worked with all their heart.

Nehemiah 4:6

HROUGHOUT THE Bible, in particular in their giving of the Ten Commandments with their emphasis on honour and honesty, God instructs us to deal fairly in the matter of buying and selling goods, and in the way we live out our lives in the world of business.

Trevor Harvey, a second-hand car salesman in Norwich, used to give no thought to God, but his life was transformed when he began to think about becoming a Christian. At the time, he had been trying to sell a property overseas, but despite having agents in Spain and England, neither had found a purchaser in four years. Trevor decided to commit the matter to God. Within five weeks, the money was in his bank, the property having been sold! Trevor says, 'I have learned since never to take the credit in business for such things, rather, to look up and thank God.'

One evening Trevor thought he would like to try church, but the suggestion caused a serious row with his wife, resulting in him noisily leaving the house. Feeling crushed and desperate, he threw himself into a ditch and cried out, 'God take my life.' Trevor recalls, 'He took it all right, but not in the way I had intended. I was finished, but God had just begun. That night the old Trevor Harvey died and a new one was born, and I was filled with the Holy Spirit. I changed dramatically straight away. Then there came an amazing transformation in my business. In the second-hand car sales business it is difficult to deal with people in a Christian way, but now God directs my affairs. Week after week He provides in a wonderful way. Sometimes we think we can't possibly be viable as a business this week; we are simply not going to sell enough cars. But on Friday night, when we complete our figures, the Lord has provided sufficient for our business to pay its way.'

Alan Storkey in his book *A Christian Social Perspective* develops the theme that 'Economic blessing, judgement, freedom and care, the meaning of work and rest are all shaped by, and shape, mankind's relationship with God.' Everything we do throws light on this central relationship between God and man, because every aspect of economic life matters to God. Psalm 65 tells us: 'O God . . . who formed the mountains by your power . . . You care for the land and water it; you enrich it abundantly . . . and bless its crops . . . The grasslands of the desert overflow.' God has provided enough food for all the nations of the world, but our greed and unjust economic practices have resulted in starvation for millions of people.

The economics of everyday life are constantly abused in the selfishness and rapidity of modern living. In His teaching on economic life, Jesus' parable of the rich fool illustrates the eternal truth that ambition for wealth will not solve man's basic problems. In the parable, the rich man's barns get fuller and he simply builds bigger ones to accommodate the increasing wealth, without considering the purpose of his life or his own spiritual position (Luke 12:15-21). Jesus stresses that the accumulation of material wealth is not the ultimate goal of our life on this earth.

Peter Vellacott is a sheep farmer in Sussex, and had gradually, over the years, come to realize that all we have belongs to God, and we are merely sharing in His wealth. Reading about the suffering of Christians in communist countries convinced him that if they could remain faithful while suffering so much for their Christian faith, they deserved support, which he was able to provide. Once, after the sale of some land, Peter planned to give a substantial sum of money to a Christian missionary organization. He writes: 'I well remember working out on the farm and feeling that I should send this money off right then. Inside I felt, "Can't you see I am busy, and there is a lot to do today?" but the inner voice was insistent, saying, "Now!" I went indoors and wrote out the necessary documents and sent them off. About a fortnight later I met the secretary of the organization and he thanked me, saying that they had a project needing funds, but could not get it off the ground unless they had the money in hand. The timing had been absolutely perfect; I found this such an encouragement.'

Paul wrote to Timothy in I Timothy 6:7–9: 'For we brought nothing into the world, and we can taking nothing out of it. But if we have food and clothing, we will be content with that. People who want to get rich fall into temptation and a trap and into many foolish and harmful desires that plunge men into ruin and destruction. For the love of money is a root of all kinds of evil. Some people, eager for money, have wandered from the faith and pierced themselves with many griefs.'

The purpose of business is gain, but Jesus said you cannot serve God and money. The excuse that you cannot afford to be honest only demonstrates a lack of faith. Peter Vellacott found this a challenge several years ago when he bought some sheep from an estate. Together with the farm manager, they agreed a price in the field. Peter recalls, 'The next day I called to collect the sheep from the yard and realized they were worth a lot more than I had paid, and that I had got a great bargain. After I had collected the sheep, my conscience began to trouble me. This would not do; but what had I done that was wrong? The vendors could much better afford to lose out than I could.' In his heart Peter knew that by doing nothing, he would be serving money, not God. Peter continues: 'I wrote to the farm manager to ask if he would like me to pay an extra £2 a head, in other words £700 to make up the difference. He replied saying he appreciated the offer as he, too, felt he had made a wrong decision about their value. We realized that the sheep had not looked their best out in the open field, and that we had both gained a false impression. On the face of it, I had given away some hard-earned money. I had even risked looking foolish, but I knew I had been honest. In this case the sheep were later resold, leaving a good profit margin in a very short time, and the farm income that year was a record by a long way!' Miracles do happen in business, for honesty is the best policy.

Someone else who made honesty a priority in his business was Harry Knight, who for several years in the 1950s was an encyclopaedia salesman in north London and Essex. He loved the job, as it involved getting out and meeting lots of people. He also believed in the product he was selling, because the encyclopaedias were well written, and they were reminders that God created our beautiful universe. When talking to a potential customer one evening, he made a sale, took a deposit and left the encyclopaedias with the gentleman.

However that night Harry's conscience reminded him that he had implied to the customer that he had had a set of encyclopaedias at home when he was a boy. In fact he did not have his own set, but used to borrow them one by one from a friend. It seemed a small thing, but it loomed so large that Harry felt he had to go back the next day and put it right. The customer welcomed him and Harry apologized that he had not told the complete truth the day before. The customer said, 'Never mind; I'm delighted with these encyclopaedias, and four of my friends would like to order sets from you.' Harry was overjoyed that his honesty had been rewarded with five orders instead of one! 'That was the only time I sold more than one set at a time,' he said.

Gordon Hickson, who now lives in Watford, used to be the

head of a company working on construction projects, and found himself in a difficult position. He was away on an assignment, seeing business clients in Seoul, Korea, when he received a phone call from his wife to say that his company was being taken to the High Court and sued for everything they owned. The reason was that he had been working for another company, but had recently set up in business on his own, running a Christian company in the same line of business. The company he had worked for were afraid Gordon would take their clients with him, although he was in fact gaining new clients, not taking advantage of any former contacts. His previous company were taking Gordon to court to prevent him from doing business in the new company, under the name he had chosen for it.

Gordon remembers, 'We had the choice of either fighting the case or just giving in to the other company. That morning I prayed a simple prayer, saying: "God, I don't know how you are going to tell me this, but I need to know whether or not I stand firm and fight this case or whether I should just ring up and concede." I went out into the teeming millions of Seoul. I got out of a taxi and walked across a bridge, when I became aware of two nuns ahead of me. Suddenly they turned round and, out of the blue, said they had a word from the Lord for me that day. One reached into a bag and took out some bookmarks bearing words by Mother Basilea Schlink, who is one of the leaders of a worldwide order of Protestant nuns, based in Germany. Holding out several bookmarks towards me, she said, "Pick one of these, it will be the Word of God for you." Taking the middle one, I looked in astonishment at the words: "Stand firm, and persevere, for I know the trials that you are going through and I have already determined the time when I will come and rescue you." '
This miracle of exactly the right word of Scripture for the situation showed Gordon that God knew all about his business and would honour his honesty. He did, in fact, go on to win the case, although God used the situation to remind Gordon of the

sin of pride, and to build up his faith in Him to do miracles in the area of his finances.

One of these miracles concerned a Christian school, which Gordon wanted to help finance by starting a new Christian company. One day, he was having lunch with a business client from Kuwait, who noticed that Gordon was wearing a Christian badge in his lapel, and asked him about his faith. Gordon was happy to talk about his commitment to Jesus and the man from Kuwait declared that he too was a Christian. During the course of the conversation, Gordon mentioned that his church was involved in setting up a Christian school, at which the man was most interested, and he asked Gordon many questions about the school. Apparently the Lord had told him to begin looking for opportunities to sow his own money into Christian education in England. As a result of this brief meeting, he sent a cheque for £20,000 to finance Gordon's company. Gordon had never been blessed with a cheque like that before, and praised God for this provision for his company and for the school.

Leslie and George were both skilled engineers who had worked for the same company in Dorset for many years. In addition to working for the company, they also owned some of their own engineering equipment which they used in their workshops at home. Sometimes the company had an urgent deadline to meet, so Leslie and George were asked to take work home to complete in their own workshops. If specialized equipment was needed for this, they were encouraged to borrow it from the company for the purpose. The arrangement worked very well, and their good work helped the company to achieve the Queen's Award for Industry.

However the company was taken over by a larger company and a manufacturing manager was put over them who, although very well qualified, had much less practical experience of precision engineering than they had. One of their areas of expertise was honing – finely grinding a piece of metal to a precision of within a thousandth of an inch. On one occasion the new manager decided the company should buy a semi-automatic machine for honing costing £30,000, but Leslie and George advised him it would not be suitable. Ignoring the advice, he had it installed, but it indeed proved to be unsuitable and had to be scrapped. Leslie and George knew it was not suitable for the required task, as they had a similar machine back home. A friend of theirs wanted to buy two grinding-machines at an auction, and the honing-machine was included in the lot. Hearing George and Leslie could use it, he sold it to them for £64! Rather than admitting he was wrong, this seemed to stir up hatred in the manufacturing manager against Leslie and George, as he took the view that they had only advised against the expensive machine because they preferred to do the extra work at home.

One Friday there was an urgent deadline to meet, so he asked Leslie and George to take the work home, which they agreed to do. However when Leslie returned with the completed work on Monday, the management had the police there to meet him, accusing him of stealing company equipment. George was also arrested, and both had their car boots and home workshops emptied of engineering equipment, much of which was their own. They were adamant that the company's equipment was required for the work they had undertaken on behalf of their employers, but the present management were not party to the informal arrangement to do work at home. Their solicitor, Andrew, was convinced of their innocence, but persuading the Crown Court was another matter.

On the morning of the trial, Andrew, Leslie and George, who are all Christians, individually prayed that they would be vindicated. Amazingly, the prosecution withdrew the charges, and the judge pronounced their acquittal. They then applied to an industrial tribunal and received damages for unfair dismissal, and all their equipment which had been seized by the police was returned to them. Most amazing was that all the managers of the company, except one who had told the truth, were dismissed for various reasons, and George and Leslie were reinstated in their jobs. All three, George, Leslie and Andrew, have told us that they were convinced God intervened on the day of the trial, since so many lies had been told against them that it seemed impossible for the judge and jury to be able to see the truth. The withdrawal by the prosecution, which had been so unlikely, brought about the miracle in response to prayer.

Another legal miracle involved William, a solicitor himself, who had prepared an affidavit for a divorce client. The client did not want his wife to know his real address. He had moved around a great deal, and William also found it difficult to keep up with him. William prepared the affidavit on the basis of the address the client had given him, but it turned out to be a false one. When the wife discovered this, she reported it to the police as perjury. During the interview, the client had made a comment which implied that William knew the address was false, so he was charged with aiding and abetting an act of perjury. As a solicitor, this was very serious, and would have meant the end of his career.

A cloud hung over him for eighteen months until the case was brought to trial. Several people who knew William's character and Christian faith were praying for a just outcome. About halfway through the morning's hearing, the judge said to the prosecution, 'You are going to find it very difficult to prove this case, aren't you?' After a short adjournment, the prosecution decided not to proceed with the case, and William was acquitted and awarded costs. Everyone involved in praying for William was convinced that God had intervened.

When someone does well in business, he or she can use their wealth to God's glory by giving to Christian work. Bob Edmiston, one of the richest men in the Midlands, gives away millions of pounds each year. He has never asked God to give him money, but he is a committed Christian who has always sought God's guidance in all business decisions. As a result, his business has flourished and he has been greatly blessed.

Bob spent much of his childhood in East Africa, where he went to a school run by monks and, although he hated church, was made to go by his devout Catholic mother. He says, 'As I grew up, my impression was that God was a guy up there with a white beard and fiery eyes, just waiting to hit me every time I did something wrong. Well, He had plenty of opportunity, because I was always doing something mischievous.' Back in England, when he was seventeen, someone dropped a card through the letterbox, inviting the Edmistons to a Christian meeting. His father decided to go, and he asked Bob to go with him. Bob went along, and later joined the youth group at the same church. One evening at the youth group, it suddenly dawned on Bob that Jesus Christ had died for him personally, and he committed his life to Him. Bob says: 'God changed my life. When I was at school I used to swear a lot, and that just stopped. My outlook changed; Jesus became a very important part of my life. On one occasion at a church meeting there was an appeal made for funds. God spoke to me, and I gave everything in my pocket. As a result, I had to walk the seven miles home. I do believe God honours those things – the Bible says He is no man's debtor.'

Bob studied to be an accountant and became a financial analyst. He was working for Jensen Motors when it hit disastrous times and was forced to go into liquidation. It was a tough period, as by this time Bob was married and had three young children. He used his £6,000 pay-off to buy Jensen Parts and Service Goods, to supply Jensen cars still on the road. Since then Bob has gained the franchise in Britain for Subaru and Hyundai cars, and is now the chairman and chief executive of IM Group Ltd. Bob says, 'Without doubt, God has been intimately involved in my business. I once heard something said at church which really struck a chord in my heart: "It's not your money; it's God's money." In business, there are many difficult decisions to be made; I endeavour to make each of these prayerfully. At times I have to make people redundant, but when I do, I try to assist them in every way possible; in many cases we have found them new jobs. One day while in prayer I had a vision. I was standing before God and He asked, "Bob, what did you do with your life?" "Well, God, I made plenty of money." So He said, "OK, what else did you do?" I was very challenged. The Bible says that much is required of those to whom much is given.'

By setting up a trust fund, Christian Vision, into which ten per cent of the company's pre-tax profits go, Bob has been able to finance Christian projects; for example, he supports a hundred church pastors in Poland, forty workers in India, and Christian radio broadcasting. He is also generous with his personal funds, believing that wealth is simply a 'tool'; but God is interested in what we do with our resources. Bob explains, 'Some people think Christians should not be rich, but the Bible says that the Lord delights in the prosperity of His servants. Abraham, Jacob, Joseph, Job: they were all rich men, but they all put God first. That is the key. When people pray for God to supply a need, the money is not going to fall out of heaven. What they are actually praying for, whether they realize it or not, is that God would bless Christians and that they would then give. Money is not the root of all evil, but the love of money is. Jesus Christ is very much involved with both my life and my business. It is as if He were my senior partner.'

A young man in Canada, Robert Brown, described himself as 'materialistic with no reliance on God'. Late in 1980 he attended a charismatic church for several weeks before responding to an altar call to receive Christ into his life. He remembers: 'In my silent prayer at the altar of the church, I surrendered my life to God for His guidance, and offered Him a partnership in the real estate company I was just setting up.' Robert promised to give ten per cent of all he earns, in return for God's guidance in his business life.

In January 1981, shortly after setting up the company, Robert's income was $550, of which he tithed $55. Only one month after that he secured a major property deal, which realized a commission of $55,000, which was a thousand times the figure he had tithed. For Robert, this was a great lesson in how much God loved him and wanted to bless him, which he has not forgotten.

God also rewards us when we make right use of our time, by increasing the amount of time we have available if we put Him first. It is easy to be tempted to think that the more days we work, the more successful we will be, but we are instructed in the Bible to rest on the sabbath, which for Christians is Sunday. This is for our benefit, to recharge our physical, emotional and spiritual batteries, and also to make Sunday a special day for God. Only necessary work should be carried out. Peter Vellacott, the sheep farmer mentioned earlier, says: 'I reserve Sunday for rest and worship, only doing essential tasks, and I have always found that my farm operations have been completed as soon or sooner than those of other farmers who do ordinary work seven days a week.'

In times of financial pressure, God can bless in other ways too. Peter remembers: 'A few years ago we had several years when profits were low, but during that time I had peace of mind, and not the stress that should have accompanied those lean years. This bears out the promise in God's Word: "He will keep him in perfect peace whose mind is stayed on Him." Whilst there was good reason to complain, I was able to have peace and to keep praising God.'

Peter discovered that this is also true of our use of time generally. He learnt a lesson when leading a boys' camp one summer. Several local Christian farmers stopped their work in the harvest fields to set up a team to play football with the boys. This impressed Peter, as he would not have volunteered to do that had he been back home; his work would have come first.

However on another occasion, at a busy time of year on the farm, Peter was asked to preach one Sunday morning. On the Saturday, he knew he should give God prime time, so he worked on the sermon all morning and part of the afternoon. When he went to work for the rest of the day, he was amazed how much work he achieved in the short time spent in the fields. He achieved more work than he would have expected to, had he spent all day on the farm!

John Lekkerkerk is a businessman in the Netherlands and runs a small construction company. On one occasion they were building a ceiling in a jeweller's shop. At the time John used to swear continuously. The jeweller invited John out to dinner, during the course of which he asked why John cursed so much. The jeweller then explained that he was a born-again Christian, and that his relationship with God brought him such great joy, that he personally felt no need to swear. John dismissed the whole idea as crazy.

Over the next few years John worked as a product manager for another company, had a heart attack brought on by stress, and then set up his own small company. He joined a yachting club, and when the yachting club chairman's son died in an accident, he attended the funeral. John recalls: 'To my astonishment, the man who led the service was the jeweller who had invited me to dinner years before! The service was wonderful – it was unbelievable – as if the sermon was addressed to me personally. There at the funeral service I committed my life to Jesus Christ. My wife joined me in starting to go to the same church as the jeweller and she, too, committed her life to Jesus. My life changed straight away. I learned to pray for every area of our lives, including my business, and every morning prayed with my employees, asking God to bless them. My neighbour asked me why she didn't hear me cursing any more; I hadn't realized, but it was completely gone!'

When John bought a piece of land to build a warehouse, he

planned, at the extra cost of 150,000 Dutch guilders, to include a building for their church. Things started to go wrong with the project, and he prayed that God would intervene. A lady at church reminded him that God will return to us sevenfold anything we give to Him. The very next week, a big company offered John a contract to build a furnace. This would produce a net profit of 150,000 Dutch guilders, and a week later they increased the order to seven furnaces. John concludes: 'God had indeed returned to me sevenfold! We are so thankful for the many miracles God has done for us.' John joined the Rotterdam chapter of the Full Gospel Businessmen's Fellowship International, and after a few years set up a new chapter in his area, south of Rotterdam. He prayed, 'God, if you want this, please provide ten members for this new chapter.' Within the first few meetings, ten members had joined, and the first two people to commit their lives to Jesus were John's sister and her husband.

Gordon Bambridge and his wife, Jacqueline, became Christians at a baptism service for their second daughter at their local Anglican church in Norwich. They had only agreed to the baptism to maintain good family relationships, as they had no belief in God up to that time. However during the baptism service, Gordon and Jacqueline realized that it was possible to have a relationship with God through His Son, Jesus. They became Christians and joined the church. Seven years later, Gordon got up early one morning to attend a Communion service and, reading his Bible beforehand, he asked God to make the scriptures more meaningful to him. The power of God came on him, and he was baptized in the Holy Spirit. From that time on, the Bible became full of meaning for Gordon, and, as a family, they started to experience miracles. Jacqueline was healed of agoraphobia and their daughter was healed of migraine headaches, which she used to get frequently.

When Gordon felt the time was right to begin his own wholesale business, they saw God do many miracles during the six months of setting it up. Gordon remembers: 'In August 1984, God told me that the figure I should pay to rent storage space was fifteen pounds per week. This was a ridiculously low amount, and every person who looked at the project criticized it. We stuck by it, believing it was from God, but finally out of desperation we agreed to a location at twenty-five pounds per week.' This was still a low figure, but the landlord seemed in no hurry to collect the rent; he kept insisting 'Pay me later.' Gordon recalls: 'Three months later, when I arranged to pay him some money, he said, "Just make it fifteen pounds per week." It was exactly the figure God had given us!'

God has held first place in Gordon's business, so it has prospered. If a product they stocked was not selling, they would pray about it, and within minutes a customer would come in to order that very product. God loves to answer our prayers when we put Him first. Gordon explains: 'At one point it became obvious that we needed some new shelving, which would cost about £3,000, but we only had £300 available. Just as we were considering the problem, a salesman arrived, trying to sell us things we did not want. As he was leaving, he showed me some photos of shelving, asking if I was interested in buying it. I offered him the £300, which he accepted!'

Some time before Gordon started his wholesale business he injured his back, and both his doctor and physiotherapist had told him he would never be able to do heavy work again. When Gordon attended a dinner held by the Full Gospel Businessmen's Fellowship International, he felt God tell him during a time of worship to put his hands above his head. Gordon asserts, 'When I did that, He healed my back. Now I am able to lift heavy loads, even up to 200-pound bales! I could tell you dozens of stories like this, about miracles which have happened in my life. God truly answers prayer!'

After some years of running the business, Gordon and his family considered selling the business so that Gordon could work as a self-employed agent. Around this time he received an offer from a larger business to take over his own. He accepted their offer, but in the end did not in fact get paid. The eventual outcome was that he was made personally bankrupt, losing almost everything, including his home and private pensions. Gordon says, 'This could well be considered a disaster, and I can understand how those without the Lord fall into despair, but God was still in control. In 1981 I had made a covenant with God when we gave all our finances into His control. When you have resources, that's an easy thing to do; when you are poor, it's not so simple. But God really does multiply our money to meet our needs and sometimes also our desires. We have lived for one year as a family with an uncertain income and no fall-back, but we lack nothing. God's people have blessed us in small ways, which has been an encouragement, but God himself has touched our very wallets and purses to see that we are not left short. If God's promises are true in the good years, it follows that they must hold fast in the bad. In over twenty years as a Christian, I have never known God to fail me, although sometimes our humanity gets in the way, and we have to learn to trust Him.'

Ambition can help us in our business lives, or it can lead us to hold the wrong priorities. Michael Fenton-Jones, who lives in Shepperton, held a high position in a leading property invest-ment and development company, having qualified as a chartered surveyor. He recalls: 'I needed to succeed – I had a deep ambition to be somebody.' A friend invited Michael to a lunch-time service at St Helen's Church in the city of London. He was amazed to see 500 people, mostly businessmen, in church on a Tuesday! He felt the message was directly relevant to him and afterwards, talking to the speaker, David MacInnes, he commented: 'I suppose you have no ambition.' David replied, 'My ambition is to grow daily more like Jesus Christ', which floored Michael. At that moment he knew that all the world's success could not begin to equal a relationship with Jesus Christ, so he asked Jesus to forgive him for rejecting Him and to come into his life.

That year his company was taken over by the Commercial Union, and he became managing director of a newly formed property subsidiary with worldwide responsibilities. He enjoyed a very successful career for the next fifteen years, but at the age of forty-nine, he felt God telling him to leave his job. Michael remembers: 'Humanly speaking it was a crazy thing to do, but I can now see that this was an essential part of God's preparation – I had to be able to trust God, and not my reputation, income or pension.' Since then Michael has been free to spend time with men in different areas of the business world, taking part in a variety of property projects. One of the largest has been the development of the vast G-Mex Centre in Manchester, an exhibition and event centre which has been created out of the old Central station. Michael comments, 'Bringing life back to this derelict part of Manchester has been, for me, a tangible illustration of what Jesus came to do – to bring new life.'

In 1987 a young man, Mike Flynn, set up a company called Christopher James, trading in furnishings and interior design. They dealt predominantly with the new house-building market. Money was very tight, as the company was founded only on a £300 loan from Mike's mother. Business commenced in two tiny offices on an industrial estate in Stoke-on-Trent, with a staff of Mike himself and a YTS junior. Within a few months of setting up the company, Mike became a Christian and started going to the local Pentecostal church. The pastor's wife, Annie, offered to do any typing that was needed, and eventually she became a paid member of staff.

Each day in Mike's office they would pray about the aims of the business and about specific contracts. The whole business revolved around the company's commitment to God, and by the end of the first year the initial £300 had returned a profit of

£79,000 with no debts outstanding. The company grew, taking on more staff, many of them becoming Christians and learning how to trust God as Mike had. Sometimes they did not obtain a particular contract they had been seeking with another company, which they had expected would be theirs. However whenever that happened, within a few months they would hear that the company had gone out of business, so they had been saved from risking their own company too.

During 1989 Mike's company sought a contract with Whelmar Homes Ltd, which built many new houses throughout the north-west of England. A new estate of houses was being built in Congleton, Cheshire, and after considerable effort on the part of Mike's company, the site agent agreed to recommend his company as suppliers of carpets to the purchasers of the new houses. The potential business to his company from this one site was £250,000. It was therefore crucial that the job was done well, as further recommendations would follow.

When the first order came for the Congleton site, there was great excitement in the office. The estimator measured up, the drawings were made, costings and carpet styles were approved by the customer and the carpet was ordered. The widest room was measured as 13' 4" and the carpet could be cut down for the narrower rooms. The manufacturers of the carpet had a loom which produced made-to-measure widths of carpet, so the order was for a carpet 13' 4" wide, 82' long, and dyed to a particular colour to match the customer's lounge suite. The carpet would take nine weeks to make, which fitted in with the completion date for the job in ten weeks.

On the Sunday evening of the week the carpet was to be fitted, Mike had an inner feeling that something was not right with the order. The next morning he asked the warehouse manager to check with the manufacturers and was told that it was ready and would definitely be with them on the Wednesday, for fitting on the Friday. Mike still felt uneasy, so he decided to drive to the site at Congleton. He felt he should check the measurements of the rooms, and he got a shock. The widest room was 13′ 7″, and the carpet ordered was 13′ 4″. Although carpet can be stretched on the length, it cannot on the width. Mike was horrified at this mistake. It was impossible to get another carpet made, the right size and colour, in the four days left before fitting. Returning to the office, Mike shared the problem with Annie, and they prayed about it. They also told the rest of the workers, and phoned some Christian friends, asking them to pray about their dilemma.

The carpet arrived as promised and was taken to Congleton by the fitters, although they had been warned of the problem. At 10.30 a.m. one of the fitters phoned Mike to say that they had unrolled the carpet in the widest room. It fitted perfectly, not an inch under, not an inch over. The carpet was exactly 13′ 7″. The loom had been set to 13′ 4″; the delivery note and invoice both said 13′ 4″; but in response to prayer, the carpet size was correct. There was much rejoicing in the office that day – God had done the impossible.

God honours us when we put Him first, whether in our churches, our home life, or our work situations.

CHAPTER THIRTEEN
Miracles of Creation

In the beginning God created the heavens and the earth

Genesis 1:1

God saw all that He had made and and it was very good

Genesis 1:31

N THE BEGINNING God created the heavens and the earth.' How simple, yet how profound is the opening verse of the Bible. The miracles of creation recorded in Genesis point us to a God who meets both our human and our spiritual needs.

One of the most thrilling miracles many of us experience is the conception and birth of a child. Something amazingly intricate and complex is being formed. Two microscopic particles from a man and a woman meet, and locked into that tiny piece of matter is all the information necessary to make the bones, muscles, nerves and organs that a child will need in order to be born and to thrive. That minute scrap of flesh, too small to see with the naked eye, even contains messages which give the baby the shape of its mother's nose, the delicate ears of its grandmother or hands just like its father's! We know that the 'laws of nature' cannot do all that — what makes it all possible is the creative power of God. A mother carries what God has created. It happens to so many people every day that it is easy to forget who is behind it. As Eve said when her first child was born, 'With the help of the Lord I have brought forth a man' (Genesis 4:1).

Jeremy Bates the tennis player, and his wife Ruth, described the excitement and wonder they felt after their son, Joshua, was born on 27 January 1994. The proud parents talked of their joy and the new sense of purpose which their 'little miracle' had brought to their lives. 'I look at his features, and I feel, well, amazed. I'm still at the wonderment stage!' enthused Ruth. Jeremy beamed, 'It's absolutely incredible, the effect Josh has had on us. Sometimes I'm hardly out of the house, and I want to come straight back and have another look at him.' At five months, Joshua made a big hit at Wimbledon sitting on his father's knee each time Jeremy gave a press conference!

Psalm 139:13–16 shows just how well God knows us. 'For you created my inmost being; you knit me together in my mother's womb. I praise you because I am fearfully and wonderfully made; your works are wonderful, I know that full well.' The birth of a baby may also be an occasion when parents acknowledge for the first time the vital place God occupies in their lives, by His creative and loving power.

Janet Singleton, a friend of ours who lives in Hertfordshire, wrote to us about the birth of her first, much wanted child. 'After two years of fertility treatment, our son was born at home and named Matthew, meaning "gift of God". It was hard to believe that this wonderful event had happened for us. The feelings were overwhelming – excitement, joy, love and immense gratitude. I felt a real need to make a special visit to church to say thank you, and was able to have a short service one evening, for "The churching of women after childbirth". Matthew was delivered by Christian midwives, who realized that many women appeared to be closer to God after childbirth, and would hold meetings for them in their homes. At my first meeting, I discovered that some members of the group had a very special relationship with God which I had not experienced before. Through these meetings and the miracle of Matthew's birth, I too found a personal faith in God.'

In the miracle of the Incarnation, God's own life-giving power acted directly upon the Virgin Mary and she conceived Jesus. There was a special reason for this. On that unique occasion, God was not just creating a man, but the Man who was to be the Son of God, fully human yet fully divine, in the person of Jesus.

The miracle of creation in the Bible reveals not a magician but a personal God, powerful and loving. Psalm 8 tells of how God has given man the highest calling, to care for His creation: 'When I consider your heavens, the work of your fingers, the moon and the stars, which you have set in place, what is man that you are mindful of him . . . ? You made him a little lower than the heavenly beings and crowned him with glory and honour. You made him ruler over the works of your hands; you put everything under his feet . . . O Lord, our Lord, how majestic is your name in all the earth!' (Psalm 8:3–9).

Sadly, we have not acted responsibly, especially in the last hundred years, in our dealings with our natural environment, causing many problems across the face of the earth, in the seas, rivers and in the earth's atmosphere. We have cut down forests, reducing rainfall, and causing drought; we have changed the natural landscape causing erosion and flooding; pollution sweeps across Western countries; great suffering and famine are caused by civil wars and political struggles.

Yet the miracle of creation is that God keeps on renewing and refreshing all that He makes. Consider some of the things we normally take for granted: the dew each night which waters and refreshes plants – without it, there would need to be far more rain; the way a tiny seed planted in the earth inexplicably grows into a fine plant, bearing flowers to beautify, fruit or vegetables to nourish; the immense variety of birds, animals and plants, new species of which are still being discovered and catalogued. The way everything bursts into life in spring, after lying dormant through the cold of winter; the instinct of birds to migrate to warmer climates and return the following year to the same nest.

A Salvation Army captain, Rachel Tickner, was working on the Island of Bute, in Scotland. Buses were infrequent, so to get to the town of Rothesay three miles away, she often walked along the coast road. One spring day in 1989, when she was experiencing some difficulties in her work, all the beauty of snow-capped hills and a great variety of sea birds were enhanced by a beautiful rainbow. Usually it is not possible to reach the end of a rainbow, but on this occasion it stretched from the other side of the Clyde estuary, right across to where Rachel was walking on the pavement. It 'walked' with her all the way into Rothesay. Rachel said, 'In its magnificence, the rainbow was not awesome; it was reassuring and pleasant.' The rainbow is a sign of God's promise; as Rachel quoted from a song she knew, 'Whenever you see a rainbow, remember God is love.' After Noah and his family had been protected throughout the flood, God said: 'Whenever the rainbow appears in the clouds . . . This is the sign of the covenant I have established between Me and all life on the earth' (Genesis 9: 16–17).

C. S. Lewis writes in his book *Miracles*: 'Each miracle writes for us in small letters something that God has already written, in letters almost too large to be noticed, across the whole canvas of nature . . . each carries the signature of the God whom we know through conscience and from nature.'

A lady called Pauline had experienced much hurt and sadness in her life. She felt guilty about some wrong choices she had made which had adversely affected not only herself but several other people. 'One day', she says, 'in sheer desperation, I just told Jesus what a mess my life had been, how selfish and wicked I was, and asked Him to take over my life and sort it out.' She didn't feel very different immediately. Five days later, on 5 May 1988, she was at home, as the school where she teaches full time was closed for the elections. At three o'clock, looking out of the kitchen window, she suddenly noticed that the leaves were *alive* with a beautiful glowing green, and she began praising God with words she remembered from church: 'My soul magnifies the Lord, and my spirit rejoices in God my Saviour.' Pauline said: 'I stopped and pulled myself up – wait a minute, I can't sing *this* – this is the Virgin Mary's song, and she was pure and I'm not. Suddenly I felt rooted to the spot. I couldn't move, and an inner voice echoed through my whole body. It said, "Yes, you can, you are redeemed."'

Pauline continues: 'A feeling of love and warmth rained down and enveloped me until I felt as if I was drowning, gloriously happy. I knew that if I died then, it wouldn't matter – I'd have just stepped out into God's glorious eternity.' Pauline had never had that assurance before, and God used His creation to catch her attention so that He could speak to her.

Someone who had a different kind of vision through a kitchen window, in the spring of 1982, was Val Robinson when she was staying with friends in New Malden, Surrey. Val was alone in the kitchen washing up after supper, when she became aware of a special stillness in the room. This made her look up and out of the window; above the garden, Val saw a vision of Jesus walking past, carrying His cross, a full-size vivid picture. Jesus turned his head towards her, looked straight at her and smiled. When the vision faded, Val was conscious of a presence in the room with her. She was so stunned that she sat down to reflect on it. Val didn't know what the meaning of the vision was, but on her return home, she noticed for the first time that her son, Mark, was not walking properly. By the December of that year Mark had been diagnosed with multiple sclerosis. However it was some time after that, when Val remembered the way Jesus had smiled at her, that she realized the vision had been given to uphold her.

The miracles of God are not isolated from each other or from their source. They focus what God does in vast ways into meaningful, small incidents. Take the occasion when Jesus turned water into wine, at a wedding feast in Cana of Galilee. Jesus and his friends and family were present at a large wedding. The hosts ran out of wine, and were not able to get any more. Jesus' mother mentioned the problem to Jesus, who replied, 'My time has not yet come.' However his mother instructed the servants to do whatever Jesus told them. This was a great act of faith on her part, considering that Jesus had never performed a miracle before. At the wedding feast were six stone water jars which could hold about thirty gallons each. Jesus told the servants to fill them with water. Then he told them to draw some out and offer it to the master of the feast. It was a brave thing for the servants to do, since presenting an important man with water could have got them into a lot of trouble. However, as it was poured, the water turned into wine; not only that, but the best kind of wine. The master of the feast called the bridegroom aside and said, 'Everyone brings out the choice wine first and then the cheaper wine after the guests have had too much to drink; but you have saved the best till now.'

Every year God makes water into wine, but it takes many months. The soil, sunlight and water nourish the vine, grapes are formed and, if tended and cared for in the right way, they can be made into wine. On that one occasion Jesus (God in human flesh) cut the process short and in a moment made choice wine. In Jewish culture, wine has always been a symbol of God's blessing. Jesus generously made one hundred and eighty gallons of wine; it was no mean wedding feast. The full story is found in John 2.

The laws of nature were set in place by God, and He has control over them. Jesus exercised this control on another occasion to turn a little bread into many loaves. Again, God does this every year. The farmer plants a few grains, and each one is multiplied into ears of wheat. When Jesus was surrounded by thousands of people who were so eager to listen to Him that they did not want to leave to go and find food, He decided to take action. His followers found one small boy with some food: five bread rolls and two small fish. Jesus thanked God for the food, blessed it and shared it out. It not only amply satisfied thousands of people (they counted five thousand men – there were women and children there too) but Jesus' disciples gathered up a large basketful of pieces each. God multiplies fish too, in the rivers and seas, which is miraculous in itself, but to multiply them in His hands in a moment was even more so.

One night on the Sea of Galilee, Jesus' disciples were out fishing; Jesus had stayed alone on land to pray . . . 'but the boat was already a considerable distance from land, buffeted by the waves because the wind was against it' (Matthew 14:24). Suddenly Jesus appears, walking on the water. The disciples are terrified, thinking it is a ghost, but Jesus calls out to them, 'Take courage! It is I. Don't be afraid.' Peter says, 'Lord, if it's you, tell me to come to you on the water.' Jesus replies, 'Come.' When Jesus walked on the water, He revealed to us a dimension of His kingdom – a vision of the new order, that Jesus was in control of all that has been made. It took absolute faith in Jesus for Peter to step out of the rocking boat and walk to Him. Peter physically walked on the water too, then realized what he was doing, and looking down at the sea, he began to sink. Only when he was looking at Jesus, not at the waves around him, could he follow Jesus' example, defying natural order. 'Beginning to sink, [Peter] cried out, 'Lord save me!' Immediately Jesus reached out His hand and caught him. 'You of little faith,' He said, 'why did you doubt?' And when they climbed into the boat, the wind died down. Then those who were in the boat worshipped Him saying, 'Truly you are the Son of God' (Matthew 14:30–33).

One day Jesus was in a boat with his followers crossing Galilee, when they were caught in a freak storm. The wind caused waves to sweep over the boat. The men with Jesus were tough, seasoned fishermen, well used to sudden storms. This must have been a particularly ferocious storm, as on this occasion they were all panic-stricken, fearing the worst. Calmly Jesus stood up in the boat and rebuked the storm. It immediately subsided. The men with Jesus were amazed, asking each other: 'What kind of man is this? Even the winds and waves obey Him!' (Matthew 8:27).

A similar demonstration of God's power over nature was witnessed by eighty-year-old Mrs Crombie. A cover protecting her garden furniture at her home in Southampton was in danger of blowing away in a gale. The tent-pegs holding it down had been ripped up by the wind and, at her age, she knew she could not stop it flying over the rooftops unless the gale died down. That Friday morning, as she looked anxiously out of the window, she remembered Jesus' power. She prayed, 'Lord, when you were on earth, you stopped the wind and waves. Do you think you could do it again?' To her amazement, He did. The wind dropped immediately. Mrs Crombie thanked God and went out to replace the tent-pegs. The gale did not return. As if to confirm the miracle three days later a woman she did not know said to her in passing: 'Funny weather we're having.' Mrs Crombie asked her what she meant and she said, 'Look at last Friday – it was blowing a gale, and it suddenly stopped and did not come back.'

Another incident involving the weather occurred at the New Wine Christian camp in Somerset in August 1992, this time witnessed by hundreds. One morning John Wright, one of the speakers, was in a large marquee talking about delivering people from the power of evil. It was pouring with rain outside, and blowing such a gale that the public address system was badly affected. People could hardly hear what John was saying. He asked: 'Why don't we pray that it will stop?' and everyone agreed. John prayed aloud: 'Lord, there is teaching here that you want to be heard. I pray now, in the name of Jesus, that this rain will stop and that this noise will die down. Lord, we ask for your provision.' Immediately the noise stopped as the storm suddenly ceased, not gradually, but instantly. Everyone gasped, laughed and then clapped, thanking God for acting so quickly in response to their prayer. As they looked through the entrance to the marquee, already blue sky and sunshine had replaced the storm of just a moment before. Sue Talbot of Ruislip was one of those who wrote to us about this: 'It is something I shall never forget, and it was much talked about.' Listening to a tape-recording of the event, we heard the gasps of amazement begin just as John said the last word of the prayer.'

There are times when the normal forces of nature can get out of hand; fire for example. The Lee Abbey estate in Devon, the Christian community we have talked about in earlier chapters, was where we met while Geoff was working there. Before his time, on the first day of an Easter house party in 1956, a fire began in the Valley of Rocks, an area of dry bracken. It advanced rapidly towards the estate. Fire brigades from miles around were called in to battle against walls of flame. The warden of Lee Abbey, Leslie Sutton, gathered together a group of people to pray that the fire would not harm the estate or endanger lives. The chaplain, Ken Pillar, and his wife Margaret, who had only been married a few weeks, were living in Top Lodge, which was the house closest to the fire. The fire officer advised them to evacuate the house, but, even as they were passing their possessions out of the windows for them to be loaded on to a trailer, Leslie carried them back in through the front door, insisting that they must have faith! Eventually the fire officer decided it was no longer safe to enter the house, but just at that moment, the wind suddenly changed direction, taking the fire away up the hillside. Ken and Margaret told us it was an incredible sight. A huge semicircle of flame came right up to the edge of the estate, but was averted just before touching any Lee Abbey property.

In Numbers 11:1–3 God sent a fire into the Israelite camp because the people had been complaining against Him about their hardships. 'Then fire from the Lord burned among them and consumed some of the outskirts of the camp. When the people cried out to Moses, he prayed to the Lord and the fire died down. So that place was called Taberah [meaning burning], because fire from the Lord had burned among them.'

On 29 August 1977, whilst living in Rwanda, something equally alarming happened to Hope. It was Geoff's birthday, but he had been away for over two weeks travelling to Mombasa to collect a vehicle that TEAR Fund, a Christian aid organization, had sent us to use in our missionary work in Rwanda. At Gahini, where we lived, a bush fire started on the hillside below our house, at the hottest part of the day, during the long dry season. It was gaining in ferocity as it swept through the bush, but as it was lunch-time there were no workers around. Normally they would have broken off branches and beaten the flames out, but it was too widespread for Hope to deal with by herself. An older lady was staying with us, who, unhelpfully, just stood there taking photographs! Hope quickly asked her to look after little Luke and Naomi while she ran up the road, calling in Kinyarwanda for help. It must have been the only time in our four years in Rwanda that there was nobody around!

Rushing back to the house, Hope grabbed a bucket and made for the water tap, but there was no water, as was often the case. She ran back round the house to discover that the flames were fiercer and higher, and rapidly approaching the house. They had reached a large stand of bamboo trees, ten feet across and about fifteen feet high. This was Geoff's favourite part of the garden, and it seemed sad to think it was going to go up in flames on his birthday! More seriously, the bamboo was as dry as tinder, and would act like a funnel as soon as the fire touched it, sweeping up and across to the roof of the house, much of which was built of wood and bamboo.

Hope felt totally helpless and remembers: 'It was only then that I realized I had been rushing about and foolishly hadn't even prayed. There and then I asked God to stop the fire; and He did, just like that. It was as if He snuffed it out. I was amazed. I walked over to the place where it had been burning furiously just a moment before. The whole fire had been unbelievably quenched right along the very edge of the bamboo stand. There was no gradual dying away. The fire was instantly, completely extinguished. It was a rebuke to my lack of faith in not having prayed sooner, and the bamboo was saved to welcome Geoff on his return the next day.'

The Bible teaches us who is behind all that has been created, rather than giving us details of how the world began; it speaks of the why and the who, rather than the how and the when. To get to grips with God and creation we need faith. 'By faith we understand that the universe was formed at God's command, so that what is seen was not made out of what was visible' (Hebrews 11:3).

This means that the universe was not made out of any pre-existent material, but directly by divine power. 'In the beginning God created . . . the earth was formless and empty . . . And God said, "Let there be light," and there was light' (Genesis 1:1–3). There was nothing in existence before God began to create; our world had a beginning and it will have an end. Meanwhile God sustains all that He has made. Colossians 1:17 tells us: 'He is before all things, and in Him all things hold together.' John Calvin, the sixteenth-century reformer, wrote that creation is 'the theatre of His glory'.

Occasionally God acts outside of the natural order and does something totally unexpected. Cecil Britnell, aged twelve, and his ten-year-old sister, Margaret, were walking home from the village of Postcombe in Oxfordshire, in the year 1919. They both saw the clouds draw apart, above a clump of trees, like curtains opening, and between them was Christ on the cross. The sky was radiant around the vision, which lasted for several minutes. They were awestruck and ran home to tell their grandfather, who was a chapel preacher. Their mother later told them that the vision had been seen by others at the same time, and it was reported in the local newspaper. Margaret, who is described by her daughter-in-law as a very down-to-earth person, described the experience as 'something you remember for the rest of your life'.

A similar vision was seen much more recently in Tansen, Nepal. On 7 September 1992 a cross appeared in the sky, with the figure of a man in front of it. His head was bowed and facing to the right, his arms were outstretched and he had a loincloth around his waist. It was clearly visible for a full hour above a hilltop, before it faded from view, and was seen by many people, most of whom were not Christians. The Hindu community of the area was greatly affected. A man called Birkha, who on becoming a Christian had been deprived of his inheritance by his Hindu parents, was able to explain to them what they had seen so clearly for themselves. On watching it they had said to each other, 'That's Birkha's God up in the sky.' The church pastor, Narayan, borrowed a tape-recorder so that he could interview the eyewitnesses. He recorded interviews with over a hundred people of all ages, whose descriptions of the cross all concurred. Many people who had not believed in Christ were challenged to do so having seen the hour-long vision.

When Dr George Newbold and friends were visiting the Dead Sea in Israel on 14 September 1974, they did not see anything unusual at the time. However when George had his photographs developed on his return, there were two symbols over the Dead Sea; a star of light in the direction of Bethlehem, and a large cross in the direction of Jerusalem, symbolizing the birth of Jesus at Bethlehem, and the crucifixion at Jerusalem. As a Protestant, George was unaware until later that in the Catholic calendar, the 14th of September is called the Exaltation of the Crosses. Many attempts have been made on rational grounds to explain away the appearance of the cross and star of light, but none have proven satisfactory. Both the photographic negative and the print were carefully examined by numerous people. One of these, the head of the photographic department at Cardiff

College of Art, declared that neither he nor any of his staff could find an explanation to account for the appearance of the symbols.

God is in control of time, but He Himself exists outside of time. 2 Peter 3:8 tells us: 'With the Lord a day is like a thousand years, and a thousand years are like a day.' There is a pattern and order in our days and seasons, but God can bypass that order if He so chooses. He did this in Joshua 10, when the army of Israel was in conflict with the inhabitants of the land in which they had settled. The people of Gibeon had made peace with the Israelites, but the kings of the Amorites did not like it, and joined forces to attack Gibeon. The Gibeonites sent word to Israel's commander Joshua for the army of Israel to come and help them. Joshua set off at once with his entire army.

Joshua 10:9–15 records: 'After an all-night march from Gilgal, Joshua took them by surprise. The Lord threw them into confusion before Israel, who defeated them in a great victory at Gibeon . . . On the day the Lord gave the Amorites over to Israel, Joshua said to the Lord in the presence of Israel: "O sun, stand still over Gibeon, O moon over the valley of Aijalon." So the sun stood still, and the moon stopped, till the nation avenged itself on its enemies . . . The sun stopped in the middle of the sky and delayed going down about a full day [about twelve hours]. There has never been a day like it before or since, a day when the Lord listened to a man. Surely the Lord was fighting for Israel! Then Joshua returned with all Israel to the camp at Gilgal.'

Something similar, albeit on a much smaller scale, happened on 6 June 1987 in Worthing, Sussex. Jean Breach, a professional photographer based in Lewes, was booked to photograph a wedding and arrived at the church half an hour before the service was due to begin. Unloading her equipment, she found that she had left behind her flash, which she would need for the reception after the service. She apologized to the bride's mother, saying that if she left immediately she could be back before the wedding party came out of the church. The mother was very gracious, knowing the importance of wedding photographs, and reminded her to drive safely. Getting back into the car, Jean prayed that the Lord would protect her journey.

It was a forty-five-minute journey at the best of times, but halfway there, at Portslade, there was a long tailback of traffic. It seemed to take ages to move as the cars nudged slowly forward. Reaching the cause of the delay, Jean saw that there had been a ghastly accident, and that someone was being cut out of a badly crushed car. She started to pray in tongues, interceding on behalf of the people in the accident, and kept praying until the ambulance left and she was able to continue her journey. Arriving home, Jean picked up the flash and returned to the church in Worthing. An usher directed her to a parking-space near the lych-gate, and Jean asked him if the wedding was over. He laughingly replied that it hadn't started yet. It was only then that she looked at her watch, finding to her amazement that the service was not running late, but that her journey had taken less than half an hour! She was able to photograph the bridegroom, best man and ushers, and be in the porch ready to photograph the bridesmaids and bride's mother when they arrived. She said to Jean, 'Oh, you had your flash all the time', to which Jean replied, 'No, I've been back to Lewes.' Looking amazed, the mother said, 'But that is impossible.' 'Not with God,' Jean asserted.

Jean assumed that God must have needed her to pray for the people in the accident, but He did not allow this to make her late for the wedding. When the bride's parents, Mr and Mrs Skelton, came to Lewes to collect the photos, it took them the expected three-quarters of an hour, and they questioned Jean again about the incident. It was a great witness to the family of the God who intervenes. Jean phoned them recently to ask if she could tell us about the occasion for this book, if they remembered it. 'We most certainly do,' they responded, 'and are willing to confirm it.'

Hope had an unusually short journey in 1972. After going

through more than a year of doubt concerning her faith in Christ, she was put in touch by Geoff, who was by then her fiancé, with a wise Christian lady he had met. Iris Innes lived at Thornton Heath, just forty minutes ride by moped from King's College Hospital where Hope was a student nurse. Hope went to see her on several occasions to pray and talk together, and she found these times very helpful. Once, whilst they prayed, God gave Hope a lengthy prophecy through Iris, which was exactly right for Hope in her situation, and included promises for Geoff and herself for the future. As Iris finished giving the prophecy, she felt she had to look up Jeremiah 31. There was exactly the prophecy the Lord had just given to Iris for Hope, contained in about two pages in the Bible. Iris did not even know the passage.

Suddenly realizing that they had forgotten the time in their enthusiasm, they found it was already 12.50 by Hope's watch and Iris's clock, and Hope had to be on duty at 1 p.m. The ward sister was rather a dragon, and Hope would be in trouble for being so late. 'I jumped up, grabbed my coat and apologized for leaving so hastily. Iris delayed me further by saying, "Let's pray that you won't be late." I thought this quite ridiculous, as it was inevitable that I would be very late, but I stood still while Iris prayed. As I went down Iris's path and started away on my moped, I looked back and waved to Iris standing at her gate. The very next moment, I was pulling up outside the hospital. I had definitely not done any of that journey, and had taken no time at all to cover a distance that usually took forty minutes. I thought my watch must have stopped, as it said 12.52, but the clock in the changing-room showed the same time. I put on my uniform and arrived on the ward in good time for duty at 1 p.m. I could hardly wait for my tea-break to phone Iris and tell her, "You'll never guess – I wasn't late!" "Well, I did pray you wouldn't be," Iris replied, delighted. I have never had a journey like it before or since, and both Iris and I still remember the special time we had together that day.'

It seemed extraordinary and yet the same thing happened to someone in the Bible. Philip, one of the evangelists of the early Church, was told by God to go south to the desert road leading from Jerusalem to Gaza. Philip could have complained that it was a very long journey and that he had plenty of work where he was in Samaria. However he obeyed and set off, no doubt wondering what was in store for him. When he got to the road he saw a chariot, and in it a man was reading aloud from the book of Isaiah. The Spirit of the Lord told Philip to go up to the chariot and speak to the man, who readily accepted Philip's offer to help him understand what he was reading. He was seeking to know more about the One who was the subject of Isaiah's prophecies. Philip explained to him that Jesus fulfilled those prophecies.

The man decided he would like to become a Christian, and asked to be baptized as a sign of his conversion. They came to a pool, and he persuaded Philip to baptize him there and then. He became possibly the first Christian in Ethiopia, and he was an important official in charge of the treasury of Candace, queen of the Ethiopians. It may well be that the Christian Coptic Church began as a result of this man's conversion. Immediately after the baptism, 'When they came up out of the water, the Spirit of the Lord suddenly took Philip away, and the eunuch did not see him again, but went on his way rejoicing. Philip, however, appeared at Azotus and travelled about, preaching the Gospel in all the towns until he reached Caesarea' (Acts 8:39–40). After Philip had completed the job he was sent to do, he was transported about thirty miles to the place where he was needed next.

Tuesday 5 January 1993 was the first day of Shetland's greatest potential crisis in living memory, which was widely reported on the national news. The *Braer* oil tanker lost engine-power at 5.30 a.m. and began drifting helplessly in a force-nine gale towards Garths Ness, Shetland. The tanker was carrying

85,000 tonnes of crude oil and 500 tonnes of fuel oil. The Sumburgh-based rescue helicopter was airborne by 6.20 a.m. By 7 a.m. a prayer network was in operation, organized over the telephone, between Christians of all denominations. United prayer meetings were held as soon as they could be set up, praying that disaster be averted. Periodically the tanker was swamped by huge waves and the Lossiemouth helicopter joined the rescue. By 9 a.m. the last of the crew had been winched to safety, and soon the oil began to leak out as the tanker ran aground.

During the course of the next six days, until the *Braer* broke into four pieces, the people of Shetland prayed. They prayed that the Isles would be delivered from the effects of the massive oil-spill. Humanly speaking, it was impossible to disperse all of the oil, yet miraculously, the oil disappeared over the course of two weeks. A local councillor and journalist, Jonathan Wills, said: 'I am not a churchgoer, but many Christians of all denominations started holding prayer meetings to pray it would go away. I have to admit, I was a bit scornful of the idea, but the wind stayed in the same direction for two weeks – it's unheard-of in January. It blew at over 70 miles an hour most of the time, and rose to 120 miles an hour. The effect of that was to corral that oil into a semicircular bay at the southern tip of the islands, and to pound it in these huge waves into something like salad-dressing.' Instead of spreading the slick on the sea, the unusual winds made the current carry it away. The Shetland Islands are renowned for their wildlife, yet there was minimal damage, instead of the expected environmental disaster. The Christians of Shetland held a day of thanksgiving to God on Sunday 17 January, for the way He had answered their prayers. By mid-1993 it had been established that there was indeed no environmental damage. The Creator God had delivered Shetland in a miraculous way.

Christianity without miracles is only religion. Through miracles of creation, God seeks to wake us up to the reality of Himself.

CHAPTER FOURTEEN

When Miracles Don't Happen

My wheelchair has pushed open doors
and pushed down barriers.
I try to help Christian leaders see the need
for balance regarding suffering and
the sovereignty of God. God does not have to
prove Himself with the spectacular.
God is God – He is sovereign.

Margie Willers

N THE SCRIPTURES, suffering is regarded as an intrusion into the world that God created. We read in Genesis 1:31: 'God saw all that He had made, and it was very good.' Suffering began when sin entered the human race through the disobedience of Adam and Eve, taking the form of human conflict, disease, pain in childbirth, corruption of the earth, drudgery in labour and ultimately death.

The primary reason that God, in His love, sent His Son into the world was to rescue mankind from sin, disease and spiritual death. True faith enables us to wrestle with the problem of suffering and the seeming lack of divine intervention. The reality is in God's love for us, His presence as promised and His goodness overcome even the problem of pain. The Psalmist writes: 'My flesh and my heart may fail, but God is the strength of my heart and my portion for ever' (Psalm 73: 26).

The book of Job in the Old Testament portrays a man in an extreme degree of suffering and perplexity. He cries out to

God because he is faced with complete disaster. A good and prosperous man, he loses his children and all his possessions, and is then struck with a hideous skin disease. Three friends come to 'comfort' him and try to help him wrestle with his terrible suffering. They assume Job must have sinned to bring upon himself so much calamity. As for Job himself, a God-fearing man, he cannot understand why he has been allowed to suffer so much.

But despite the lack of heavenly intervention, Job is still able to say: 'I know that my Redeemer lives' (Job 19:25); for Job believes that God will ultimately vindicate him in all his troubles. Finally God responds to Job's challenge by appearing to him, speaking great words of wisdom and showing him His overwhelming power. Job comes to realize that God is bigger than his problems. Eventually his health returns, plus a large measure of material goods, and the Lord makes him prosperous once again.

God is still with us in power, even if we do not see a miracle, and cannot find a reason for our suffering.

We received a very moving letter from Alyn Haskey of Nottingham, who wrote to us on the theme of 'When Miracles Don't Happen'. He was born severely disabled and had extreme communication difficulties. Yet Alyn writes: 'As somebody who has been disabled all their life, and a Christian for a good part of that time, I am faced with the dilemma of miracles. People often ask me why God hasn't healed me. I want to say first of all that I believe in miracles, not only in the past but for today. However I think that sometimes our definition of a miracle is not realistic, and that this is part of the problem.

'For me, being alive is a miracle; having God's resources day by day is a miracle; having opportunities to serve God is a miracle. Yet I'm aware that for some, a miracle would be me jumping to my feet and leaving my wheelchair behind! OK, yes,

I've experienced miracles like this. I was born with cerebral palsy and severely disabled, with no control over my speech or limbs, written off educationally speaking at the age of nine. I became a Christian at the age of fourteen, and in the years since then, God has done tremendous things, including improving my speech and coordination out of all recognition. This means that today I can live independently, have a life that includes academic and sporting achievements, and now I am serving God in the power of Jesus. Yet I am still in a wheelchair, so has God failed? Am I beyond that miracle?

'Over the years I've listened to many reasons why I haven't received complete healing. They include lack of faith, undeclared or unforgiven sin, disobedience. They all sound OK, except that I do believe in the power of God to change – I've experienced it. As for sin, I confess my sins as often as I'm aware I've committed any, and as for disobedience, well in no way do I claim to be perfect, but I do try to listen to what God says. So why no miracle? I believe this is the wrong question to ask, for there are miracles in my life as I've already mentioned, but to me the greatest miracle is being at peace with God, knowing that I'm forgiven and that I'm in His will. Speaking of will, it just might be that God is choosing to use me where I am, hopefully to bless many people in that. Miracles like this are not easy to discern, but they are nevertheless real.'

Alyn gained a degree in Sociology and History at York University, and another from the Open University, and a Licentiate in Theology which, as he says, is 'not bad for someone who was classified as educationally subnormal!' He is also an Olympic medallist, a songwriter and author, and has achieved bronze, silver and gold Duke of Edinburgh awards.

Alyn continues: 'The miracle of trusting God's grace day by day is just as powerful as getting out of my wheelchair. God has said to me that one day I will stand on my feet. When it happens, I'll praise the Lord! Until then, I will continue to trust

God for each day. When we think miracles don't happen, maybe it's because we're not looking in the right places.'

To have a vibrant faith in God is not a protection against suffering. Cases of illness among Christians during the apostolic age are well documented. For instance, we learn that Timothy had a long-term stomach complaint, in I Timothy 5:23. The ability these early Christians knew to perform miracles could not simply be used to keep themselves or their friends free from disease.

Paul's 'thorn in the flesh' illustrates this most strikingly (2 Cor 12:7), often assumed to be a chronic eye complaint. For him of all people we could have expected a miracle of healing. Paul has been honoured as the second greatest man in history after Jesus Christ, yet physical healing did not come. 'Three times I pleaded with the Lord to take it away from me. But He said to me, "My grace is sufficient for you, for my power is made perfect in weakness"' (2 Cor 12:8).

A young man in a similar position to Alyn is Simon Hollingworth, who lives in Huddersfield. Simon was also born with cerebral palsy which, in his case, causes his muscles frequently to go into spasm. He explains that his condition means that his muscles cannot be controlled as they should, but doesn't affect the part of his brain that he thinks with. He says: 'When I try to talk, my limbs start moving at the same time, so I am strapped into my wheelchair with belts round my arms, hips and feet, and a set of cushions. No, I don't mind being strapped in, since it controls the spasms, which then means I can control my head. This is the best part of my body, which enables me to operate a computer with a special letter-board, an electric wheelchair and a portable communicator.'

Simon, like Alyn, has not allowed his condition to defeat him. He invited Jesus into his life at the age of thirteen and the Bible started to make sense to him. He really believed God would heal him and now, at the age of twenty-nine, he sometimes wonders why he has not received physical healing. He knows God has healed him emotionally, and has prepared him to fulfil a role for Him. Simon knows God has called him to train as a local preacher in the Methodist church. It has required a great deal of time to do all the study; for example, each three-hour exam paper took him twenty hours to type. Friends and family have helped him with reading and assignments.

During the training, he had to preach a number of sermons. It takes him about thirty hours to prepare a sermon, and another local preacher stands beside Simon to deliver it. Although Simon can communicate on a one-to-one basis, he cannot be adequately heard in a congregation. In July 1994 he was recognized as a fully accredited local preacher, and he finds spreading the love and power of God to people both inside and outside the Church an exciting responsibility. His faith in God has remained strong and he says, 'God was with me right from when I was a baby; God planned my life, and life with Him is a fantastic experience. I thank Him for it.'

Dr Hugh James and his wife, Vivien, spent several years at a mission hospital in Burundi, Africa. Later, after becoming a consultant anaesthetist in Leicester, Hugh developed multiple sclerosis. Hugh writes: 'As a family we had known God's answers to prayer before this catastrophe hit us. As soon as we knew the diagnosis, it was natural for us to seek God's healing. Our vicar came to our home group, laid hands on me, and all the group united in prayer for healing. At church we have healing services twice a month. I repeatedly asked for prayer, but sadly I have not been physically healed; but for now I have peace that God wants me as I am.'

Hugh recounts: 'I have encountered the full range of reactions from other people. One was, "You lack faith." As we are all pygmies in faith, this is undoubtedly true. How often, though, did Jesus heal people with very little evidence of faith. I know of no suggestion in Scripture that we can earn our healing by having remarkable faith any more than we can make ourselves right with God by doing good deeds. One Baptist minister asked me, "Hugh, are you sure there is no unconfessed sin in your life?" I am sure he did it with great concern, seeking the best for me, but it was still a cruel question. My reply was, "No, there is not," but maybe I should have said, "Yes, probably, what about you?" To others I am a disappointment. They had believed God would heal me, and when He did not, they avoided me. Disability tends to cut you off from people anyway, so the added isolation is especially cruel. To remain physically in the Church today is emotionally more difficult than it was a few years ago, since greater emphasis has been placed on that part of the Gospel message in recent times. If it is not God's will to heal me, the natural question is, Why?'

He reflects on his previous responsibility, running an intensive care unit. There he was called on to offer support to grieving relatives, especially those of young children. Hugh says, 'As I studied the Scriptures, I never found a pat answer. However I did find a God who, in Jesus, did not throw suffering at mankind from far away, but entered into it, suffering Himself as horribly as is possible. I found the question to ask was not "Why should we suffer?" but rather, "If Jesus had to suffer, why should we not suffer?" At the time I found that all I could do for those relatives was to put my arm around them and weep with them. But it satisfied my need for understanding when my MS was diagnosed years later.

'Does my illness have any benefit for other people? I know I am prepared to use my pen and voice in support of the needs of the disabled – regarding access for them, and helping to change people's attitude towards them, both locally and on a wider scale. Only when you find your way to a door totally barred by three steps with no handrail do you realize the importance of minor planning details. I am conscious that day by day, my Lord does provide me with the strength I need. Several people have told me, "We find you a real encouragement." That is encouraging to me; perhaps the family of God does benefit.'

Another doctor, Richard Rowland, a general practitioner, writes: 'We must face the fact that much of what happens in our world, including sickness, is *not* God's will. Otherwise why would Jesus have taught us to pray "Your will be done on earth as it is in heaven"? Although it may break His heart, one of God's ways of testing us is to allow us to live with the consequences of the broken, spoilt choices of our rebellious race. One day, when He returns, Jesus *will* put everything to rights, but meanwhile it seems He wants to do another sort of miracle for those who suffer. If He doesn't deliberately choose suffering, He can use it to turn the dross to gold in us. Every day we need to hear His promise, "Do not be afraid or discouraged . . . For the battle is not yours, but God's" (2 Chronicles 20:15). I can pray this for my friends who suffer.'

The whole concept of a miracle-working God is put to the test when a situation needs a miracle, but none occurs. Does this mean that God has withdrawn His love and compassion? This question is most commonly asked in connection with the illness and death of those whom we love. C. S. Lewis, in *The Problem of Pain*, writes:

> God whispers to us through our laughter
> and shouts to us through our pain.

Our bishop, Keith of Lichfield, whose wife has Alzheimer's disease, wrote a moving article entitled 'God Still Speaks' in the diocesan letter of February 1994. 'I have just been sitting by my wife's bed in our small local hospital. She has been suffering from a serious illness for some time. Today, as I left for a Shropshire confirmation, she collapsed on to our kitchen floor. When I managed to get back to the hospital, her eyes were shut. Her white face aroused in me the pain of anxiety. I felt helpless.

'Last year things were just as difficult. After being transferred to different hospitals, her confusion got worse. At the time, she seized my hand: "Please take me home", she pleaded. But by the doctor's orders, I could not do so. I drove home with my heart torn in a thousand pieces.

'Very early the next morning, while I was trying to pray, the telephone rang. It was the ward sister. She wanted to tell me that Jeannie was eating her breakfast, that she had slept well and that there was no cause for alarm. This article is a tribute from my own heart to that ward sister. After a long night of duty, her act of loving communication brought light into my darkness. And that is a wonderful picture of the light of the Gospel. In a world where people die and suffer, Jesus – by His birth and baptism, by His teaching and healing, by His death and resurrection, by His gift of the Spirit – is God's own act of loving communication. He shows us how to live. The ward sister spoke. In desperate need, I listened. God speaks – do we listen?'

Sickness and suffering are a mystery. What we do know is that God entered our world of suffering in His Son. Through suffering, persecution, scorn, torture, weariness and rejection, identifying Himself with us, Jesus took our fallen humanity to the cross. Even He questioned the whole purpose of suffering in the Garden of Gethsemane: ' "Father, if you are willing, take this cup [the cup of suffering and death] from me; yet not my will, but yours be done." An angel from heaven appeared to Him and strengthened Him' (Luke 22:42–3).

In July 1967 Joni Eareckson, then only seventeen years of age, dived into Chesapeake Bay in her native state of California. Unaware there was a rock under the water, she hit her head and broke her neck. Since that accident, Joni has been confined to a wheelchair as a quadriplegic, but she has written several books, including *Joni*, an autobiographical account, and *A Step Further*, in which she explains her feelings when healing does not occur.

Through her open and honest account of her bouts of despair, depression and loneliness, she has received thousands of letters from all over the world. Her readers have identified themselves with her suffering, and also with the extraordinary way God has strengthened her. Joni writes in *A Step Further*: 'It's hard enough for someone who's always been an indoor bookworm sort of person to adjust to a wheelchair lifestyle, but most people agree that it's even harder for someone such as myself who's been very active . . . When I was on my feet, I couldn't sit still for a minute . . . I often tell people "Now I have to sit still for the rest of my life" . . . Either I must be mad, or there is a living God behind all of this who is more than a theological axiom. He is personal and He works and proves Himself in my life . . . I wasn't the brunt of some cruel divine joke. God had reasons behind my suffering, and learning some of them has made all the difference in the world.' Joni is now happily married [she is known as Joni Eareckson Tada] and has a worldwide ministry helping disabled people. She remains unable to use her hands or feet, but she writes, types and paints beautiful pictures with her mouth.

We must always bear in mind that though apparently inactive, God is working out His purposes. When Hope was very seriously ill with active chronic hepatitis and diabetes, and was likely to die, we did not know whether there was a future for us as a family. But we found great comfort in the following verse in Jeremiah 29:11 which someone gave us at the time: 'For I know the plans I have for you,' declares the Lord, 'plans to prosper you and not to harm you, plans to give you hope and a future.'

We believe God has total control over all that He has created, and that in His Wisdom He does not always intervene. Yet how can a God of love allow the innocent to suffer? We understand from Scripture that God has given man a choice, to choose to follow Him or not to follow Him.

God's Son lived a perfect life, yet He suffered. We read in the Gospels that His pilgrimage to the cross was one of suffering as well as joy. He lived out the life of the suffering servant spoken of in Isaiah 53:3–5, written hundreds of years before Jesus was born:

> He was despised and rejected by men,
> a man of sorrows and familiar with suffering.
> Like one from whom men hide their faces
> he was despised, and we esteemed Him not.
> Surely He took up our infirmities
> and carried our sorrows,
> yet we considered Him stricken by God,
> smitten by Him, and afflicted.
> But He was pierced for our transgressions,
> he was crushed for our iniquities;
> the punishment that brought us peace was upon Him,
> and by His wounds we are healed.

The Hebrew word for 'sorrows' expresses both physical and mental pain. The Old Testament looked towards someone who would be the One anointed (Messiah) and would suffer.

God enters into suffering, and can give it new meaning. Through pain God can work out His redemptive purposes. He did it with the Israelites, and He did it with His Son. Jesus suffered on behalf of the whole world.

Today we fight shy of this kind of thinking, even within the Church. Success is the key word. Rejecting all affliction as evil, and putting the physical condition right, seems to be the top priority. Yes, of course, we ultimately want to be whole in mind, body and soul, but so often God allows us to wait, to be tempered by suffering and to trust Him. 'And we know that in all things God works for the good of those who love Him, who have been called according to His purpose' (Romans 8:28).

Jennifer Rees-Larcombe has proved the truth of this Scripture. In the prime of life she was struck down in February 1982 by a severe, nearly fatal illness. She suffered acute attacks of inflammation of the brain, meninges and nerves, which were prolonged and life-threatening. Between the acute bouts, it was found that the inflammation affected her muscles, causing continuous pain, loss of balance, muscular weakness, fatigue and lack of coordination, blurred vision, distorted hearing, loss of sensation in the limbs and lack of bowel and bladder control. The DHSS awarded her an attendance allowance, a mobility allowance and a severe disability allowance, and after two years they said she had deteriorated to the point where regular assessments would no longer be needed. This was a polite way of saying they had no expectation of her condition improving.

For eight years of disability and constant pain, Jen wrestled with the issue that God was not intervening to heal her. Nevertheless through the illness, which deeply affected not only herself, but also her husband Tony and their six children (the youngest was only four when she was taken ill), Jen's relationship with God changed and deepened as she learnt to suffer with Him.

In her book *Beyond Healing*, Jen records with great courage, humour and disarming honesty how the whole family entered into a pilgrimage of living with a mum in a wheelchair. Jen had many feelings of frustration. She describes a few of them: 'I became acutely conscious that I was a physical wreck . . . I hated the humiliation of wheelchairs. Have you ever realized that when you are in a wheelchair, you are not considered a person by most people? . . . I was utterly shattered . . . The pain was sometimes worse than I felt it was possible to live through; I felt angry and desperate . . . I was told things like: "It is never God's will for us to be ill even for one minute." "You must be harbouring some secret, unconfessed sin, or you could walk out of here." "Your trouble is, you're just accepting this, and not fighting." "You brought all this on yourself, you know, you have been doing far too much." "Sometimes we cling on to illness as a way of feeling important and being noticed. Are you willing to be healed?" I had positively shaken with rage after that man had spoken to me, but really he did me a great deal of good.'

Jen continues: 'That night I realized the danger of the illness becoming the centre of my life, ruling me. I prayed, "Lord, help me to put you in the very centre of my life" . . . I wanted to be healed so badly I twisted myself into mental and spiritual knots, trying to take all this conflicting advice. So it seemed a positive relief when someone said "Stop praying for healing – just praise the Lord" . . . Surely, I thought in desperation, we should be able to praise God whether He brings us good or bad, and go on praising Him even when our circumstances do not change.'

Some moments were particularly hard. Jen wrote: 'I shall never forget Richard's first morning at school . . . As we reached the school gates, I felt pierced by the stares of other children and their mums. They gazed at my emaciated body.' Depression also came to Jen – 'a terrible black cloud descended over my head, tangible and suffocating' – which she found worse than anything. 'No pain or illness is as bad as depression, and you cannot believe it will ever end.'

Many people prayed for healing for Jen, in addition to her own heartfelt pleas. In the midst of her suffering she wrote: 'When we belong to Him, He is with us whether or not we feel it or even believe it. All through that dark valley His "everlasting arms" were underneath me (Deuteronomy 33:27) even when I did not *realize* it. His presence with us does not depend on our feelings or our faith, it just happens to be fact!' Jen was thrilled when she was healed of depression. She recorded in her diary: 'Felt groggy physically all day but not *one bit depressed*!' Jen was healed physically after those eight difficult years, but that's for another chapter.

There is a relationship between a person's expression of faith and God's healing. For example, we read in Matthew 13:55: 'Isn't this the carpenter's son? Isn't his mother's name Mary? . . .

And they took offence at Him ... And he did not do many miracles there because of their lack of faith.' Thinking they knew Jesus' background, some of the people from his home town refused to believe He could perform miracles.

However healing does not depend upon the faith of an individual. The sick person has plenty to contend with, without being told they haven't enough faith! When the paralysed man was healed in Mark 2:3–12, it was the faith of his friends who brought him to Jesus that enabled his healing. The breakdown of care in local communities has resulted in many people becoming isolated and lonely. God intends that we should draw together and strengthen and care for one another.

In the Western world we attempt to insure ourselves against all eventualities and cushion ourselves from suffering as much as possible. We resent illness and difficulties when they strike. In many parts of the world people accept pain and suffering much more as part of everyday life. This has been true of the West in past years, and people were led to greater dependence on God. As C. S. Lewis put it in *The Problem of Pain*: 'Pain is God's megaphone to rouse a deaf world.' A prayer commonly made at the time of the plague in the seventeenth century reads: 'Have pity upon us miserable sinners, who now are visited with great sickness and mortality.' The emphasis was on asking for God's mercy rather than 'Why is this happening?'

Suffering may have a valuable purpose that we cannot perceive at the time. For instance, if St Paul and John Bunyan had not been imprisoned for long periods, the world would have been deprived of their fine writings. Neither of them would have chosen imprisonment, and yet their lives were so fully occupied that without this enforced curtailment of their activities, they probably would not have written much at all. Our ultimate goal is not that we should be physically perfect, but that we should become the person God intended us to be.

Tony Melendez was born in Nicaragua on 9 January 1962. He had no arms, eleven toes and a severe club-foot. His mother had been prescribed the drug thalidomide by a trusted family doctor for nausea and dizziness during pregnancy. She took only two weeks of medication. Around 1959 onwards, over ten thousand babies around the world were born without arms or legs, until the connection was made with the drug thalidomide and it was banned.

At Tony's birth, the nursing staff were reluctant to tell his mother what was wrong with the baby, and his father sobbed as he broke the news to her. Recently she told Tony about that moment: 'I lay back on the pillow, feeling God's presence in the room. The journey ahead was uncertain, but arms or no arms, I knew that God would be with you and with us every step along the way.' Tony has needed many operations and plaster casts for his foot. The family had to move to California to get the medical help Tony needed, and his father took any jobs he could.

Life has not been easy for Tony, but his autobiography is entitled *A Gift of Hope*. At the age of three he learnt to hold a crayon and draw pictures with his feet. Whenever he drew people, he always drew them with arms. His mother frequently said to him as he was growing up: 'Don't worry. God has something wonderful in mind for you. Trust God and don't get impatient.' Tony taught himself to play his father's guitar using his feet. He has played to audiences of many thousands, including a huge televised gathering in front of the Pope. As one badly deformed young woman in a wheelchair said to him: 'Tony, because of you, we all have hope!'

We asked friends of ours, Quentin and Jenny Dawe, to write about their youngest daughter: 'When Penny, our fourth child, was born in October 1981, she had Down's syndrome and was in heart failure. Although the doctors expected her to live only a few weeks, we never doubted that she would grow up with us. We were right about that, and we resolved to treat her the same as our other three children. Sarah, aged nine, Catherine, eight, and Bob, three, were all involved right from the moment Penny was born. She has been teased, pushed around and had the corners knocked off her, just like any child in a large, busy family.

'Penny's life and character have brought much joy and happiness to many people. She has taught us all that life is for living now and enjoying, even if you have to look hard at times to find the good bits. Society might see her life and condition as a disaster, something to be made the best of or endured. We do not see her in that light. She is perfect in God's sight, like anyone else, and who are we to see her any differently? We would not have changed anything about her. She is as God intended her to be, and we feel privileged that we have had the experience of being her parents and learning from her. It is only our society and education system that see intellect as important. There are many more sides to a person than that.

'Penny's sensitivity, kindness, astuteness, canniness, sense of fun and lovable nature are all important in making up her complete character. Never have we seen her as a problem – although sometimes she is a challenge. She is very precious, no more and no less than our other children.'

It is wonderful when someone we know is miraculously healed, but how do we respond when a loved one dies? Naturally we ask where *was* God in all this? Why did it have to happen? Russell Chiswell was a fine preacher and the loving pastor of a church in Hirwaun, South Wales. He was greatly loved and respected there, but knowledge of his gifts had reached Oxford, where he had just been invited to be Vice-Principal of Wycliffe Hall Theological College. In the new year, a few months before this appointment, Russell became ill. A tumour was found in his bowel and an operation in April apparently removed it completely. He was told by his consultant that there was not likely to be a recurrence of the cancer for several years.

However, at a routine follow-up examination in early August, when his only complaint had been 'some indigestion', a CT scan showed conclusively that the tumour had returned, the liver was already severely affected, and there were secondaries throughout the abdomen, as if it were 'shot through with holes'. Having felt well and excited about his imminent move to the new job in Oxford, Russell and his family suddenly had to face the fact that he had perhaps only weeks to live. The moving sermon he gave on 7 August 1992, only two days after hearing the news, is an incredible testimony to his trust in God. He quoted Samuel Johnson's words: 'Knowing you have a short time to live greatly concentrates the mind.' Russell said, 'I can see more clearly than at any other time what is really important and what isn't; what, at the end of the day, matters and what doesn't.' He knew that his priorities now were to spend time with God and with his family.

Of course, Russell and his family and hundreds of others in various parts of the country prayed for his healing. As Russell said: 'We don't understand why – there are lots of questions we can't answer. We know why there is evil and suffering in the world, but we don't know why one person gets it and another doesn't.' Russell quoted the verse in Philippians 3:14 which says: 'I press on towards the goal to win the prize for which God has called me heavenwards in Christ Jesus.' He concluded his sermon by saying: 'It is a prize; I've always looked forward to it. I just hadn't imagined the prize-giving would come so soon.'

Russell, his wife Julie and their children, Susannah, aged ten, and Evan, aged six, made immediate plans to vacate the vicarage as they were already packed up for the planned move to Oxford. With the help of the church, they were able to buy a house in Hirwaun, so they would be near the friends with whom they had shared the past twelve years. As Russell said of the church there, 'The warmth, love and affection in which I hold them and in which they hold me is something special.'

Russell was interviewed on BBC Radio Wales later in August 1992, making clear his continuing faith in God. His trust in God remained unshaken, despite his situation. Asked if he felt angry, Russell replied: 'I'm only forty, but I have a great deal to be grateful for in my life so far. I don't feel angry, but I feel enormous sadness at the thought of not spending the future with my wife and missing the precious years of seeing my children grow up. I have no sense of being abandoned by God. I'm surrounded by an enormous amount of love and support in prayer.'

The interviewer asked, 'Do you think God has lost control in this situation?' Russell replied, 'God has not lost control, but there is a battle going on between the powers of darkness and the powers of light. One thing about evil is that by its very nature it hits people at random. If I could explain why this has happened, it would not be so bad and evil and nasty as it is. The Christian vision is not that everything will work out smoothly for those who trust in Christ, but that ultimately God will triumph.'

The interviewer continued: 'You've ministered as a vicar to many people who are dying; is it different from the inside from what you assumed?' Russell answered: 'The main thing in ministry that you really notice is the difference between those who die with a clear, firm faith and those who don't. I thank God I don't feel the sense of despair and hopelessness I've seen sometimes, and I don't. I have no doubts that I'll have a place in heaven; not because of anything I have done, but because of God's grace to those who believe in Jesus.'

The family moved house while Russell was still well enough to do so, and they made the most of their time left together. Russell's mother, Dorothy, was staying with them for a few days around her birthday when Russell's health suddenly deteriorated. He died at home on 25 October. His wife Julie said: 'Russell showed a great deal of courage. People who stand up and speak out sometimes get shot, and he was a casualty in the spiritual battle. His spirit survived although his life was ended. I can't pretend that God brought the pain or death, but He helps us to get through it.' His brother Peter, to whom he was very close, said: 'We're sometimes given the impression that when a Christian dies we should only rejoice because they are going to a better place, but there is still grief for the family and friends. The wider Church has also lost a dynamic man with many gifts. We can't see why, but we trust God in it.'

Death for the Christian is not the end. It is the beginning of a new dawn in terms of a spiritual life, since at Easter Christ put death to death. Stephen Verney wrote in the *Listener* in 1977 about 'the mystery of the Resurrection'. 'Three years ago my wife died . . . Some part of yourself has been torn out, and you fall to pieces, and gradually – very gradually – you have to be reformed in a new pattern. The process of mourning is not just pain. It is also the discovery of new strength and new happiness, so that it can be not only the most terrible anguish but, at the same time, the greatest privilege. The heart of this privilege has been the gradual unfolding of the mystery of the resurrection . . . The story of the resurrection of Christ helped me to understand my wife's death, but, at the same time, her death helped me to understand the resurrection of Christ.'

The miracle in death for the Christian is that God gives us the assurance that 'the best is yet to be' in the life to come. Dying is just a journey with God for the Christian, because, as St Paul says in Romans 8:38–9: 'For I am convinced that neither death nor life, neither angels nor demons, neither the present nor the future, nor any powers, neither height nor depth, nor anything else in all creation, will be able to separate us from the love of God that is in Christ Jesus our Lord.'

The death of a child brings immense pain for parents. The parents of twenty-year-old Bruce Goodrich received a night-time call that Bruce had been rushed to hospital in Texas, where he died the same night, in August 1984. He had just started his first semester at Texas A & M University, training in the corps of cadets. It was customary for existing students to push new entrants to physical extremes. In this instance, having been forced to get up during the night to run for an hour, do sit-ups and push-ups, Bruce suffered heatstroke and did not recover consciousness when attempts were made to resuscitate him. After his death, fellow cadets said, 'Bruce was enthusiastic about his new school.' 'In my eyes there wasn't anything about him I didn't like.' 'The first thing that comes to my mind is that Bruce was probably the best Christian in the outfit.'

Bruce's father, Ward Goodrich, wrote to the university: 'I would like to take this opportunity to express the appreciation of my family for the great outpouring of concern and sympathy over the loss of our son, Bruce. We were deeply touched by the tribute paid him in the battalion and were particularly pleased to note that his Christian witness did not go unnoticed during his brief time on campus. To those who may be burdened by guilt or remorse over their involvement in the incident and to their families, I hope it will be some comfort to know that we harbour no ill will in the matter. We know that God makes no mistakes. Bruce had an appointment with His Lord, and is now secure in his celestial home. When the question is asked 'Why did this happen?', perhaps one answer will be that many will consider where they will spend eternity.'

There is only one way in which, with the world as it is, God shows Himself in respect of man's suffering, and that is by not asking anything of us that He is not prepared to endure Himself. He shares in the loneliness, the bafflement and the pain, even the death. He is a God we can respect, a God who made himself a servant and became one of us. When we cry out in our misery

'Why has this happened to me?' God can answer truthfully: 'It happened to Me too.'

To try to cope with the pain of bereavement Anne Townsend, a missionary doctor in Thailand, wrote in *Suffering Without Pretending*: 'The inexplicable thread of bereavement ran through the life I was so busy living. God did not allow me to evade unpleasant issues. The biggest blow came when five adult missionaries, seven children (and three nearly full-term unborn babies), most of whom were close friends of mine, were killed at Manorom (Thailand) in a road accident in 1978.'

Anne and her husband, John, also a doctor, were on leave in England at the time, and she explains: 'John flew to Thailand to see if he could bring some kind of comfort to the bereaved. He arrived at Manorom, the car door swung open, and he fell into the arms of those who had all lost someone they had loved. One face above all shines in his memory. A Swiss missionary mother had lost her youngest son in the accident. Her brown hair framed a pale face, ravaged by grief. John was at a loss. What could he possibly say to comfort her? His words would be empty phrases. But her voice rang with conviction: 'John, God is good.'

Such words from such as she can never be erased from John's heart. A mother whose youngest son had been killed needlessly was certain that God was good. This mother holds the key which can unlock much of our searching and perplexity. She believes that, despite everything appearing to the contrary, God is still good. As we look at children who die, we need to see through eyes like hers. We theorize, but she has walked barefoot along this path. She has emerged believing against all odds. A Son hung on a cross and cried in agony to His Father – His Father was one with the Son and suffered with Him as He died. God knows what it is like to be human and to be hurting. God suffers when we are hurt. He suffers with each child and adult who suffers.'

Those who have suffered a miscarriage or stillbirth experience a very real bereavement, but may not receive from others the sympathy they need because the baby has never lived. One bereaved mother, Pam Vredevelt, in her book *Empty Arms*, wrote: 'On days when I wanted to hibernate like a hermit, I made myself talk or write. Sometimes I'd talk to John [her husband] or friends. Other times I'd talk out loud to God. John and I had to recognize that there are things in life beyond our control because sin is corrupting our world – one outflow of this is death. But our doubts caused tremendous growth in our lives. Even though it's hard to see now, I trust that God will work something good out of this situation. No matter what "hell" I have to walk through, God will be there with me. He never separates Himself from me. God will get me through this.'

The pain of stillbirth can haunt a family if the child born dead is never talked about, and the parents feel they have not been allowed to work through their grief. Friends of ours, Steve and Heather, were very much looking forward to the birth of twins, their first children. When the twins were stillborn, they were never shown to the parents, and were 'disposed of' by the hospital. Steve and Heather felt totally empty, having no opportunity for the grieving which a funeral allows. In the wider family too, the birth and death of the twins was never talked about by relatives, and when they raised the subject, it was quickly changed or ignored. Steve and Heather kept their grief to themselves, but they continued to ache for their twins.

We did not meet and become friends with Steve and Heather until twelve years later, when Geoff was a curate at the church they attended. By this time they had a ten-year-old daughter and an eight-year-old son. One Friday, after a general conversation with Geoff, Heather said, 'Please say a prayer for the twins on Sunday. It is their twelfth birthday.' Geoff said he would, but walking home, he was puzzled, because he didn't know they had twins and he wondered if they were away at boarding-school. When we talked about it, we phoned Heather to ask what she meant, and she confided that her twins had been stillborn, and that she felt the situation was unresolved because they had never been named or committed to God. Geoff discussed the matter with his vicar, Jim, and decided what to do.

We invited Steve and Heather round the next day to talk and pray. Then we all decided that the best plan would be to meet in church with Jim on the Sunday afternoon, together with our children and theirs, who were great friends, to lay the matter to rest. That short service in church, on the twins' twelfth birthday, was a very special time. Heather was invited to name the twins, and in prayer they were committed to God. They were named Caroline and Louise. It was like a mini-baptism and funeral all in one. Geoff gave thanks for the whole family, asking God's blessing on them all. Steve and Heather then decided to buy a gift for the church, a sound-system to relay the service to the crèche area, and a picture for their home, both in memory of their twins.

Heather told me later that this short ceremony had totally changed her memory of the twins. Throughout the twelve years she had grieved every day for her children. Now, although she still thought of them each day, it was with joy and thanks, and without the ache in her heart.

In April 1965, Philip Leonard-Johnson was at theological college in Lincoln. His wife Mary was at home looking after four-year-old Ruth, three-year-old Deirdre and the new baby, Mark, who was just two months old. Mary remembers: 'I gave Mark a breast-feed at 4 a.m., revelling in his closeness. When Philip and I got up at 7 a.m., Mark was awake but content. He gave us a gentle smile; I kissed him, turning him on his side. I dressed the girls, we had breakfast together, and I got them ready for nursery school. I asked Ruth to see if Mark was awake, as it was time for his next feed. She came back looking worried, saying he was on his tummy.

'I dashed in and found that he was dead; it seemed

impossible. I tried to give him artificial respiration for a few seconds, then scooped up him and the girls, rushing to a doctor's surgery near by. A kind motorist offered to help, and I asked: "Could you look after the children; I think my baby's dead." The doctor gently gave him "the kiss of life" while I feverishly prayed for a miracle. When he said "It's no good – he's gone", I felt nothing but a sickening numbness. I allowed myself to be led to the car, where the girls were waiting. The motorist kindly drove us to the nursery school while I explained to Ruth and Deirdre that Mark had gone to be with Jesus. Then I went to find Philip.'

Philip takes up the story: 'I was writing my first sermon to preach in a church outside the college, on the subject of suffering. I had finished writing it, so was reading it aloud to myself, timing how long it would take. I had reflected on the creative use of suffering, such as Christians in prison camps accepting suffering and death, allowing love to turn a crucifixion into resurrection. I then applied it to our own experience of suffering and had just read aloud "from nearer home – maybe *at* home", when two students came to my room with the news: "Mark has died."' Philip and Mary went together to the doctor's, had a few minutes with Mark, then talked to the doctor. The post-mortem was completed the same morning, revealing viral pneumonia, which often produces no symptoms. Later that morning, a friend helped Mary to pack up Mark's things and put them away in a trunk, while Mary wept freely.

At lunch-time, the college warden lent them his car while his wife gave lunch to Ruth and Deirdre. Philip and Mary drove into the countryside, leant against some straw bales in the sun, and talked and talked. Mary remembers: 'We were full of questions – why had this happened? No one could have longed for this son more than we had, or loved him more. His birth had been so thrilling somehow – an easy one, although he weighed eleven pounds. Ruth and Deirdre adored him too, and our family had felt complete and perfect. Just then we felt God was very close, and that in a very real way He was mourning with us. Afterwards, we learnt that the whole college had gone into the chapel at that time to pray for us.

'We couldn't believe God had *intended* Mark to die. But we wondered why there should be a dangerous virus. Later, we delved into science a little and discovered, to our surprise, that viruses are necessary, and that they are related to the simplest form of life. Therefore it was just misfortune that Mark was the target of this particular virus. We realized that no blame could be attached to God, and were left without bitterness. We believe that the love a parent has for a child is only a reflection of God's love for us, so He must grieve even more deeply than we do at such a tragedy.'

In times of suffering God can, if we let Him, comfort our hearts and renew our lives. He is on our side.

CHAPTER FIFTEEN

The Greatest Miracle of All

One short sleep past, we wake eternally,
And death shall be no more; Death, thou shalt die.

John Donne

OGETHER WE HAVE learnt that a miracle is beyond the power of mere man to perform. The miracles of Jesus of Nazareth are object lessons, addressed to the eye as well as to the ear, giving us overwhelming evidence that He is God, and God is good.

Thirty-six miracles are described in the New Testament, integral to Jesus' ministry, the feeding of the five thousand being recorded in all four Gospels. Who was such a man to whom, at the end of His earthly life, the 'greatest miracle of all' happened – the resurrection of His crucified body? It is important to have historical facts verified when we consider the miracle of the resurrection of Jesus.

New light has recently been shed, giving greater authenticity to the recorded life of Jesus. *The Times* printed an article on 24 December 1994 in which Matthew D'Ancona wrote of the astonishing discovery made by Dr Carsten Thiede on three fragments known as the Magdalen Papyrus: 'The casual observer would not look twice. Yet these ancient scraps of papyrus, which have been locked away in an Oxford college library for most of the century ... may transform our present understanding of Christianity and the Gospels. Dr Thiede was taken aback by what he found ... the strong possibility that the Gospel according to St Matthew is not the second-century version of an oral tradition, but an eyewitness account. The New Testament, in other words, may have been written and read by men who walked with Christ through Galilee.'

Matthew D'Ancona continues: 'Since the Magdalen fragment was dated four decades ago, important research has been carried out which enabled Dr Thiede to estimate far more accurately the years in which the papyrus was likely to have been written. His conclusions were bold. In the course of four trips to Oxford, it became clear to him that the papyrus was written in a distinctive script common in the first century BC, but petering out by the middle of the first century AD. The hand, he gradually realized, was a hundred years older than was previously thought. He will not deny the extraordinary implication of his analysis. If the new dating is accurate, the Magdalen papyrus would turn out to be not only the oldest known fragment of Matthew, but the oldest of *all* listed New Testament manuscripts.'

Whatever the outcome of this investigation, it is of great interest to note that whether the earliest copy of the New Testament was dated AD 130, as it has been thought, or is contemporary with the events themselves, the recording of the events is very much closer to their happening than it is with regard to other commonly accepted ancient manuscripts. For example, Caesar's *Gallic Wars* are taken by historians to be a correct account of events; yet the earliest copy in existence is dated AD 900, which is 950 years after the events the manuscript records, which occurred in 58–50 BC, and only nine or ten copies have been found. In contrast, the events recorded in the New Testament took place around AD 40–100. The earliest known copy, before Dr Thiede's discovery, was AD 130, and five thousand copies in Greek and ten thousand in Latin exist today from those early years. There have been thorough investigations into the authorship of the New Testament, resulting in the most critical research made on any writing in history. It is apparent that the writers of the New Testament were contemporary with, or writing very soon after, the resurrection of Jesus. This is important to know, considering that this miracle of all miracles is central to Christian belief.

Jesus' resurrection is foreshadowed in John 11, when His friend Lazarus dies. Jesus declares to the sisters of Lazarus: 'Your brother will rise again . . . I am the resurrection and the life.' Jesus is deeply moved as He approaches the tomb of Lazarus, and shows his emotion at losing someone close to Him. Jesus commands that the stone laid across the tomb be removed. The sisters, Mary and Martha, complain that the smell of death would be awful, as Lazarus has already been dead for four days. Jesus challenges their lack of faith. As the stone is taken away, Jesus prays to His Father to intervene 'that they may believe that you sent Me'.

After praying Jesus shouts out: 'Lazarus, come out!' To everyone's astonishment, the grave shrouds still wrapped around him, the dead man walks out. Jesus says to those near by, 'Take off the grave clothes and let him go.'

For the Christian, death is the dawn of a new day. The miracle of the resurrection of Jesus takes away the fear of death. In the West today, death is not widely talked about; its uncertainty and finality leave many in fear and silence. Jesus had the power to take the sting of death away from Lazarus.

C. S. Lewis wrote the following inscription on his wife's memorial:

Here the whole world (stars, water, air, field and
forest, as they were reflected in a single mind)
Like cast-off clothes was left behind
In ashes yet with hope that she,
Reborn from holy poverty,
In Lenten lands, hereafter may
Resume them on her Easter Day.

In these words lies the victory that our Lord gives to the Christian; hope and life beyond the grave. Even Lazarus had to die again, to inherit the world beyond this one.

Not many have come back to life to tell us about the experience of life after death. However we have received the remarkable account of a man who did just this. Captain Edmund Wilbourne of the Church Army wrote a booklet entitled *Life after Life*. Edmund was twenty-one years old when he had the following profound experience: 'As a young Church Army student in a field placement in Manchester, I developed pneumonia and pleurisy. Rushed into Crumpsall Hospital, I was placed on the danger list. It was nearly forty-five years ago, before the discovery of today's miracle drugs, so my relatives were called to my bedside. Although unconscious for much of the time, I was aware of a great deal of activity around me and could hear conversation. After a time, I seemed to stop fighting and stood outside my body. I died and was certified as dead. Having been raised by my grandparents, my grandfather was the one told to make preparations for my funeral. However a cord linked my soul to my body; I watched from outside my body as a nurse shaved me following death and I saw the mortuary attendant stand by with his trolley.'

Edmund continues: 'I came to in Heaven, where there was light and peace, music and beauty, joyful activity and love. It was this *love* of which I was supremely conscious – the loving welcome for believers – glory beyond human description. The light was so intense I could hardly see at first, but then I perceived great joy and purposeful activity. I felt truly alive as I had never been, before or since. My past made sense, the dark and light strands of life's tapestry revealing a perfect pattern. Then I saw the Lord Jesus, with the scars of the crucifixion on His body, and I can hear my laughter now at the thought that those scars were the only man-made things in Heaven. Jesus, who was my Saviour on earth and was now my Lord in Heaven, laughed too. I wanted to stay for ever.

'Heaven was a place of perfection. Somehow I *knew* people; in almost the same way as I recognize the presence of my wife coming into a room, without turning round and actually seeing her. Heaven is a place where human characteristics are identifiable. In Heaven there is no sense of time, and because of this, everyone enters there after death at the same moment. Everyone was at a perfect age – not old or young.'

The amazing account continues: 'It was at this point that I heard resounding through Heaven a voice, at first a whisper, which grew louder and louder. A voice praying, "O God, don't let him die, he has work to do for you. O God, don't let him die!" I recognized it as the voice of Daisy Green, my landlady. Then Jesus just smiled, turned me round by the shoulders and gave me a slight push. I felt as if I was falling through space and I came to again on a slab in the mortuary at the hospital. I sat up, asking where I was; the attendant nearly had a heart attack! In fact I had to comfort him and look after him. The next thing I knew I was back in the hospital ward. I had been dead for three hours, and here I was, back again in answer to Daisy Green's prayer. I learnt later that she had knelt to pray for me at the side of my bed in her home, in the Harper Hay area of Manchester, nowhere near the hospital, saying, "Oh God, don't let him die, he has work for you to do. O God, don't let him die!"'

Edmund Wilbourne has been in active ministry for forty-five years since then. Edmund writes of those who have come back from the dead, 'There is much agreement in these so-called "out of body" experiences. Nearly every account speaks of the sensation of leaving the body and from a new position being able to see and hear what is going on around at the time. They speak of peace, of lack of pain, of golden light. Many tell of how the light radiates love without the use of words. Most of the accounts are quite adamant that the experience is not a dream, but reality, a series of real events. They also speak of being so far outside earthly restraints that none feels capable of giving a true picture of it. As one woman says: "Our world is three-dimensional, but the next one definitely isn't." Whatever explanation we would like to give, these experiences are very real.'

Another man's restoration to life was observed by several hundred people. At the Easter Gathering conference held in Jerusalem in 1986, people were lining up in several queues to register for the conference in the large reception foyer of the International Conference Centre. One of those checking people in was Esther Vera Lever, who told us what happened. A pastor had brought a group from his church. Esther noticed that his closeness to God seemed to shine out of his face. Just as he approached the registration table, he collapsed on to the floor. Esther rushed round, calling for first-aid assistance.

Two nurses, who did not know each other, came from their positions behind the registration tables, intending to attempt resuscitation. Both these nurses have told us what happened next. One, Yael Bar-shov, is an American Jew who has accepted Jesus as her Messiah and has been living in Jerusalem since 1985. As a local believer, she had been helping with the practical arrangements at the conference for Christian leaders the previous week, which was held on Mount Carmel. She therefore immediately recognized the man on the floor as Peter van Woerden, whom she had met at that leaders' conference. A Dutchman, he was working as a pastor in Switzerland. Yael is a skilled paramedic who teaches emergency techniques to others. The other girl who came forward to help was Georgina Wray, who is English, and is trained in general and paediatric nursing, with plenty of experience in emergency procedures. As she realized help was needed and made her way across the foyer, she heard God say to her: 'There is hardness of heart; there is a need for people to soften their hearts.' Her silent response was 'Lord, take me and use me.'

The two came from different directions and knelt down, one either side of him. Yael said, 'Please keep the people back. Call an ambulance.' Peter was still breathing slightly when they reached him, but then he stopped breathing completely. They both tried to find his pulse, but there were no radial, carotid or inguinal pulses. Yael asked Georgina, 'Do you know CPR?' (a resuscitation technique). Georgina replied, 'Yes, I'm a nurse.' But then, amazingly, without saying anything further, they both knew that they must not begin the resuscitation. They both felt God's presence very strongly, restraining them from taking action. All their instincts and training as nurses and first-aiders was to begin at once, yet they both heard God say 'Don't touch him.' It was as if they became oblivious of everything around them.

Esther tells us that it was an extraordinary moment. Hundreds of people were there, most of them praying or spontaneously singing 'Jesus is Lord'. A New Zealander came over and said 'I'm a doctor – he's dead – leave him.' Esther says that she felt quite desperate, as the minutes ticked by, knowing that brain damage would be inevitable if resuscitation was begun too long after he stopped breathing. For several minutes Yael and Georgina knelt beside Peter. They both heard the words 'Rend your hearts and not your garments', which they later learnt was from the book of Joel in the Bible. Afterwards they learnt the significance of this message, as a Jewish rabbi tears his clothing as a sign of death or separation. It is normal, before beginning resuscitation, for first-aiders to tear open the patient's coat and shirt to reveal the chest and get into the exact position to perform heart massage. People around them could not understand why they were slowly and gently unbuttoning Peter's shirt. It was contrary to everything they had been taught, yet neither of them felt any freedom to do otherwise.

After several minutes had passed, both nurses simultaneously felt God say to them 'Now!' Yael and Georgina knew at the same moment that it was the right time to begin cardiac massage, although there was no exchange of communication. Yael moved to Peter's head and gave him two breaths. Georgina did the heart massage, then they both did the next set of breaths and heart massage. Peter was a large man and Yael is quite small. Although she was breathing into him correctly, with maximum effort, it was having no effect at all. As they began the resuscitation technique, Esther earnestly prayed, 'Lord, raise this man up.' When Yael began the third set of breaths, Georgina prayed, 'Lord, please put your breath in her.' As she breathed in, Yael felt as if God was breathing into her, through the top of her head, and out into Peter's mouth. His chest rose powerfully. At that moment Peter came back to life and began praying aloud in tongues. Yael raised one arm and said 'Alleluia.' Peter opened his eyes, looked straight at Yael and said 'Yael, this is intercession.' Then he closed his eyes and carried on praying in tongues.

The ambulance crew arrived. Before being moved to hospital, Peter said that he had had a meeting with Jesus, who had sent him back to this life. One of the girls needed to go with him in the ambulance, and Georgina told Yael to go. Georgina felt she must return to her work of registering conference delegates, although she was feeling quite overwhelmed, having been in God's presence and heard Him speaking to her. She continued with the registrations all morning and into the afternoon. At about 3 p.m., the husband of her friend Joan Wilson came to collect a packet from her. When he heard what had happened a few hours before, he insisted she go and talk to Joan, although Georgina was reluctant to disturb her, hearing she was praying. The other registration staff encouraged Georgina to take a break, so she made her way to the hotel where Joan was staying.

On meeting Joan, Georgina was surprised to hear that she knew all about what had happened with Peter. Then she learnt that Yael had been there for quite a long time, talking and praying with Joan. She had only just left the hotel, and she wondered how the other nurse, whose name she did not know, was coping following this amazing event.

At the hospital, Peter had told Yael that during the wonderful meeting with Jesus, He had told him many things, one of which was a message for Yael. Since coming to live in Israel, Yael had asked God to show her the true meaning of intercession. She had only recently met Joan who had a ministry of intercession, that is, deep prayer on behalf of others. Joan regularly gets up very early and is quiet and still; she spends hours at a time in prayer. Yael is a very active person, so she did not consider being an intercessor was appropriate for her. Her message from Jesus addressed all that she had been thinking about: 'You don't have to be quiet and still, or get up at 5 a.m. and spend hours every day in prayer. Your whole life is a prayer – that's what intercession is.' This fitted in exactly with Peter's first words to Yael, as he was being restored while she was busily involved in trying to resuscitate him.

After Georgina had shared with Joan her feelings of that morning and been prayed for, she went back to the conference centre and met Yael properly for the first time. They hugged each other and talked about their experience. They became good friends, and over the following years, also with Peter and his wife Inga. Peter was the nephew of Corrie ten Boom, a lady well known in Christian circles for her message of forgiveness to the Nazis after she had been badly treated in Ravensbruck concentration camp. The whole family had been active in rescuing Jews from Nazi persecution throughout the war, and in helping them after the war. Peter said, 'Isn't it just like our Lord, after the help I gave to Jews in Holland during the war, that a Jew should save my life in Israel?' Yael replied: 'Not only a Jew, but two believers – a Jew and a Gentile, united in Jesus.'

Peter had a great love for Israel and the Jews. He and his family spent much time in Israel; they all spoke and sang in Hebrew. He organized prayer groups throughout Switzerland

and France to pray for reconciliation between Jews and Arabs. For many years he brought groups of Christians to Israel to meet with Arab and Jewish Christian believers. After a few more years of valuable ministry, Peter died around 1990.

At the time of Peter's being raised to life, a man who was ninety per cent blind was waiting in the conference queue for registration. He was completely healed at the same moment that Peter was restored. Yael and Georgina are convinced that, if they had started resuscitation any earlier than God showed them, so much would have been lost. Peter would have been deprived of the wonderful conversation he had with Jesus. Yael would not have learnt that valuable lesson about prayer. Georgina would have been deprived of a wonderful closeness with God which she experienced. The blind man would not have been healed, and nor would anyone witnessing that momentous event have seen God at work.

Jesus, God's Son, taught His friends about Heaven: 'Do not let your hearts be troubled. Trust in God; trust also in me. In my Father's house are many rooms; if it were not so, I would have told you. I am going there to prepare a place for you. And if I go and prepare a place for you, I will come back and take you to be with me that you also may be where I am. You know the way to the place where I am going.' Thomas said to Him, 'Lord, we don't know where you are going, so how can we know the way?' Jesus answered, 'I am the way and the truth and the life. No one comes to the Father except through me' (John 14:1–6).

The ultimate message for the Christian is the resurrection of Jesus. As early as AD 100 a Christian creed states: 'I believe in Christ Jesus . . . crucified under Pontius Pilate and buried; the third day He rose from the dead; He ascended into Heaven.' Jesus did not give His disciples a creed. He gave them actual evidence. He lived, taught, performed miracles, died and rose again from the dead by the power of God.

In Luke 24 women, men and angels share in the discovery that Jesus has conquered death. 'Very early in the morning the women . . . found the stone rolled away from the tomb, but when they entered, they did not find the body of the Lord Jesus. While they were wondering about this, suddenly two men in clothes that gleamed like lightning stood beside them . . . the men said to them, "He is not here; He has risen! Remember how He told you, while He was still with you in Galilee: "The Son of Man must be delivered into the hands of sinful men, be crucified and on the third day be raised again." Then they remembered His words. When they came back from the tomb, they told all these things to the Eleven and to all the others . . . But they did not believe the women, because their words seemed to them like nonsense . . . Two of them were going to a village called Emmaus . . . As they talked . . . Jesus Himself came up and walked along with them; but they were kept from recognizing Him . . . When He was at the table with them, He took bread, gave thanks, broke it and began to give it to them. Then their eyes were opened and they recognized Him, and He disappeared from their sight . . . They got up and returned at once to Jerusalem. There they found the Eleven and those with them, assembled together saying, "It is true! The Lord has risen and has appeared to Simon." Then the two told what had happened on the way, and how Jesus was recognized by them when He broke the bread. While they were still talking about this, Jesus Himself stood among them and said to them, "Peace be with you." '

After the resurrection Jesus was seen by hundreds of people, and not only His disciples. He spoke and ate, wore ordinary clothes and showed the marks of the crucifixion on His hands and feet. It was a very important time, because His very presence, and not only what they saw and heard, prepared them to receive the coming Holy Spirit, when the Christian Church would be born. Each generation of Christians since then, including the witnesses in this book, have been conscious of the presence of

Jesus with them, and the power of the Holy Spirit. Transformed lives have resulted, changed in thought, word and deed, vital and exciting. Tolstoy described how Russian peasants would greet one another and respond joyfully at Easter with the words 'Christ is risen!' 'He is risen indeed', as though this momentous event had only just happened.

For sceptics the personal encounter of Jesus with Thomas must be one of the most revealing interviews ever given. Remember that Thomas had insisted he touch Jesus' wounds before he would believe the resurrection had really happened, since he had not been present when Jesus appeared to the other disciples.

'A week later his disciples were in the house again, and Thomas was with them. Though the doors were locked, Jesus came and stood among them . . . Then he said to Thomas, "Put your finger here; see my hands. Reach out your hand and put it into my side. Stop doubting and believe." Thomas said to Him, "My Lord and my God!"' (John 20:26–8). Jesus then drew upon that significant distinction between those who, like Thomas, believe because they can touch and see, and those whose faith is stronger, since, neither touching nor seeing, they believe.

The miracle of the resurrection is of historic importance. An Apostle was first and foremost a man who could say he had seen with his own eyes the resurrected Jesus. This is borne out by the nomination of two candidates to fill the post left by the suicide of Judas after he had betrayed Jesus. Their qualification was that they had personally known Jesus before and after His death and so were able to offer a first-hand account of His resurrection to others (Acts 1:22). Each instance of preaching in the book of the Acts of the Apostles had the miracle of the resurrected Jesus as its central theme.

If the story of Jesus ended on the cross, then He would simply have been a good man who had lived for others. The resurrection of God's Son gives to us not only the greatest

miracle of all, but a miracle that through the Holy Spirit, lives
in the hearts and lives of countless people today.

Life after Life
and the
Death of Death.

BIBLIOGRAPHY

All Bible references are from the New International Version. The titles that follow are listed in the order in which reference is made to them within the text.

CHAPTER ONE

Divine Intervention

'God moves in a mysterious way', William Cowper, *The New English Hymnal*, Norwich, Canterbury Press

Angels, Hope Price, London, Macmillan, 1993

Miracles, C. S. Lewis, London, Collins, 1947

'There is a Redeemer', Melody Green, Word Music (UK) Copy Care Ltd

Your God is too Small, J. B. Phillips, Epworth Press, 1952

Story of a Soul, ed. Mother Agnes of Jesus, Wheathampstead, Herts, Anthony Clarke, 1973

'They lived not only in ages past', L. Scott, 1898

The Way of Peace, Cecil Kerr, London, Hodder & Stoughton, 1990

CHAPTER TWO

Who Needs a Miracle?

Everyman's Guide to the Holy Spirit, the End of the World and You, John and Christine Noble, Eastbourne, Kingsway, 1991

In the Face of Fear, Harvey Thomas, Marshall Pickering, 1985

Miracles, C. S. Lewis, London, Fount Paperbacks, 1982

From Prison to Praise, Merlin Carothers, London, Hodder & Stoughton, 1972

Requiem Healing: A Christian Understanding of the Dead, Michael Mitton & Russ Parker, London, Daybreak, 1991

Deliverance, Michael Perry, London, SPCK, 1987

Healing the Family Tree, Dr Kenneth McAll, Sheldon Press, 1982

[315]

BIBLIOGRAPHY

Healing the Haunted, Dr Kenneth McAll, London, Darley Anderson, 1989

A Book of Beliefs, eds. Langley, Butterworth & Allan, Tring, Herts, Lion
    Publishing, 1981

The Church in the Market Place, George Carey, Eastbourne, Kingsway, 1984

One Step at a Time, David Waite, Eastbourne, Kingsway, 1989

Dancer off her Feet, Julie Sheldon, London, Hodder & Stoughton, 1991

CHAPTER THREE
Miracles in our Family

A Feast for Advent, Delia Smith, The Bible Reading Fellowship, 1983

Excerpt from *Sweet Reprieve*, Frank Maier & Ginny Maier, New York, 1991,
    Crown Publishers Inc., printed in *Reader's Digest* 1991

CHAPTER FOUR
The Miracle of Changed Lives

Smoke on the Mountain, Joy Davidman, London, Hodder & Stoughton, 1959

Making Men Whole, J. B. Phillips, Highway Press, 1952

CHAPTER FIVE
Miracles in the Bible

God Our Contemporary, J. B. Phillips, Hodder & Stoughton, 1960

The Lion Concise Bible Encyclopaedia, ed. Pat Alexander, Tring, Herts, Lion
    Publishing, 1980

The Young Church in Action, J. B. Phillips, Geoffrey Bles Ltd, 1960

Jesus, the Man who Lives, Malcolm Muggeridge, London, Fontana, 1975

The Illustrated Bible Dictionary, Inter-Varsity Press, 1980

CHAPTER SIX
Miracles of Healing

The Christian Healing Ministry, Morris Maddocks, London, SPCK, 1981

Questions of Life, Nicky Gumbel, Eastbourne, Kingsway, 1993

'I Do Not Know What Lies Ahead', Alfred B. Smith, United Nations Music
    Publishers, 1947

That You May Believe, Colin Brown, Eerdmans, 1985

BIBLIOGRAPHY

What's the Point!, Norman Warren, Lion Publishing, 1986

Good News Bible, The Bible Societies, 1976

Unexpected Healing, Jennifer Rees-Larcombe, London, Hodder & Stoughton, 1991

Holy Bible, King James Version

Article by Dr Rex Gardner, *British Medical Journal*, vol. 287, 1983

Healing Miracles, Dr Rex Gardner, Darton, Longman & Todd, 1986

Heal the Sick, Reg East, Mowbray, 1977

CHAPTER SEVEN
Miracles in Places of Conflict

The Way of Peace, Cecil Kerr, London, Hodder & Stoughton, 1990

Marie, Gordon Wilson, London, Marshall Pickering, 1990

Rees Howells: Intercessor, Norman Grubb, Cambridge, Lutterworth Press, 1952

We have a Guardian, W. B. Grant, London, The Covenant Publishing, 1952

Candles in the Dark – Six Modern Martyrs, Mary Craig, London, Hodder & Stoughton, 1984

Saints, Lord Longford, London, Hutchinson, 1987

A Tramp for the Lord, Corrie ten Boom, London, Hodder & Stoughton, 1974

The Dancing Sun, Desmond Seward, London, Macmillan, 1993

Partners Together, magazine of Mid-Africa Ministry, Autumn 1994

CHAPTER EIGHT
Miracles in Holy Places

The Medieval Church in England, Dorothy Meade, Churchman Publishing, 1988

Healing Miracles, Dr Rex Gardner, Darton, Longman & Todd, 1986

Bede (A History of the English Church and People), Leo Sherley-Price, London, Penguin, 1970

The Meaning of Walsingham and *The Story of Walsingham*, Hubert Box, The Guardians of the Shrine, 1990

The Dancing Sun, Desmond Seward, London, Macmillan, 1993

From Where I Sit, Alison Davis, London, SPCK, 1989

Gumfreston Church Guide

Source: the Holy Wells Journal, ed. Tristan Gray Hulse, 1994

BIBLIOGRAPHY

Fatima Shrine Guide

Medjugorje – The War Day by Day, Sister Emmanuel, Florida, Florida Centre
for Peace, 1993

Realities – The Miracles of God Experienced Today, Basilea Schlink, Lakeland,
1981

The Eyelids of the Dawn, Jack Winslow, London, Hodder & Stoughton,
1954

Growing in Faith, Richard More, London, Hodder & Stoughton, 1982

CHAPTER NINE
Miracles in History

The Lion Concise Bible Encyclopaedia, ed. Pat Alexander, Tring, Herts, Lion
Publishing, 1980

The New International Dictionary of the Christian Church, ed. J. D. Douglas,
London, Paternoster Press, 1974

The Medieval Church in England, Dorothy Meade, Churchman Publishing,
1988

Miracles, Michael Poole, London, Scripture Union, 1992

Miracles and the Critical Mind, Colin Brown, London, Paternoster Press,
1974

The Story of Christianity, Tim Dowley, Tring, Herts, Lion Publishing,
1981

The Lion Concise Book of Christian Thought, Tony Lane, Tring, Herts, Lion
Publishing, 1984

Bede (A History of the English Church and People), Leo Sherley-Price, London,
Penguin, 1970

George Fox's Ministry of the Miraculous, article by David Allen for *Renewal*
magazine, October 1994

Joy Unspeakable, Martin Lloyd-Jones, Eastbourne, Kingsway, 1984

The Welsh Revival of 1904, Eifon Wales, Evangelical Press of Wales, 1969

When God Stepped Down from Heaven, Revd Owen Murphy (privately published
booklet)

Miracles, C. S. Lewis, London, Fount Paperbacks, 1982

Pensées, Blaise Pascal, London, Penguin, 1966

BIBLIOGRAPHY

CHAPTER TEN
Miracles in Relationships

A Tramp for the Lord, Corrie ten Boom, London, Hodder & Stoughton, 1974

Healing the Family Tree, Dr Kenneth McAll, Sheldon Press, 1982

The Living Bible, Illinois, Tyndale House Publishers, 1971

Something's Happening, Eileen Vincent, Marshall Morgan & Scott, 1986

CHAPTER ELEVEN
Miracles in the Local Church

Divine Landscapes, Ronald Blythe, London, Viking, 1986

Asian Report, from Asian Outreach International, Report 201, September 1993

Make Your Faith Work, Paul Yonggi Cho, Eastbourne, Kingsway, 1989

A Way for Healing, Robert A. Gillies, The Handsell Press, 1995

CHAPTER TWELVE
Miracles in Business

A Christian Social Perspective, Alan Storkey, Inter-Varsity Press, 1979

A Dictionary of Christian Theology, ed. Alan Richardson, London, SCM Press, 1969

CHAPTER THIRTEEN
Miracles of Creation

Joy and C. S. Lewis, Lyle Dorsett, London, HarperCollins, 1993

Miracles, C. S. Lewis, London, Collins, 1947

CHAPTER FOURTEEN
When Miracles Don't Happen

Awaiting the Healer, Margie Willers, Eastbourne, Kingsway, 1991

The Problem of Pain, C. S. Lewis, London, Collins, 1961

A Step Further, Joni Eareckson, Melbourne, Interbac, 1979

Beyond Healing, Jennifer Rees-Larcombe, London, Hodder & Stoughton, 1986

A Gift of Hope, Tony Melendez, Word Publishing, 1989

BIBLIOGRAPHY

'The Mystery of the Resurrection', Stephen Verney, the *Listener*, 3 March 1977

Suffering Without Pretending, Anne Townsend, London, Ark Publishing, 1980

Empty Arms, Pam Vredevelt, Eastbourne, Kingsway, 1984

New International Dictionary of the Christian Church, ed. J. D. Douglas, London, Paternoster Press, 1984

The Christian Healing Ministry, Morris Maddocks, London, SPCK, 1981

The Lion Concise Bible Encyclopaedia, ed. Pat Alexander, Tring, Herts, Lion Publishing, 1980

CHAPTER FIFTEEN
The Greatest Miracle of All

Jesus, the Man who Lives, Malcolm Muggeridge, London, Fontana, 1975

Miracles, C. S. Lewis, London, Fount Paperbacks, 1982

'Eyewitness to Christ', article by Matthew D'Ancona in *The Times*, 24 December 1994